THE SCHOOLS HISTORY PROJECT · S·H·P · OFFICIAL TEXT

BRITAIN
1815–1851

a study in depth

CORE TEXTS FOR GCSE

DAVE MARTIN

Series Editors:
Ian Dawson
Chris Culpin

JOHN MURRAY

D0417669

The Schools History Project

This project was set up by the Schools Council in 1972. Its main aim was to suggest suitable objectives for History teachers, and to promote the use of appropriate materials and teaching methods for their realisation. This involved a reconsideration of the nature of history and its relevance in secondary schools, the design of a syllabus framework which shows the uses of history in the education of adolescents, and the setting up of appropriate examinations.

Since 1978 the project has been based at Trinity and All Saints' College, Leeds. It is now self-funding and with the advent of the National Curriculum it has expanded its publications to provide courses for Key Stage 3, and for a range of GCSE and A level syllabuses. The project provides INSET for all aspects of National Curriculum, GCSE and A level history.

The SHP website can be found at www.tasc.ac.uk/shp.

Series consultant
Terry Fiehn

Note: The wording and sentence structure of some written sources have been adapted and simplified to make them accessible to all students, while faithfully preserving the sense of the original.

Words printed in SMALL CAPITALS are defined in the Glossary on page 163.

© Dave Martin 2000

First published in 2000
by John Murray (Publishers) Ltd
50 Albemarle Street
London W1X 4BD

Layouts by Eric Drewery
Artwork by Art Construction, Linden Artists, Tony Randell
Typeset in 10.5/12 pt Walbaum Book by Wearset, Boldon, Tyne and Wear.
Colour separations by Colourscript
Printed and bound in the United Kingdom at the University Press, Cambridge

A catalogue entry for this book is available from the British Library.

ISBN 0 7195 7478 1
Teachers' Resource Book ISBN 0 7195 7479 X

Contents

INTRODUCTION

It all begins with Waterloo!

ON 18 JUNE 1815 the British army, led by the Duke of Wellington, and their allies, the Prussians, defeated the Emperor Napoleon at the Battle of Waterloo.

SOURCE 1 An extract from the memoirs of Sergeant John Douglas, First Regiment of Foot, who fought at Waterloo

> 66 *The British, so long on the defensive, were impatient for close quarters, longing and even calling out for the order to advance, eager to put an end to this glorious day of destruction, in which the patience, bravery and fortitude of the British soldier was put to the utmost trial. Four deep we advanced with three British cheers, while the sun, hitherto obscured, now shone forth, as if smiling on the last efforts of Britain for the liberties of Europe.* 99

Home come the heroes

Waterloo marked the end of nearly twenty years of war against France known as the Napoleonic Wars. The French monarchy was restored and the FRENCH REVOLUTION of 1789 was finally reversed. Britain's soldiers and sailors could return home victorious.

But the Britain they returned to had changed forever. This book is about those changes and how the people of Britain reacted to them.

Here are snapshots of four of Britain's heros. How did life turn out for them in the period 1815–1851?

Arthur Wellesley, first Duke of Wellington (1769–1852)

The victorious general at the Battle of Waterloo, Wellesley was rewarded with a pension, lands and the Dukedom. He went on to enjoy a successful political career, which included serving as Prime Minister. He was an opponent of PARLIAMENTARY REFORM and on 27 April 1831 a stone-throwing mob broke the windows of his home, Apsley House. As Commander-in-Chief of the British army he personally planned the measures to protect London from the CHARTISTS in April 1848.

Captain Thomas Hardy (1769–1839)

Hardy served as flag captain to Admiral Nelson, who won a famous victory against the French at the Battle of Trafalgar in 1805. In 1815 Hardy returned to Britain and was knighted. He continued to serve in the navy and reached the rank of Admiral. In his retirement he was governor of Greenwich Hospital, a home for retired sailors.

John Lees, soldier

John Lees fought in Wellington's army at Waterloo. He survived the battle and at the end of his term of enlistment left the army. He returned home to live and work in Oldham. He was sabred and killed at the PETERLOO reform meeting in 1819.

George Armstrong, seaman

George Armstrong had been caught by a press-gang and forced to join the navy. At the end of the war his ship was PAID OFF and he returned to civilian life. He returned to his Dorset home where he worked as an agricultural labourer. He avoided becoming involved in the SWING RIOTS but in old age fell into poverty and died in the WORKHOUSE.

What was Britain like in 1815?

Old Britain

Royalty and nobility
(3,000)

Baronets, knights and squires
(50,000)

Upper clergy, merchants and bankers
(40,000)

Upper civil servants and lawyers
(40,000)

Independent gentry
150,000

Upper doctors and other professionals
(20,000)

Army and naval officers
(70,000)

Lesser clergy
(75,000)

Upper freeholders
(300,000)

Shipowners, lesser merchants, shipbuilders, engineers, builders
(200,000)

Lesser professionals, civil servants and dissenting ministers
(250,000)

Innkeepers
(375,000)

Shopkeepers and hawkers
(600,000)

Master craftsmen and manufacturers
(450,000)

Lesser freeholders
(900,000)

Farmers
(1,300,000)

Teachers, actors, clerks and shopmen
(320,000)

Artisans and other skilled workers
(4,500,000)

Agricultural labourers, miners, seamen, road and canal workers
(3,500,000)

Personal and household servants
(1,300,000)

Soldiers and sailors
(800,000)

Paupers, vagrants, prisoners and lunatics
(1,900,000)

SOURCE 1 Patrick Colquhoun's estimate of the social structure of the United Kingdom *c.* 1815

The monarchy

At the top of the political system was the monarchy. King George III had a disease that produced similar symptoms to a form of insanity, so his son George had been Prince Regent since 1811. The Prince Regent was lazy and incompetent and took very little interest in government. He had the power to appoint the Prime Minister and to have a say in the appointment of other ministers, but he also had to take notice of Parliament. Without its support he could not influence policies or raise the taxes he needed.

SOURCE 2 A portrait of King George IV (1820–30), who acted as Regent from 1811

The aristocracy

Below the King was the ARISTOCRACY, a group of about 300 families. Their political power was based upon their ownership of land. Their income came largely from farming their vast estates. Servants and tenants depended on them for work. They acted as the king's ministers and sat in the HOUSE OF LORDS. In 1815 nearly half the 658 Members of Parliament in the HOUSE OF COMMONS owed their seats to the influence of the aristocracy. The aristocracy also filled all the top positions in the Church, the lawcourts and the army and navy.

On a local level they also dominated politics. At the head of each county was the Lord-Lieutenant. Usually the largest landowner, he was the king's representative in the county. Below him were the JUSTICES OF THE PEACE or magistrates who were responsible for maintaining law and order and preventing crime.

SOURCE 3 Francis Russell, seventh Duke of Bedford (duke from 1839–62). As a duke, he automatically sat in Parliament in the House of Lords. Allied to him was the local clergyman, the representative of the Church of England. Together they were looked up to by the population of the area.

The gentry

The Justices of the Peace or magistrates were appointed by the Lord Chancellor, usually having been nominated by the Lord-Lieutenant. Most were landowners or clergymen, drawn from the class known as the GENTRY, who owned smaller estates than the aristocracy. As Justices of the Peace they had the power to arrest, fine and imprison people. Their strong influence in the local area as landowners and employers, together with these legal powers, made them the dominant force in rural society. If they were faced with local disorder they could call on three sources of support:

- the YEOMANRY or militia, a mounted volunteer force made up of property owners like themselves
- special constables, ordinary men sworn in by the magistrates and armed with staves
- the army.

Changing Britain

These three groups – monarchy, aristocracy and gentry – represented Old Britain. Between them they had held political control for hundreds of years. But in 1815 New Britain threatened their position. New Britain was made up of the growing number of people whose income came not from land but from industry and mining. These new groups wanted a greater say in the running of their own lives and, ultimately, in the running of the country.

The middle classes

This was the name being used to describe the bankers, merchants, industrialists and mine owners who emerged from the INDUSTRIAL REVOLUTION. They controlled the business life of the towns and cities they lived in but often had very little political influence. Some of them used their new wealth to buy land. They all wanted parliamentary reform to give them political power. People in the professions, such as doctors and lawyers, could also be described as belonging to the middle classes. Many members of the middle classes also became involved in charitable work and tried to improve the lives of the working classes and the poor.

SOURCE 4 Elizabeth Fry (1750–1845). The daughter of a banker, mother of ten children and devout QUAKER, Elizabeth Fry spent much of her life working to improve prison conditions. She first visited Newgate Prison in 1817 and was shocked by the conditions there for prisoners, particularly the women and children. She visited frequently from then on and worked to improve conditions.

The working classes

These were divided into two main groups, urban workers and rural workers. In the towns there were the skilled and unskilled industrial workers in the mines, cotton mills and iron works. In the countryside there were the agricultural labourers. They all wanted better living and working conditions and some believed that they would only get these if they had political power.

SOURCE 5 An engraving of men working near the High Level Bridge, Newcastle upon Tyne, 1849

The poor

Below all these groups were the poor – those who had no work and depended on POOR RELIEF to live, and those who were in work but so poorly paid that they also had to seek help.

■ **ACTIVITY**

1. Work with a partner. Look at the people identified by Patrick Colquhoun in Source 1. Which of the five groups – aristocracy, gentry, middle classes, working classes or the poor – do they fit into?
2. What are the:
   a) advantages
   b) disadvantages
   to the historian of using labels like middle class?

What changes were affecting Britain in 1815?

PERHAPS THE LEADERS of Old Britain looked with some envy at France in the years immediately after Waterloo. With the restoration of the French monarchy it seemed as though France had been able to 'turn back the clock'. Old Britain could not do the same. Over the previous fifty years the country had undergone enormous changes, changes so great that historians sometimes describe them as 'REVOLUTIONS'.

■ **ACTIVITY**

As you read this section think about the following questions:

1. How do you think the five 'revolutions' described here would have affected the power and influence of Old Britain?
2. How did these 'revolutions' help to create New Britain?

Discuss your ideas with a partner.

The agricultural revolution

In the eighteenth century there were a series of developments in agriculture. Farmers developed new methods, grew new crops, used new tools and machines and bred new breeds of cows, pigs and sheep. These developments continued into the nineteenth century and the result was an increase in efficiency and productivity. This produced CAPITAL that landowners could invest in the new industries, as well as the extra food required by the growing population.

The Industrial Revolution

The industrial changes in the early years of the nineteenth century were so great in comparison to other years that they are sometimes called the Industrial Revolution. The greatest changes were in the cotton industry, where imports of raw cotton trebled between 1815 and 1830; in the coal industry, where production rose from 16 million tonnes in 1815 to 30 million tonnes in 1830; and in the iron industry. By 1820 the water wheel had been improved, making water a highly efficient source of power for industry. Although still in its early stages, steam power was also making an impact. The development of industry drew people into the towns to find work. For example, in 1820 there were 66 cotton mills in Manchester and by 1832 this had increased to 96 cotton mills.

The population 'revolution'

In the first half of the nineteenth century there was a dramatic growth in population. For the first time in history the rise in population was not held back by famine and starvation. Between 1801 and 1851 the population almost doubled. This meant that there were more mouths to feed but also more hands to do the work.

1. Look at Source 1. How does the population pattern for Ireland differ from that of England, Wales and Scotland?
2. Can you suggest any reasons that might explain this?

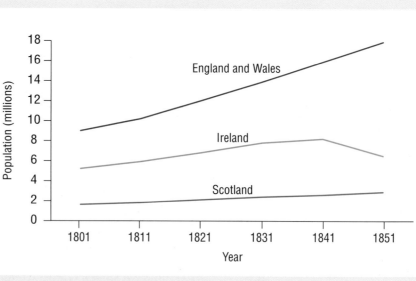

SOURCE 1 Population figures, 1801–51

The transport revolution

In the eighteenth century there were major improvements in transport that continued into the nineteenth century. Roads were improved by the TURNPIKE TRUSTS. This enabled people to move about the country more quickly. In 1750 there were 4800 km of turnpike road. By 1800 this had increased to 32,000 km. Similar developments with the building of canals allowed heavy goods to be moved more quickly and easily. The first canal was built in 1757. By 1840 there were over 4800 km of canal. The first railway powered by a steam locomotive opened in 1824. By 1850, there were 9791 km of railway. All these developments supported the growth of industry in the period.

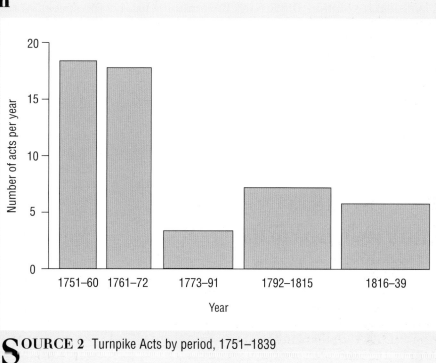

SOURCE 2 Turnpike Acts by period, 1751–1839

The urban revolution

In 1801 only 17 per cent of the population lived in towns of more than 20,000 people. By 1831 this figure had risen to 25 per cent and by 1851 over 50 per cent lived in towns. This was an urban revolution. It led to a series of problems. The historians Sidney and Beatrice Webb described these as 'the massing of men in urban districts, the devastating torrent of public nuisances, the catastrophic increase in destitution and pauperism and the consequent prevalence of crime and SEDITION ...' You will look at these problems in more detail on pages 70–75.

SOURCE 3 An illustration of Leeds, *c*. 1840

Why was the French Revolution so important?

THE OTHER GREAT revolution at this time was a political revolution, the French Revolution. On 21 January 1793 Louis XVI, King of France, was sent to the GUILLOTINE by his own people. Nine months later his wife, Queen Marie Antoinette, met the same fate. Their son and heir, the Dauphin, died in prison two years later. Thousands of their subjects were also killed in disturbances, guillotined or murdered. These events followed the French Revolution of 1789. The turmoil in France shocked the other European rulers. They feared the threat to their own authority and position. They were terrified of revolutions in their own countries and of meeting the same awful fate as the French royal family.

British reactions to the French Revolution

The majority of the ruling classes in Britain were afraid of revolution by the working classes and this affected how they acted. They did their best to stop the spread of revolutionary ideas through such measures as the Proclamation against Seditious Publications in May 1792. They believed that anyone who suggested change or reform was really threatening revolution and the breakdown of society.

There were others in Britain who admired what had happened in France. To them the revolutionary ideals of Liberty, Equality and Fraternity were very attractive and they wanted to see these ideals put into practice in Britain. They included writers like Thomas Paine (1737–1809) who wrote *The Rights of Man* in 1791–92. In this book he argued that all men should have the right to vote. Under threat of arrest in Britain he fled to France in 1792, was convicted of seditious libel in his absence, and died in EXILE in the USA in 1809. Support for the views of people like Paine declined after the execution of Louis XVI and the newspapers became much more hostile to the French Revolution.

SOURCE 1 *Massacre of the French King*, a contemporary English poster depicting the execution of Louis XVI

SOURCE 2 A British cartoon depicting the revolutionaries, or *Sans-culottes*, published in 1792. The *Sans-culottes* was the name used to describe the common people of France. Its literal translation is 'without trousers'

SOURCE 3 A British cartoon of the French Revolution by James Gillray, published in February 1793

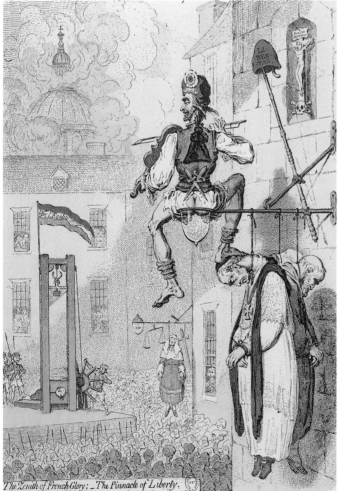

The Zenith of French Glory; _ The Pinnacle of Liberty.

Look for the caps of liberty. These were a very important symbol of the French Revolution and when people in Britain wore them they were giving a very clear message to the authorities. The term 'Liberty, equality and fraternity' was also an important slogan.

1. How can you tell that Source 1 is hostile to the French Revolution?
2. In Sources 2 and 3, both cartoonists are hostile to the French Revolution. How do they make their point?
3. What crimes are the revolutionaries accused of?

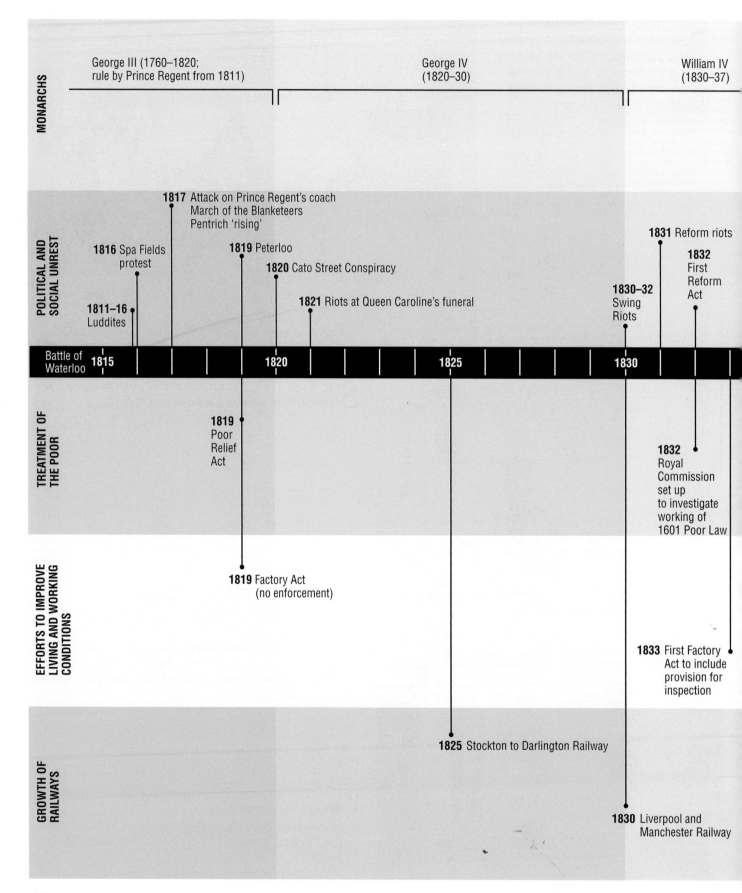

MONARCHS

George III (1760–1820; rule by Prince Regent from 1811)

George IV (1820–30)

William IV (1830–37)

POLITICAL AND SOCIAL UNREST

1817 Attack on Prince Regent's coach
March of the Blanketeers
Pentrich 'rising'

1831 Reform riots

1816 Spa Fields protest

1819 Peterloo

1832 First Reform Act

1820 Cato Street Conspiracy

1811–16 Luddites

1821 Riots at Queen Caroline's funeral

1830–32 Swing Riots

Battle of Waterloo | 1815 | 1820 | 1825 | 1830

TREATMENT OF THE POOR

1819 Poor Relief Act

1832 Royal Commission set up to investigate working of 1601 Poor Law

EFFORTS TO IMPROVE LIVING AND WORKING CONDITIONS

1819 Factory Act (no enforcement)

1833 First Factory Act to include provision for inspection

GROWTH OF RAILWAYS

1825 Stockton to Darlington Railway

1830 Liverpool and Manchester Railway

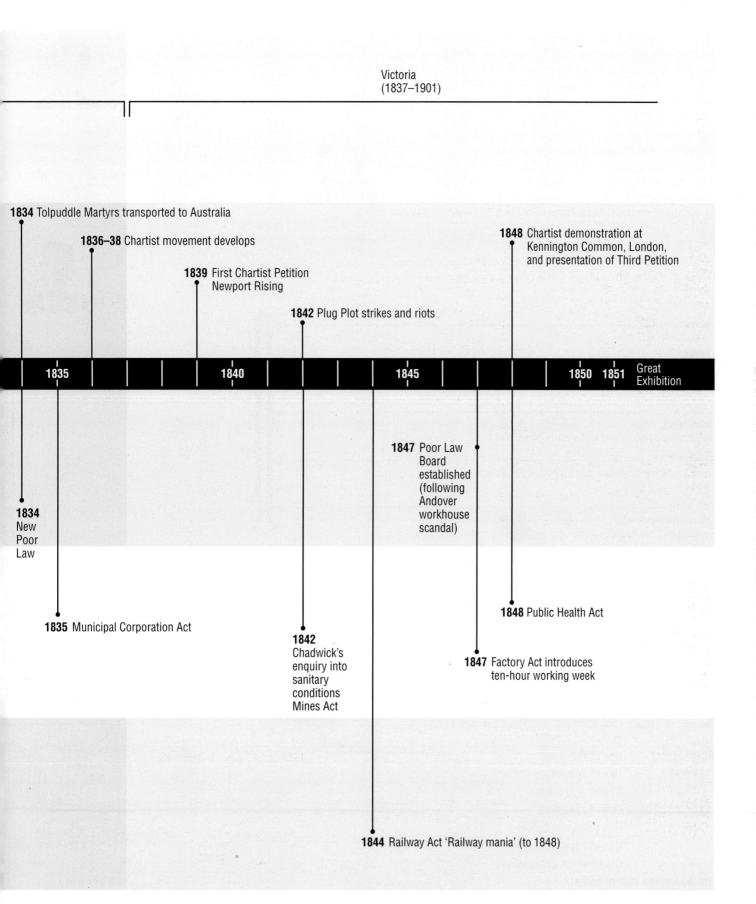

Victoria
(1837–1901)

1834 Tolpuddle Martyrs transported to Australia

1836–38 Chartist movement develops

1848 Chartist demonstration at Kennington Common, London, and presentation of Third Petition

1839 First Chartist Petition Newport Rising

1842 Plug Plot strikes and riots

1835   1840   1845   1850   1851   Great Exhibition

1847 Poor Law Board established (following Andover workhouse scandal)

1834 New Poor Law

1835 Municipal Corporation Act

1848 Public Health Act

1842 Chadwick's enquiry into sanitary conditions Mines Act

1847 Factory Act introduces ten-hour working week

1844 Railway Act 'Railway mania' (to 1848)

Your enquiry: why wasn't there a revolution in Britain?

YOU CAN SEE from pages 8–9 that many people in Britain feared revolution. Some even expected it. So, the rest of this book is about the key question: why wasn't there a revolution in Britain? Some modern historians argue that there was never any real danger of a revolution but at the time the monarchy and the aristocracy believed that the threat of revolution was very real indeed.

At various points in this book you will be asked to 'take the revolutionary temperature' using the diagram below – to make your own judgement on how close Britain was to revolution at a particular time.

In order to do this you will be asked to look at the actions, methods and aims of the various groups of protesters and decide if they were revolutionaries . . .

Were they asking for change or for things to stay the same? Were their actions peaceful or violent? Were they attacking property or people?

You will also be asked to look at the actions of the ruling classes . . .

How did they maintain control? Was it by using the power of the law, the courts and the army? Did they pass new laws? Did they use harsh punishments? Was it through the ruthless use of imprisonment? Was it through making concessions?

Finally, you will need to look at the rest of society . . .

Did they support the protesters? Were they quite happy with their lives and the way society was run?

Very hot! Boiling!
Revolution now

Hot! Watch out!
People are getting angry
Great danger of revolution

Getting warm!
Tricky times
Got to tread carefully and make the right decisions

Comfortable!
Some problems as always, but they are under control

Very cool!
Total peace, total calm
No danger of revolution

The heat of revolutionary ideas

In order to help you do this, you will need to create a table like the one below and continually add to it during your studies.

Protesters:	Demands		
	Actions		
	Character (links to French Revolution in words, symbols or actions)		
Government response:	Use of the army		
	Use of special constables		
	Changes to the law		
	Use of execution		
	Use of imprisonment		
	Use of TRANSPORTATION		
	Government concessions		
Attitude of the rest of society			

1

PRESSURE FOR POLITICAL REFORM

chapter 1

HOW NEAR TO REVOLUTION WAS BRITAIN AT THE END OF THE NAPOLEONIC WARS?

FOR ORDINARY SOLDIERS and sailors returning from the Napoleonic Wars it was a strange homecoming. Britain was in a state of unrest in 1815. There were few jobs. Bread prices were high. Riots had broken out in some areas. In the Midlands and the north-west the LUDDITES had been carrying out attacks on stocking-making machines for the past four years. Troops had been called in to deal with them. People were growing desperate and the authorities were afraid.

This spread summarises the problems.

■ TASK

Your task is to construct a timeline of the events in the decade 1810–1820 that are covered in this chapter. For each event you should note:

a) what happened
b) how it mirrored events in the French Revolution
c) how it added to the fears of the ruling classes.

Rising unemployment
Over a third of a million soldiers and sailors were DEMOBILISED and this added to the problems of unemployment caused by a SLUMP in industry and agriculture. At the same time, the population was increasing.

Falling agricultural prices
A series of good harvests flooded the markets with produce. Food prices fell and so, as a result, did the incomes of the landed aristocracy and gentry. They responded to this first by cutting wages and then, through their influence in Parliament, by passing the Corn Laws in 1815. By banning the import of foreign corn until the cost of home-grown corn had reached £4 per quarter-hundredweight (12.7 kg), these laws kept the price of corn high. This protected the landowners' income from farming but also led to high food prices.

Economic depression
Those industries which had been stimulated by the war – textiles, iron and armaments – were set back by peace. There was also a cut in government spending. The post-war boom only lasted three years at most in some industries. Many European states were short of money as a result of the Napoleonic Wars and could not afford to buy British goods.

Rising cost of Poor Relief
A combination of rising unemployment and falling wage levels led more people to claim Poor Relief, thus increasing the costs.

SOURCE 1 Problems in Britain at the end of the Napoleonic Wars

The Spa Fields protest

Protest meetings were held in many places and most were entirely peaceful. But on 2 December 1816 a protest meeting at Spa Fields in London ended when a group of approximately 200 men broke away from the main demonstration and marched on the Tower of London. On the way they broke into some gunshops. However, when they got to the Tower the marchers did nothing and were easily dispersed by troops.

In response to this incident the Government decided to pass a new law to make protest meetings illegal and suspended the Habeas Corpus ACT. This meant that people could now be arrested and imprisoned without trial.

High taxes
The cost of fighting the wars left Britain with a national debt of £861 million. This debt had to be paid off through high taxes. Over 70 per cent of these were indirect taxes, that is, taxes that you pay when buying goods. These taxes hit the poor hardest.

The Luddites
On 11 March 1811 several hundred people attended a protest meeting in Nottingham market place. Later that evening, 63 stocking frames used in the local hosiery industry were smashed. This was the start of Luddism, a protest against pay cuts and attempts to introduce new ways of working. Between 1811 and 1816 there were many incidents of frame-breaking by the Luddites. The Government sent troops to the worst-affected areas and introduced the death penalty for those convicted of frame breaking.

Attack on the Prince Regent

In January 1817 the Prince Regent got a very hostile reception from the crowd as he returned from the state opening of Parliament. They hissed and threw stones at his carriage, smashing its windows. It was even said that someone had fired at him with an air-gun. This reminded people of the attacks by the Paris mob on the coaches of the French aristocracy. Certainly the Prince Regent was very unpopular. At a time of economic difficulty, when many of his subjects were living in poverty, he lived an extravagant life and was massively in debt. One slogan painted on the wall of his house read, 'Bread or the Regent's head'. Soldiers escorted his carriage on the rare occasions when he appeared in public.

The March of the Blanketeers

In March 1817 a protest march, which became known as the March of the Blanketeers, was put down by troops. The marchers, who were unemployed cotton workers, got their name from the blankets that they carried for shelter at night. They were protesting against the Government's new law banning meetings. They planned to march from Manchester to London but were stopped at Stockport and the leaders arrested. Without their leaders the rest got no further than Macclesfield. Again, their march reminded people of the protests in France.

The Pentrich 'rising'

In June 1817 the Pentrich 'rising' took place in Derbyshire. Led by Jeremiah Brandreth, the rebels, armed with pikes and guns, marched to Nottingham believing they were part of a national rebellion. A government agent, Oliver, had encouraged the rebels in order to get them arrested. In Nottingham, the pre-warned soldiers easily put them to flight. Three of their leaders were hanged and 30 were sentenced to transportation. Despite its failure, this rising also reminded people of the peasants' risings in France, when aristocrats were murdered and their châteaux burnt down.

'Peterloo Massacre' or 'Riot at St Peter's Field'?

AS YOU HAVE already seen, Britain faced a number of problems at the end of the Napoleonic Wars. One group, known as the RADICALS, felt that part of the solution to these problems would be a fairer political system. The way to achieve this, they believed, was through parliamentary reform. If all men were represented in Parliament then the government would be run in their interest. They wanted all men to have the right to vote, as well as annual elections and votes cast in secret. There were a number of leading Radicals.

The Radicals

Major John Cartwright (1740–1824)
He argued for annual Parliaments, payment for MPs, secret ballots and for all men to have the right to vote. Between 1813 and 1815 he toured and addressed meetings in the Midlands and the north of England. He set up Hampden Clubs for his supporters. Hampden Clubs were named after John Hampden, the seventeenth-century MP who, in 1635, challenged Charles I's right to levy the tax of Ship Money without parliamentary approval. These clubs flourished until the REPRESSIVE legislation of 1817.

Sir Francis Burdett (1770–1844)
He was MP for Westminster 1807–37 and MP for Wiltshire 1837–44. He spoke in favour of reform at meetings and in the House of Commons. He was the first chairman of the London Hampden Club, set up in 1812 to promote parliamentary reform. He was imprisoned for a time in the Tower of London.

Francis Place (1771–1854)
He was involved in the reform campaigns from the 1790s onwards and was particularly influential in the years leading up to the Reform Act of 1832. He later helped draft the 'People's Charter' (see pages 142–43).

William Cobbett (1763–1835)
He was in favour of parliamentary reform and published a cheap weekly newspaper, the *Political Register*, putting forward his ideas from 1816 onwards. In 1817 he fled to America to avoid arrest. He returned to Britain and was later tried for supposedly stirring up the Swing Riots (see pages 44–51). He was MP for Oldham from 1832.

SOURCE 1 A comment by the WHIG politician Lord Grey on the Radical leaders. Whig politicians had close links with industrialists and supported limited social and political reform

66 Is there one among them with whom you would trust yourself in the dark? 99

1. Do you think it likely that these men were directly influenced by the French Revolution?
2. What methods of campaigning did these Radicals have in common?

Henry 'Orator' Hunt (1773–1835)
The son of a Wiltshire farmer, he was in favour of parliamentary reform and was often asked to speak at large outdoor meetings. He tried to work up popular feelings but backed off when it seemed there was a threat of violence breaking out. He offered not to speak at Peterloo. He was imprisoned for his role at Peterloo and on his release wrote an exposé of prison conditions. He was to become MP for Preston in the years 1830–32.

The activities of these men and their supporters frightened the Government. To the Government and its local representatives, the Justices of the Peace, it seemed that the Radicals and their ideas could lead to revolution. One government tactic was to employ spies, the most famous of whom was known as 'Oliver'. Their job was to join groups suspected of revolutionary plotting and to gather evidence about them. In the case of the Pentrich 'rising' (see page 15) Oliver acted as an *agent provocateur*, that is, he had encouraged the men to break the law.

The Government's fears also affected how they tried to deal with protest meetings. The Radicals called a number of large meetings in towns that did not have MPs to represent them. They then encouraged the people to choose their own representative. This was both illegal and a deliberate attack upon the Government. The most famous example is the meeting in St Peter's Field in 1819.

What happened at Peterloo?: the author's version

In your study of history so far you will have come to realise that there is not one narrative of the past but many narratives. Nowhere is this more obvious than in descriptions of a controversial event such as Peterloo. So you will start with my version, which attempts to describe **the facts** as I understand them.

Overview
On 16 August 1819 a great meeting assembled in St Peter's Field, Manchester. Estimates of the numbers vary from 30,000 to 153,000. Men, women and children dressed in their Sunday best had marched into Manchester from the surrounding towns and villages. They had come to listen to the main speaker, Henry 'Orator' Hunt, talk about parliamentary reform. They marched in organised groups behind their leaders, carrying banners with slogans such as 'Liberty and Fraternity' and 'Unity is Strength'. They also carried caps of liberty. All these were revolutionary symbols. Their actions were a challenge to the authorities.

The local magistrates, who had banned an earlier meeting planned for 9 August, were watching the marchers (see Source 4). They were worried that the meeting was illegal and feared what it could lead to. After most of the people had arrived the magistrates decided it would be sensible to arrest Hunt before he could speak. The local constables said they could not arrest him without military protection. So they were given an escort of Manchester and Salford Yeomanry. The Yeomanry were mounted volunteers drawn from the property-owning classes. They were not well trained in dealing with large crowds.

The constables and their Yeomanry escort made their way through the crowd to the HUSTINGS and arrested Hunt. Then they were trapped; they could not get back through the crowd. The magistrates saw this and sent in the Fifteenth Hussars, a unit of regular troops, to rescue them. As these disciplined troops forced their way through the people, panic broke out among the crowd. There is some evidence to suggest that the Yeomanry also panicked and struck out with their swords. Certainly by the end of the day eleven people had been killed and over 400 injured.

Timeline

8.00   Roughly 6000 reformers met at Middleton to hear a speech from Samuel Bamford.

8.30   The Fifteenth Hussars paraded in Manchester.

9.00   Oldham reform groups began their march to Manchester.
The Cheshire Yeomanry assembled on Sale Moor and then began the march to their position in St John Street.
The first people began to gather at St Peter's Field.

10.00   The Fifteenth Hussars took up their positions in Byrom and Lower Mosley Streets.
The magistrates met at the Star Inn.

10.30   George Swift and a group of men started to put up the hustings.
John Tyas, a reporter for *The Times*, estimated the crowd to be about 250 people at this point.

11.00   The magistrates moved to Mr Buxton's house in Mount Street overlooking St Peter's Field.

Timeline continued

11.30 About 5000 marchers from Stockport arrived at St Peter's Field. Some marchers were carrying standards and caps of liberty, others sticks and brickbats.
Members of the Manchester and Salford Yeomanry were seen drinking in nearby public houses.

12.00 John Tyas estimated that there were now about 80,000 people in St Peter's Field.
George Swift and Robert Wild addressed the crowd.
About 400 special constables marched into St Peter's Field. They formed two rows between the hustings and Mr Buxton's house.

12.30 The crowd sang the National Anthem.

1.20 Henry Hunt, Richard Carlile, John Knight, Joseph Johnson and Mary Fildes arrived at the hustings. Elizabeth Gaunt was taken ill in the crowd and lifted onto the hustings.
John Tyas, Edward Baines of the *Leeds Mercury* and John Smith of the *Liverpool Mercury* joined the speakers on the hustings.

1.30 John Moorhouse from Stockport arrived at the hustings.
The magistrates decided to arrest Henry Hunt, John Knight, Joseph Johnson and John Moorhouse. Warrants were signed. The special constables said they were too few to arrest Hunt and the others. Messages were sent to Major Thomas Trafford and Colonel L'Estrange.

1.35 Rev. Charles Ethelston read the RIOT ACT from Mr Buxton's window.

1.40 Henry Hunt began to speak to the crowd.
The Blackburn reform group arrived at St Peter's Field.
The Manchester and Salford Yeomanry knocked down Ann Fildes and her two-year-old son William, on the way to St Peter's Field. William Fildes was killed and his mother badly injured.

1.45 Major Trafford ordered Captain Birley and the Yeomanry to arrest the four leaders on the hustings.
Richard Carlile, John Smith and Edward Baines saw the Yeomanry approaching and left the hustings. The Yeomanry got caught up in the crowd.

1.50 Colonel L'Estrange and the Fifteenth Hussars were ordered to rescue the Yeomanry from the crowd.
Captain Birley arrested Hunt, Johnson, Swift, Knight, Saxton, Moorhouse, Tyas, Gaunt and Wild.

2.00 Except for the dead and wounded the crowd had left St Peter's Field.

3. Read the Timeline. What was it about the crowd that would have led the magistrates to fear revolution?
4. What clues are there to suggest that the Yeomanry might panic and use violence?
5. What evidence can you find in Source 2 that the magistrates feared trouble at the meeting?

■ ACTIVITY

What happened at Peterloo?: your version
Now its your turn. What will your interpretation of Peterloo be? You've got the facts from pages 17–19. Now you need an angle or a story.

Source 3 is a modern artist's interpretation of what the scene might have looked like at the start of the meeting in St Peter's Field. It is the first in a series of six storyboards for a short film about the event. Your task is to produce the next five storyboards to complete the film outline. To help you do this you should study Sources 5–15.

You will need to choose which viewpoint you want to give. Will you be for the protesters, against the protesters, or will you try to give an impartial view? You decide.

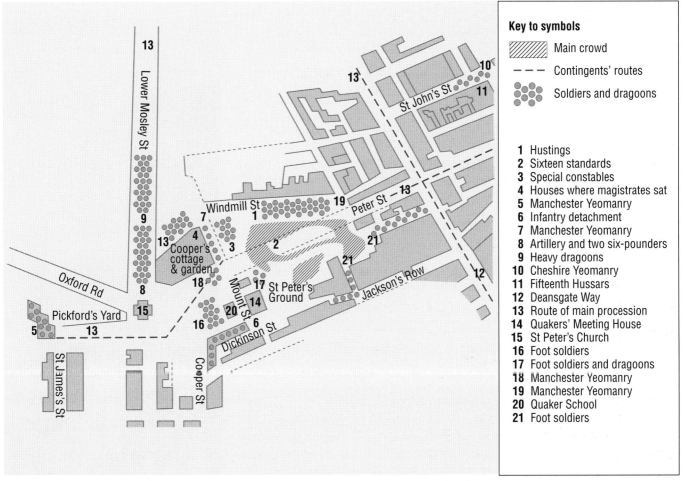

SOURCE 2 A map to show the positions of the people and groups at Peterloo, with the original key and labels that appeared in the *Manchester Observer* on 23 October 1819

Key to symbols

- Main crowd
- Contingents' routes
- Soldiers and dragoons

1 Hustings
2 Sixteen standards
3 Special constables
4 Houses where magistrates sat
5 Manchester Yeomanry
6 Infantry detachment
7 Manchester Yeomanry
8 Artillery and two six-pounders
9 Heavy dragoons
10 Cheshire Yeomanry
11 Fifteenth Hussars
12 Deansgate Way
13 Route of main procession
14 Quakers' Meeting House
15 St Peter's Church
16 Foot soldiers
17 Foot soldiers and dragoons
18 Manchester Yeomanry
19 Manchester Yeomanry
20 Quaker School
21 Foot soldiers

SOURCE 3
A modern artist's illustration of the scene at the start of the meeting

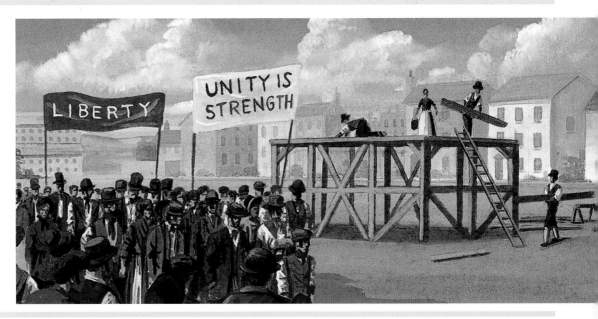

What happened at Peterloo?: sources from the time

■ SOURCE INVESTIGATION

Sources 4–15 describe the events at Peterloo from a variety of viewpoints, including those of the magistrates and those of the reformers.

1. Copy the table below and list the sources. Tick the appropriate column if you think a source describes the event from the point of view of the magistrates or the reformers.
2. In the final column make a note of any useful information you think you can take from the source.

Source	Pro-magistrates?	Pro-reformers?	Information you can take from this source

SOURCE 4 William Hulton, Chairman of the Magistrates, speaking at the trial of Henry Hunt, March 1820

“ I observed the arrival of Hunt. He was in a carriage, in which I believe were also Johnson, Moorhouse and Carlile. I had a view over the whole of St Peter's area. The number of persons assembled was estimated at 50,000 and the meeting did undoubtedly inspire terror in the minds of the inhabitants. Many gentlemen stated to me they were greatly alarmed, and looking to all the circumstances, my opinion was that the town was in great danger. ”

SOURCE 5 Extracts from the official report of Colonel L'Estrange, commanding officer of the military forces at Peterloo. The report was written at 8pm on 16 August 1819

“ Early in the afternoon, the civil power [magistrates] finding it necessary that the troops should act in aid of them, it was deemed expedient [thought necessary] that the cavalry should advance; and ... two persons, Hunt and Johnson, were arrested; as were also two persons named Saxton and Sykes who were active, as I am told, on the hustings. This service was performed with the assistance of the cavalry.

I have, however, great regret in stating that some of the unfortunate people who attended this meeting have suffered from sabre wounds, and many from the pressure of the crowd. One of the Manchester Yeomanry, if not dead, lies without hope of recovery; it is understood he was struck with a stone. One of the special constables has been killed. The Manchester Yeomanry, under Major Trafford, and the Cheshire Yeomanry under Lieutenant-Colonel Townsend, who had come on very short notice from the county magistrates, many of them from a great distance, were most active and efficient in discharge of their duty. ”

SOURCE 6 An extract from a letter, dated 19 August 1819, from Robert Mutrie of the Manchester and Salford Yeomanry to his friend Archibald Moore

“ The crowd had pelted us with stones for an hour or two. Captain Booth gave the word and we then charged the crowd. My horse grew quite mad and carried me over the backs of many poor devils. I think the reformers will not call another meeting. ”

6. Does Robert Mutrie (Source 6) sound sorry for the deaths at Peterloo?

SOURCE 7 *The Peterloo Massacre, a cartoon by George Cruikshank published in October 1819*

7. How does Lieutenant Jolliffe (Source 8) justify the actions of the Hussars?

SOURCE 8 An account given by Lieutenant William Jolliffe of the Fifteenth Hussars, in an interview for a book which was published in 1847

❝ *We arrived at St Peter's Field with Colonel L'Estrange. It was then for the first time that I saw the Manchester troop of Yeomanry; they were scattered singly, or in small groups over the greater part of the field, literally hemmed up and hedged into the mob so that they were powerless either to make an impression or to escape. The small body of horsemen was entirely at the mercy of the people by whom they were, on all sides, pressed upon and surrounded. It only required a glance to discover their helpless position, and the necessity of our being brought to the rescue.*

The Hussars drove the people forward with the flats of their swords, but sometimes, as is almost inevitably the case when men are placed in such situations, the edge was used, both by the Hussars and, as I have heard, by the Yeomen also; but I believe nine out of ten of the sabre wounds were caused by the Hussars. I still consider that it is an indication of the humane behaviour of the men of the Fifteenth that more wounds were not received, when the vast numbers are taken into consideration with whom they were brought into hostile collision; beyond all doubt, however, the far greater amount of injuries were from the pressure of the routed multitude [fleeing crowd]. ❞

SOURCE 9 An extract from a speech by Henry Hunt at St Peter's Field on 16 August 1830

The last time I had the honour to meet you in this field of blood was eleven years ago this day. We met for the purpose of offering up our prayers and petitions to Parliament for a repeal of the Corn Laws, and a reform in the House of Parliament. We were peaceably and legally assembled to perform a constitutional duty when we were attacked by bands of drunken Yeomanry, who rushed among the unarmed multitude, of whom 14 were killed and 618 badly wounded. This was the way in which our prayers were answered.

SOURCE 10 John Tyas, a reporter for *The Times*, describing what happened immediately after Hunt had been arrested. Although *The Times* supported the Government Tyas himself was arrested

As soon as Hunt and Johnson had jumped from the wagon, the cavalry made a cry, 'Have their flags'. They immediately dashed not only at the flags which were in the wagon, but also at those which were posted among the crowd, cutting most indiscriminately to the right and left in order to get at them. This set the people running in all directions, and it was not until this act had been committed that any brickbats were hurled at the military. From that moment the Manchester Yeomanry Cavalry lost all command of their temper.

8. How is Source 10 supported by the Timeline on pages 17–18?

SOURCE 11 An extract from a letter written by Lord Sidmouth, Home Secretary, to his wife on 18 August 1819

The proceedings were not of an ordinary character, but they will I trust, prove a salutary lesson to modern reformers. Hunt and his associates are in custody, and their flags etc. have been seized and destroyed by the special constables and soldiery, all of whom have behaved with the greatest spirit and temper, but forbearance [restraint] became impossible.

SOURCE 12 John Smith, a journalist for the *Liverpool Mercury*, speaking at the trial of Hunt, March 1820

In no case whatever did I see any attempt to resist nor any encouragement to resistance given by Mr Hunt, or any other person, either by word, look, or gesture. I saw no sticks lifted up against the military. I saw no brickbats or stones thrown till the [crowd had been broken up], when I saw one stone thrown. If any stones or brickbats had been thrown, or any sticks raised in defiance of the military, I must have seen it. I am more than six feet high, and therefore was able to see all that took place. I neither heard any offensive expressions uttered, nor saw any acts of violence committed by the people, from the time of their assembling to the time they left the field.

SOURCE 13 A list of those who died at Peterloo, or shortly afterwards. The inquest on the death of John Lees attracted considerable publicity as he had fought in the Duke of Wellington's army at the Battle of Waterloo and survived. The reformers exploited this.

Name	Town	Cause of death
Joseph Ashworth	Manchester	shot
Thomas Ashworth*	Manchester	sabred and trampled
John Ashton	Oldham	sabred and trampled
William Bradshaw	Bury	not recorded
Thomas Buckley	Chadderton	sabred and trampled
James Crompton	Barton	trampled
William Dawson	Saddleworth	sabred and trampled
Edmund Dawson	Saddleworth	sabred
William Fildes	Manchester	trampled
Mary Heys	Manchester	trampled
Sarah Jones	Manchester	not recorded
John Lees	Oldham	sabred
Arthur O'Neill	Manchester	trampled
Martha Partington	Manchester	trampled
John Rhodes	Hopwood	not recorded

*one of the special constables

SOURCE 14 Elizabeth Healey, whose husband was arrested and subsequently imprisoned for one year. After feeling sick she watched events from a house in Windmill Street. This interview took place a few days after the event

66 *By this time Mr Hunt was on the hustings addressing the people. In a minute or two some soldiers came riding up. The good folks of the house, and some who seemed to be visitors, said 'the soldiers were only to keep order, they would not meddle with the people'; but I was alarmed. The people shouted, and then the soldiers shouted, waving their swords. Then they rode amongst the people, and there was a great outcry, and a moment after a man passed without a hat, and wiping the blood off his head with his hand, and it ran down his arm in a great stream. The meeting was all in tumult; there were dreadful cries; the soldiers kept riding amongst the people and striking with their swords. The front door opened, and a number of men entered, carrying the body of a decent, middle-aged woman, who had been killed.* 99

SOURCE 15 Edward Baines, a reformer on the hustings. He saw himself as impartial since he disapproved of the meeting and was only there as an observer

66 *On 16 August 1819, when seventy or eighty thousand persons were collected at Manchester, on St Peter's Field, to petition for parliamentary reform, and when Henry Hunt was addressing the meeting, a troop of Manchester Yeomanry was ordered by the magistrates to take Hunt and others into custody; and in carrying out this most unwise and improper order, the Yeomanry dashed furiously into the midst of an unarmed multitude, whom they trampled down and struck with their sabres, till they surrounded the hustings, which they threw down, and took all the persons who had been upon them into custody. Then, galloping over the field, they dispersed the immense assemblage, who fled in every direction. Several persons were killed and hundreds wounded by this military outrage.* 99

The aftermath of Peterloo

The fact that British troops had attacked unarmed people at a public meeting shocked many, and the Radicals began to call it the Peterloo Massacre. This was an ironic reference to the Battle of Waterloo of 1815. Although the government was privately unhappy with the Manchester magistrates' handling of the situation, it had little choice but to back them. The Prince Regent congratulated the magistrates on their 'prompt, decisive and efficient measures'. Henry Hunt was sent to prison for two years.

The Government blocked attempts to hold an enquiry into Peterloo and instead passed the Six Acts. These helped to stop the Radical movement.

9. Look back at your answer to question 2 on page 16 where you explained how the Radicals campaigned. How would the Six Acts make campaigning difficult for them after 1819?

The Six Acts 1819

The Six Acts, passed in 1819, had a number of specific terms, all of which were intended to make life more difficult for the Radicals. They:

■ banned unofficial military training
■ gave magistrates the power to search houses for arms
■ ordered that political meetings could only be held with the permission of a magistrate
■ increased the tax on newspapers in order to make them too expensive for the working classes
■ made it easier to suppress publications that were regarded as seditious
■ made it easier for magistrates to bring people more quickly to trial.

It is worth noting that the Six Acts were not as harsh as some legislation in other European countries. Some of the measures were no more than temporary and the Government did not possess the necessary police force to enforce them.

Even so, the Six Acts was probably an over-reaction. There were only a few parts of Britain, mainly towns and cities, where there were sufficient concentrations of working men to give the Radicals hopes of success; it was never a national movement. It is also important to remember that at this time the events of Peterloo were an isolated incident of violence.

The Cato Street Conspiracy

Peterloo and the Six Acts were not the end of the troubles. Soon afterwards an event occurred that seemed to justify government fears – the Cato Street Conspiracy. A group of militant reformers, led by Arthur Thistlewood, planned to murder the entire Cabinet. Unknown to them, one of their number, George Edwards, was a government informer. He supposedly recruited members and suggested the plan. What is certain is that he passed on details of the plot, and the conspirators were arrested. Thistlewood and four others were convicted and sentenced to be hanged, beheaded and quartered, the executions taking place on 1 May 1820. This was the last public beheading in Britain.

A few weeks earlier, on the night of 11 April, a group of armed men, thinking they were part of a national uprising, had marched from Barnsley to Huddersfield. When it became apparent that there were no other risings the men slipped away; but both events frightened the authorities. There was certainly some evidence to justify the belief that groups of revolutionaries were in existence in the early part of 1820.

SOURCE 16 The arrest of the Cato Street conspirators. The conspirators resisted arrest and one of the Bow Street Runners (a police force) was killed. This drawing was published in March 1820

■ REVIEW ACTIVITY

At a number of places in this book you are going to 'take the revolutionary temperature' of Britain to decide how great the danger of revolution was. This is the first point, 1820.

1. Look back over the Introduction and Chapter 1 to remind yourself of what Britain was like between 1815 and 1820. You should also look at the timeline on pages 10–11.

2. Make your own judgement as to how great the danger of revolution was in 1820, and shade in your own copy of the thermometer accordingly. If you think the danger of revolution was very high, you'll shade in all the way up to the top. If you think the danger was not so serious, you won't shade so far.

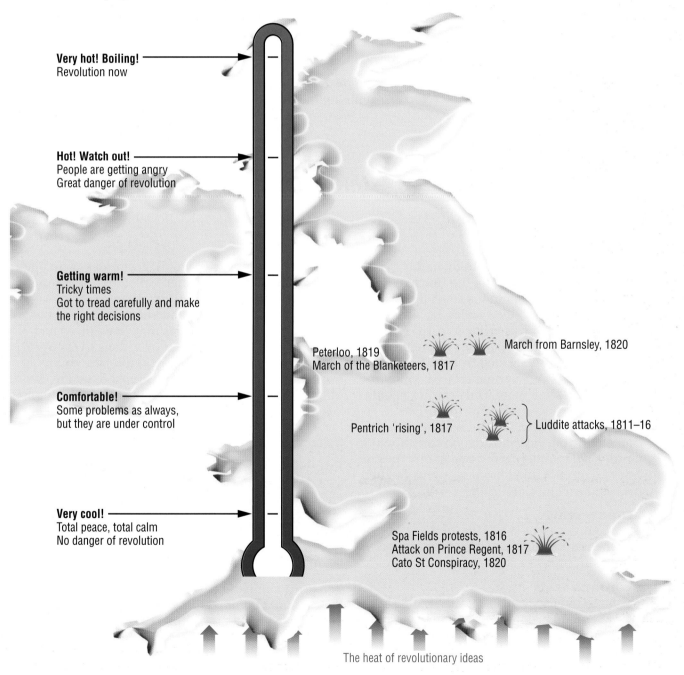

Very hot! Boiling!
Revolution now

Hot! Watch out!
People are getting angry
Great danger of revolution

Getting warm!
Tricky times
Got to tread carefully and make
the right decisions

Comfortable!
Some problems as always,
but they are under control

Very cool!
Total peace, total calm
No danger of revolution

Peterloo, 1819
March of the Blanketeers, 1817

March from Barnsley, 1820

Pentrich 'rising', 1817

Luddite attacks, 1811–16

Spa Fields protests, 1816
Attack on Prince Regent, 1817
Cato St Conspiracy, 1820

The heat of revolutionary ideas

chapter 2

WHY DID SO MANY PEOPLE DEMAND ELECTORAL REFORM?

THE ELECTORAL SYSTEM of the early nineteenth century was very different from the one we have today. In our current system:

- Members of Parliament (MPs) each represent a CONSTITUENCY and each constituency has roughly the same number of voters
- MPs are paid a salary so that anyone can afford to become an MP
- every man and woman over the age of eighteen is eligible to vote (with some exceptions)
- MPs are only allowed to spend a small amount on their election campaign to make sure the contest is fair
- when voters actually cast their votes they do so in secret, so they do not feel threatened by pressure to vote for a particular candidate.

We see all these things as necessary for our system to be a fair parliamentary DEMOCRACY. In this chapter you are going to find out how the system worked in the period we are studying and why so many people demanded change.

How did the electoral system work before 1832?

The House of Commons

Britain was governed by a combination of the monarchy, the House of Lords and the House of Commons. The House of Commons controlled finances and was central to the system. Its authority came from the fact that it was elected. In 1831 there were 658 elected MPs. Three-quarters of them were English MPs; the rest represented Ireland, Scotland and Wales. The voters in a particular area, known as a constituency, elected them. Only certain people held the FRANCHISE (were allowed to vote). The poorest people had no vote. Nor did women. The people who could vote varied from one constituency to another. In England there were two main types of constituency – counties and boroughs – plus the two universities, Oxford and Cambridge.

English county seats
The English counties elected 82 MPs. In these counties all the men who owned FREEHOLD property worth over 40 shillings a year were allowed to vote.

English borough seats
The boroughs or towns elected 394 MPs. In these there were several different types of franchise. Over half of the boroughs had fewer than 600 voters and the majority were in southern England. Many of the new industrial cities such as Birmingham and Manchester had no MPs to represent them.

Those boroughs with small electorates were open to corruption and were often called rotten boroughs. Others, which were under the influence of aristocratic landowners who either employed the voters, owned the properties they lived in, or had some other economic power over their lives, were called pocket boroughs. For example, the county of Cornwall had twenty boroughs represented by 40 MPs in 1830. All of these boroughs had fewer than 200 voters and members of the aristocracy or other local landowners influenced every single one of them.

English universities
The members of Oxford and Cambridge universities elected two MPs. In each case there was an electorate of 500.

■ ACTIVITY

You are a young man who wants to get into Parliament. You have some money but not a huge amount. In which of the different types of parliamentary seat would you choose to stand for election? Make a list of the possibilities and comment briefly on how you could get elected in each.

How were elections conducted?

General elections, in which every constituency voted, had to be held after seven years. In some constituencies, the pocket boroughs, there was no need for a campaign because the local landowner was so influential that no one would stand against his candidates. Uncontested elections were common in this period. In other constituencies electoral campaigns could be influenced by bribery. It was considered quite acceptable, although actually illegal, for voters to sell their vote to the highest bidder. The price of a vote varied depending on the number of voters in a constituency. Often candidates provided treats and free drinks for voters, and paid the expenses of those who had to travel some distance to cast their vote. Voting was not secret – voters had to announce in public who they were voting for. This could lead to physical intimidation (see pages 30–33).

Who were the MPs?

All of the 658 Members of Parliament were men. They were unpaid, so they had to have an independent income. This meant that they were drawn from the land-owning ruling classes. Roughly half of them owed their seats to the influence of members of the House of Lords or were actually related to them.

These MPs did not all belong to a political party in the way that our MPs do today. There were two main groups, the Whigs and the TORIES, to which some MPs belonged. Those who always supported the Government were known as 'placemen'. They gave their support in return for posts, pensions or sinecures (jobs with a salary but no work). The majority of MPs would vote for one side or the other depending on how their own interests were affected in each case.

SOURCE 1 A scene from the BBC Television serialisation of George Eliot's novel *Middlemarch*. Mr Brooke is standing for election and is making his first speech to the voters

The types of franchise for English borough seats

Burgage boroughs

The right to vote was directly linked to owning a particular property or 'burgage plot'. When such properties were put up for sale they would be advertised as including a vote. None of the 29 boroughs in this category had more than 400 voters. 23 had fewer than 200 voters. The worst example was Old Sarum, the original site of the city of Salisbury. Here two MPs represented just seven voters.

Corporation boroughs

The right to vote belonged to any member of the corporation or council. Such corporations were not elected; the members selected new members. All of the 25 boroughs in this category had fewer than 70 voters.

Freeman boroughs

The right to vote was given to any freeman of the borough. How someone became a freeman varied from place to place. In some the freeman had to live there in order to vote. In others it was enough just to turn up and vote in elections. Of the 92 boroughs in this category, 40 had 200 voters or fewer. An extreme example was Dunwich. The 30 freemen could not live in the borough because it was under the North Sea, a victim of coastal erosion.

Potwalloper boroughs

The right to vote was directly linked to owning a property with a hearth (fireplace) and lockable door, proof of which could be given by rattling your key in your cooking pot, or 'potwalloping'! Of the twelve boroughs in this category, five had 200 voters or fewer.

I'm the only taxpayer here, so I'm the only voter. I elect you as my MP. I'm sure you'll do as I tell you.

Scot and Lot boroughs

The right to vote was directly linked to paying certain local rates and taxes. What these were varied from place to place. Often the electorate was large. Westminster had 11,576 voters in 1831. However, eighteen boroughs in this category had 200 voters or fewer. Gatton was the worst example. It consisted of six houses and their owner had the right to elect two MPs. In 1830 the owner sold them for £180,000.

Two modern judgements on the electoral system before 1832

It is often said that one of the major problems with the electoral system was that large towns and cities like Birmingham and Manchester were not represented. The historian Professor Norman McCord has pointed out that owners of property worth more than 40 shillings in those cities were entitled to vote in county elections. So Birmingham voters had an important influence in the Warwickshire county election and the voters of Manchester could similarly not be ignored in the Lancashire county election.

The historian Frank O'Gorman has pointed out that great activity surrounded elections. Yes, local élites tried to keep their position in the community by getting their nominees elected, but they still needed the support of the local interests, as represented by the voters. Elections also involved the participation of non-voters who could express their views in the public meetings and on polling days. The voters themselves could not all be bought.

O'Gorman has argued that, 'The attitudes and behaviour of the voters are not those of people who were just mindless idiots, ready to be corrupted.' Over the next few pages you will be finding out what happened in the Shaftesbury election of 1830. You will decide whether the events in Shaftesbury support O'Gorman's view?

■ TASK

1. Old Britain said the existing electoral system was fine because it kept power in the hands of those who owned land and so had a big stake in Britain.
   a) What would New Britain say to that?
   b) What do you say to that?

Case study: the Shaftesbury election of 1830

SHAFTESBURY IS A small town in Dorset, with a population of 8518 in 1830. It was entitled to send two MPs to Parliament and was a Scot and Lot borough (see page 29). All male householders who had paid rates and taxes for six months prior to the election qualified to vote. This amounted to roughly 315 voters in 1830. In 1820 Robert, Lord Grosvenor, had bought about two-thirds of the houses in the town. From then on he owned 282 properties with 294 tenants and his estate dominated the town. He controlled the town corporation through his ownership of land and houses and through the economic influence of his estate. Local tradespeople were under pressure to vote for his nominees if they wanted to keep his favour and business. In the three parliamentary elections following his house purchases his nominees were elected unopposed.

In 1830, on the death of King George IV, a further election took place. Grosvenor put forward his two nominees, Edward Penrhyn and William Stratford Dugdale. As usual he expected his nominees to be elected. However, this time his opponents put forward another candidate, Francis Charles Knowles. Their opposition was as much to do with local issues, in other words electoral issues, as it was to do with national issues.

■ TASK

Draw up a table like the one below. Use the diary of events and Sources 2–5 to make notes showing how the events in Shaftesbury reflect what was wrong with the electoral system.

	Examples in Shaftesbury election of 1830
Bribery	
Corruption	
Intimidation	
Violence	
Lack of representation	

Let us imagine it is midsummer in Shaftesbury. An election meeting is in progress. Here is what happened.

This diary is made up, but it is very carefully based on evidence about the actual election. You can read some of that evidence on pages 32–33.

SOURCE 1 A modern artist's illustration of Mr Penrhyn, Mr Dugdale and Mr Knowles addressing the crowds in Shaftesbury on Monday 26 July

Monday 19 July 1830

The election campaign began.

Monday 26 July

There was a public debate between the two sides in the Market Place, one of several during the campaign. Knowles challenged the Grosvenor side to allow tenants to vote according to their consciences, without fear of eviction. At one point there was a scuffle between the supporters of the two sides. Many of the crowd were Grosvenor farming tenants carrying heavy sticks and organised by Lord Grosvenor's head gamekeeper. At the end of the day the Grosvenor nominees retired, having had the worst of the debate. Mr Knowles' supporters tried to dine at the Grosvenor Arms but were refused service. The landlord dared not serve them, for fear of '…giving offence to Lord Grosvenor's agent, which might lead to a notice to quit'.

Tuesday 3 August

Voting began at the town hall. Some voters complained of the treatment they had received from the Grosvenor agents. Mr Hiskins, a butcher, complained that these agents had taken the bed from under his wife and children because he was late with the rent of £3.

Voters had to stand before the poll bar and declare their vote out loud. Either side could challenge their right to vote and it was the job of the returning officer to decide whether to accept their vote. The returning officer was the Mayor, William Swyer, who was also Grosvenor's rent collector. Some were refused the vote because they had received Poor Relief, because they were not residents, or because they did not pay rates. Knowles' supporters feared that they were unfairly being refused the right to vote. 25 votes for Knowles were disallowed.

Thursday 5 August

When the poll closed on the third day the numbers were Penrhyn 153, Dugdale 133 and Knowles 115. That evening Knowles addressed a crowd estimated to number 10,000. Later, a crowd of 200 or 300 attacked the Grosvenor Arms, broke into the inn-yard, threw objects through the windows and battered the doors. None of Lord Grosvenor's supporters were injured. The crowd then went on to attack the houses of other Grosvenor supporters in the town. Mayor William Swyer sent for the military.

Friday 6 August

In the morning 44 men of the Second Dragoons arrived from Blandford. A hostile crowd later surrounded them but no violence occurred. Voting finished on this fourth day when the Mayor had decided on the eligibility of the disputed votes. The final poll stood at Penrhyn 169, Dugdale 145 and Knowles 121. Lord Grosvenor's two nominees were both elected as MPs for Shaftesbury. There was uproar at this result. Knowles' supporters believed that 'had justice been done he would have been elected'.

Monday 9 August

Mayor William Swyer, in his capacity as magistrate, sent four young men to Dorchester prison to await trial for their part in the attack on the Grosvenor Arms.

Wednesday 1 September

The four young men imprisoned in Dorchester prison since 9 August were brought home. They had been freed on bail. They were greeted on the way by church bells and large crowds celebrating their 'liberation'.

Thursday 2 September

In the morning the Grosvenor party organised a victory parade which was blocked by a street barricade. There were further disturbances in the afternoon. William Swyer swore in 100 special constables and armed them with short, heavy staves. When the MPs tried to dine at the Grosvenor Arms that evening another disturbance broke out which led to fighting and window-breaking. The Riot Act was read.

Tuesday 19 October

At the Dorchester QUARTER SESSIONS three bills of indictment were made against 33 inhabitants of Shaftesbury for alleged riots on Thursday 5 August and Thursday 2 September. The cases were to be tried at the Dorchester ASSIZES in March 1831.

SOURCE 2 Extracts from the speeches on 26 July

66 *Mr Knowles: 'The honourable gentleman states that Lord Grosvenor is at liberty to let his houses on whatever terms he pleases; this I deny. He has a right to exact, and to be paid, a fair rent for his houses, but he has no right to use them as the means of biasing or of corrupting the people in the way they choose to vote, and as to property, his deeds [legal documents of ownership] conveyed to him the bricks and mortar, but not the souls and bodies of their inhabitants. I will now make an appeal. I ask my opponents whether they will release from their promises those of Lord Grosvenor's tenants who have promised from fear of the consequences of a refusal, and in violation of their consciences? A promise under such circumstances cannot be binding.'*

Mr Penrhyn, to the voters: 'I do not think you ought to break your promises.' 99

1. From your reading of Source 3, in what ways did Francis Charles Knowles try to persuade men to vote for him?

SOURCE 3 A list of Mr Knowles' bills for the 1830 election

Mitre Inn	£139. 14. 2
Ship Inn	£113. 0. 0
Key Inn	£5. 9. 11
Crown Inn	£57. 12. 9
Ox Inn	£94. 9. 8
Cider House	£4. 5. 11
Half Moon Inn	£3. 4. 9
Black Dog, Ludwell	£3. 0. 0
Carpenter	£1. 5. 6
Milliners for ribbons	£1. 0. 0
Shirts	£1. 1. 1
The band (12 shillings per day per man)	£148. 12. 0
Sundry payments	£180. 2. 5
Beer and cider	£29. 13. 0
Reporters for writing election addresses and posters	£23. 0. 0
Clerk of the Peace, witness on disputed votes	£10. 0. 0
Lawyer's retainer fee	£20. 0. 0
Agents' fees	No charge
Printers (for 15,000 addresses and posters)	£48. 15. 0
Flags	£5. 0. 0
Cost of public dinner and tea, 17 and 18 August	£234. 5. 11
Total	£11,246. 12. 1

■ ACTIVITY

You are now going to take part in a mock election campaign. The two candidates will be CANVASSING for votes. What you have to do will be printed on the card that your teacher gives you. Remember, at this time it was considered acceptable for voters to sell their vote to the highest bidder (despite the fact that it was illegal). Just remember that the vote is in public. Everyone will hear whom you are voting for and it will be recorded in a pollbook – a list of the voters in a constituency and who they voted for.

LIST OF THOSE WHO HAVE RECEIVED
NOTICES TO QUIT,
WHICH NOTICES ARE SIGNED
By Mr. P. Chitty, on behalf of the Earl Grosvenor;
UP TO OCTOBER 18th, 1830.

K. at the end of the names, means that the elector voted for Mr KNOWLES; P. that he voted for his landlord's nominee, Mr. PENRHYN; and P. & K. that he gave one vote to his landlord's nominee, Mr. PENRHYN, and one to Mr. KNOWLES. The words Three or Six Months indicate the length of the notice.

IN ST. PETER'S PARISH.

H. NORTON . . . . *Shopkeeper* . . . . . *Six Months* . . . . K.
B.H. NORTON . . *Common Carrier* . *Three Months* . . . . K.
J. GARRETT . . . . *Cooper* . . . . *Six Months* . . . . . P. & K.
T. DUNHAM . . . . *Tailor & Draper* . . *Three Months* . . . . P.
C. WHITMARSH . *Mason* . . . . *Six Months* . . . . K.
FRAN. HOSKINS . *Labourer* . . . . *Six Months* . . . . K.
GEORGE FRY , , *Boot & Shoemaker* *Six Months* . . . . . P. & K.
I. MULLETT . . . . . *Saddler* . . . . *Six Months* . .DID NOT VOTE.

IN THE PARISH OF HOLY TRINITY.

H. FRICKER . . . . *Dairyman* . . . . *Six Months* . . . . . . P. & K.
C. WILMOTT . . . . *Labourer* . . . . *Three Months* . . . . K.
JOSEPH BOWN . . *Painter & Glazier* . *Three Months* . . . . .P.
HENRY CHITTY . . *Gentleman* . . . . . . *Six Months* . . . . . P. & K.
WM. ANDREWS . . *Cheese Dealer* . . . . *Three Months* . . . . K.
JAMES WHITE . . *Tailor & Draper* . . *Three Months* . . . . P.
R. BENNETT . . . . *Shirt-Wiremaker* . . *Three Months* . . . . P.
T. HIGGINS . . . . *Baker* . . . . *Six Months* . . . . K.

IN ST. JAMES' PARISH.

G. DOYLE . . . . . . *Gentleman* . . . . . . *Six Months* . . . . K.
R. BRICKELL . . . *Schoolmaster* . . . . *Six Months* . . . . K.
R. TANSWELL . . *Labourer* . . . . *Six Months* . . . . . P. & K.
JOHN MATHEWS . *Labourer* . . . . *Three Months* . . . . P. & K.
JAS. ANDREWS . . *Cheese Dealer* . . . . *Six Months* . . . . K.
JOHN DEAN . . . . . *Gardener* . . . . *Three Months* . . . . P. & K.

J. RUTTER, PRINTER, SHAFTESBURY.

LIST OF PERSONS INDICTED.

FIRST INDICTMENT,
For assaulting one William Swyer, one William Patteson, and one Thomas W. Nicholls, on the 2nd of September, 1830.
William Garrett, *one month.*
Stephen Dean, *discharged.*
Charles Hoskins, *discharged.*
James Upjohn, jun. *discharged.*
John Elkins, *one month.*
Elizabeth Dicketts, *one month.*
Philip Hopkins, *four months.*

Witnesses against them, Messrs. William Swyer, Patteson, *and* Nicholls.

SECOND INDICTMENT,
For a riot and assaulting the Special Constables, on the 2nd of September, 1830.
James Brockway, *two months.*
John Bugden, *one month.*
Thomas Dowding, jun. *discharged.*
George Elkins, *tried before.*
George Elkins, jun. *tried before.*
John Elkins, *one month.*
Charles Foot, *two months.*
William Garrett, *discharged.*
John Hiskins, *three months.*
Charles Hoskins, *discharged.*
Charles Mullens, *discharged.*
James Perry, *not tried.*
Thomas Read, *acquitted.*
Thomas Roberts, *not tried.*
Charles Stone, *one month.*
James Upjohn, jun. *not tried.*
Thomas Willmott, *two months.*
George Elkins, jun. *acquitted.*

James Andrews, jun. *acquitted.*
James Erle, *one month.*
Philip Hopkins, *four months.*
William Brickle, *acquitted.*
Robert Brickle, *acquitted.*
Mark Woodcock, *acquitted.*

The Second Indictment was supported by the evidence of William Swyer, James Lush Buckland, Jesse Targett, Jeremiah Wilkins, Thomas Imber, William Brockway, William Gatehouse, Thomas Brickle, John Gatehouse, Thomas King, Robert Warren, Caroline Colbourne, Betsey London, *and others.*

THIRD INDICTMENT,
For a riot and breaking windows on the 5th of August, 1830.
Charles Willmott, *discharged.*
William Andrews, *discharged.*
Stephen Dean, *discharged.*
Charles Hoskins, *discharged.*
Charles Jenkins, *discharged.*
Charles Terry Short, *discharged.*
Thomas Alford, *discharged.*
Jeremiah Davidge, *discharged.*
John Rutter, *postponed until next assize.*

The Third Indictment was supported by the evidence of William Edwards, Thomas Burridge Chitty, William Swayne, John Short, John Short, jun. Robert Burridge, Wm. Jay, Patience Hurd, Philip Ring Hurd, Charles Shepherd, *and others.*

NOTE.—Those who were discharged were fined 1s. each, and bound in their own recognizances to keep the peace for one year.

It is intended shortly to publish, from short-hand notes, a more full account of these trials, including the Judge's remarks on the Earl Grosvenor and his Agents.

SOURCE 4 A list of Lord Grosvenor's tenants who received notice to quit and who they voted for, published by John Rutter, printer, Shaftesbury. John Rutter was the leader of the group who had put forward Francis Charles Knowles for election

SOURCE 5 A list of those indicted for (charged with) riot in 1831, published by A. B. Rutter, bookseller and printer, Shaftesbury

What was wrong with the electoral system?

■ **ACTIVITY**

There were a variety of opinions about what was wrong with the electoral system. Sources 1–3 are cartoons that show some of these. What can you learn from them? Some points have already been made on Source 1. Record your own ideas about Sources 2 and 3. You can get enlarged copies of each from your teacher.

George Cruikshank (1792–1878)

Cruikshank first worked as an illustrator of children's books and song sheets. In the 1830s and 1840s he illustrated Charles Dickens' novels, his best-known work being for *Oliver Twist* (see page 62). From 1811 onwards he drew political cartoons satirising politicians and events. He was deeply shocked by the Peterloo Massacre and his response was the drawing *The Peterloo Massacre* (see pages 20–21).

Each year from 1835 until 1854 he published *George Cruikshank's Comic Almanac*. This gave his view of each year's events and forms an invaluable source for the historian trying to get an overview of our period. He did not hold strong political views and so as well as pro-Radical prints he also produced anti-Radical prints. He produced over 15,000 drawings during his life but never became rich.

The value of cartoons like those by Cruikshank is that through their content they tell us which people and events were considered important at the time. Their treatment also gives us clues to the opinions some people held.

SOURCE 1 *The System That Works So Well!*, a cartoon by George Cruikshank

34

S**OURCE 2** *A Show of Hands for the Whig Candidate as He Distributes 50,000 Reasons for Voting for Him*, a cartoon by George Cruikshank published *c.* 1840

S**OURCE 3** *Old Sarum*, a cartoon by George Cruikshank published in 1832

Problems with the system: a summary

As you have already learnt from your work on cartoons and the earlier enquiries in this chapter, there were a number of problems with the electoral system. These are summarised in the spider diagram.

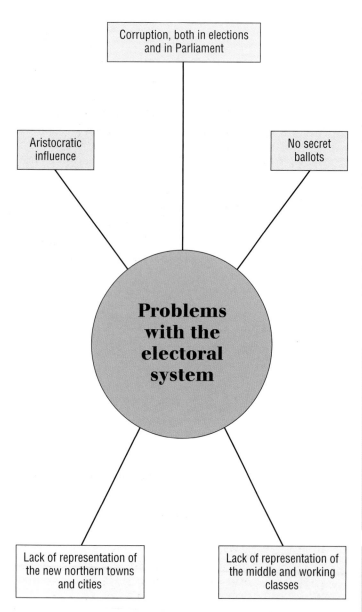

Corruption, both in elections and in Parliament

Aristocratic influence

No secret ballots

Problems with the electoral system

Lack of representation of the new northern towns and cities

Lack of representation of the middle and working classes

How did some people defend the existing electoral system?

Most opponents of reform were upper-class landowners. There were three strands to their argument.

Firstly, some argued, 'If it ain't broke, don't fix it!' At any time in history there will always be those who are against change simply because it is change. They argued that the system had worked well for a long time and that those with a stake in the country, the landowners, were the best people to run it.

Secondly, they pointed to events in France as an example of what would happen if things were changed. They felt that reform would lead to revolution.

Thirdly, they were unwilling to change a system they controlled to their own advantage. They didn't want to lose power.

The Duke of Wellington was the most influential voice in this group. In 1830 he resigned as Prime Minister because he and his Tory Government were unwilling to reform the electoral system. The House of Commons represented the landowners, the City of London, the universities, the boroughs and the Church. If these important elements of society, or 'interests', were represented then, they argued, the people of the nation were represented.

SOURCE 4 An extract from a speech by George Canning, published in the *Quarterly Review* in 1820

66 *If the boroughs of Knaresborough, Tavistock, Horsham, Winchelsea, Peterborough were disenfranchised [lost the right to elect MPs], and the right of election were transferred to more populous places, to Birmingham, Manchester, Sheffield, Leeds . . . I should regret that the House of Commons should be deprived of so many great lights [distinguished and able MPs].* 99

SOURCE 5 Part of a speech by Sir Robert Inglis in the House of Commons, 2 March 1831

66 *The House of Commons is now the most complete representation of the interests of the people which has ever assembled in any age or country. It includes within itself those who can urge the wants and defend the claims of the landed, the commercial and the professional classes of the country.* 99

Why did some people want to change the system?

Upper-class reformers

These were men who had come to realise that the changes in society required a change to the electoral system. They feared that without reform there could be revolution. Earl Grey, a wealthy landowner, belonged to this group. On Wellington's resignation in 1830 he led the new Whig Government which introduced the Reform BILL.

Middle-class reformers

The banker Thomas Attwood founded the Birmingham Political Union in 1829. Its purpose was to press for political reform (see Source 7). By 1832 it had over 25,000 members – this in a city with a population in 1831 of 144,000 and no MPs! Similar political unions were started in towns and cities all over the country. Most wanted representation for the new manufacturing and trade interests, essentially the middle classes.

Working-class reformers

Other political unions wanted representation for all men. It was from these groups that Chartism was later to develop (see pages 142–56).

SOURCE 6 Sir Philip Francis, MP for Appleby, describing his election

The fact is that yesterday morning between 11 and 12am I was unanimously elected by one voter to represent this ancient borough in Parliament. There was no other candidate, no opposition, no poll demanded … On Friday morning I shall quit this triumphant scene with flying colours and a noble determination not to see it again in less than seven years. "

SOURCE 7 An extract from the Declaration of the Birmingham Political Union, commenting on the House of Commons in 1830

That honourable House, in its present state, is too far removed in habits, wealth and station from the wants and interests of the lower and middle classes of the people to have … any close identity of feeling with them. The great aristocratic interests of all kinds are well represented there … But the interests of Industry and of Trade have scarcely any representatives at all! "

SOURCE 8 An extract from a letter from John Wilson Croker to the then Prime Minister, George Canning, 3 April 1827

I think it right to send to you a memorandum which will show you, in one view, how impossible it is to do anything satisfactory towards a government in this country without the help of the aristocracy. I know that you must be well aware of this, yet the following summary may not be useless to you, though I know that it is imperfect.

Numbers of members returned to the House of Commons by the influence of some of the peers:

__Tories:__ Lord Lonsdale 9, Lord Hertford 8, Duke of Rutland 6, Duke of Newcastle 5, Lord Yarborough 5, Lord Powis 4, Lord Falmouth 4, Lord Anglesey 4, Lord Aylesbury 4, Lord Radnor 3, Duke of Northumberland 4, Duke of Buccleugh 4, Marquess of Stafford 3, Duke of Buckingham 3, Lord Mount-Edgcumbe 4, total 70; besides at least 12 or 14 who have each two seats, say 26.
__Total: 96.__

__Whigs:__ Lord Fitzwilliam 8, Lord Darlington 7, Duke of Devonshire 7, Duke of Norfolk 6, Lord Grosvenor 6, Duke of Bedford 4, Lord Carrington 4, total 42; with about half a dozen who have each a couple of seats 12.
__Total: 54.__ "

■ ACTIVITY

You are going to produce a newspaper article on the issue of parliamentary reform.

1. Decide whether you are going to argue:
   a) for reform or
   b) against reform.
2. Look back at Sources 1–8 in this enquiry and at previous enquiries in Chapter 2. Make a note of the sources and examples that support your argument.
3. Make a note of any sources and examples that support the opposite point of view. How could you argue against them?
4. Now use the information you have gathered to write your article.

Why was the 1832 Reform Act passed?

THE REFORM MOVEMENT did not disappear after the events of Peterloo and the government crackdown that followed. It had too many supporters for that to happen. Despite the opposition from the aristocracy and the upper classes, the reformers eventually got what they wanted, the 1832 Reform Act. We are now going to look at the reasons why that Act was passed.

■ TASK

Here are some factors which led to the passing of the Reform Act:

- ■ support for reform from the middle classes in political unions
- ■ the press
- ■ fear of revolution
- ■ the fall of the Tory Government led by the Duke of Wellington in 1830 and their defeat in the 1831 general election
- ■ working-class riots, 1830–32
- ■ the activities of reformers such as Francis Place.

1. a) As you read the following three pages, make notes using the table your teacher will give you.
   b) Use your notes to help you write your answer to question 2.
2. 'All six factors were equally important reasons why the 1832 Reform Act was passed.' Do you agree?

A new king

In 1820 King George III died and was succeeded by his unpopular son, the Prince Regent. The new King George IV wanted to take the opportunity to divorce his wife, Queen Caroline, for adultery. The very public divorce case led to great popular sympathy for the Queen and hostility towards the Government. She died in 1821 and at her funeral the crowds rioted and forced the authorities to allow her funeral procession to pass through the city of London.

During the 1820s there were attempts by the Whig party to promote reform but the Tory Government defeated them all. The pressure for reform came from a number of groups. The industrial manufacturers were largely based in towns and cities in the north of England, which did not have MPs to represent them. They realised that their interests were not always those of the landowners who dominated Parliament. As they grew in confidence, through their business success and their involvement in local government, they began to press for reform.

Political unions

In 1828 the banker Thomas Attwood founded the Birmingham Political Union. Its aim was to campaign for reform by organising public meetings and petitions. The organisers claimed that 15,000 people attended the first meeting in January 1830. By 1832 the membership had reached roughly 25,000.

The working man has no need of the vote! The interests of the manufacturer and the men he employs are the same. It is the manufacturer and men like him whose voice must be heard in Parliament.

Francis Place, founder of the National Political Union

The interests of the workers and the employers are not the same. All men should have the vote!

A member of the National Union of the Working Classes

SOURCE 1 Different attitudes among members of political unions towards reform

These figures show how many people supported reform in Birmingham. The success of Attwood encouraged others to set up political unions in towns and cities all over Britain. These represented a powerful force that the Government could not ignore.

While the political unions all wanted reform they did not all want exactly the same kind of reform. The middle-class manufacturers within them wanted their interests represented in Parliament by people like themselves. This was the line taken by Francis Place who organised the National Political Union. The working-class members and more radical thinkers like William Lovett wanted more. Lovett, with Henry Hetherington, founded the National Union of the Working Classes. Inevitably, because of their higher status in society, the views of the middle classes carried more weight.

The press

An important place for the reformers to argue their case was in the press. By 1830 national newspapers like *The Times* were certainly in favour of some sort of reform. At a local level, particularly in the unrepresented towns and cities, newspapers such as the *Leeds Mercury, Manchester Guardian, Newcastle Chronicle* and *Sheffield Independent* were much stronger in their support. Their editors, men like Edward Baines of the *Leeds Mercury*, commented upon what was said in Parliament and wrote articles and editorials arguing in favour of reform. They helped to form opinion, as well as giving voice to local views. In some cases they were closely linked with the political unions.

Growing pressure for reform

In the period 1829–32 a number of events combined to increase the pressure for reform. Poor harvests in 1828, 1829 and 1830 led to higher food prices and hardship for the poorer members of rural and urban society. There were economic slumps in 1829 and 1831 that led to increased unemployment for the working classes and financial difficulties for the middle classes. The first great CHOLERA epidemic swept Britain from 1831–32. In rural southern England there were disturbances known as the Swing Riots (see pages 44–51), while in France in July 1830 there was another revolution. Fear of revolution in Britain grew.

In June 1830 King George IV died and was succeeded by his brother, William IV. In the general election that followed many pro-reform candidates were elected. In November 1830 the Tory Government of the Duke of Wellington fell from power. The new Whig Government of Earl Grey was in favour of reform. Before accepting the post of Prime Minister, Earl Grey insisted that the King agree to a Reform Bill. To some historians this is the turning point in the period we are studying.

Attempts to pass the Reform Bill

The Whig aristocrats drafting the Reform Bill had a simple brief. They were to draw up a Bill that would deal with all the legitimate objections to the existing system whilst preventing any threat of revolution in Britain. One of their fundamental reforms, Lord Durham's proposal for vote by secret ballot, was rejected at the drafting stage on the grounds that it would undermine landowners' control of their tenants' votes. (Look back at the events in Shaftesbury in 1830 on pages 30–33.) The reformers did deal with other criticisms but when the Bill was debated in Parliament it faced great opposition. This produced a political crisis and the Whig Government insisted on another general election. This was fought on the issue of reform and the Whigs were successful. Once again the Bill was debated and this time the House of Lords blocked it on 8 October 1831.

The immediate consequences of this were working-class riots and disturbances in many places, most seriously in Derby, Nottingham, Merthyr Tydfil and Bristol. (See Source 2 on the next page.)

Political crisis

The Bill was debated for the third time and again the House of Lords resisted. The King did not back Earl Grey's threat to create 50 new peers to get the Bill through, so in April 1832 Earl Grey resigned. Once again there was a political crisis, the 'Days of May'. Some historians regard this as the moment when Britain hovered on the brink of revolution. Even Thomas Attwood in Birmingham talked of taking up arms. The Whigs had resigned but the Tories were unable to form a government.

Reformers like Francis Place held public meetings and organised petitions. Place even suggested that investors should withdraw all their money from banks to create a financial crisis, with the slogan 'To stop the Duke [of Wellington], go for gold'. This was effectively the middle classes threatening force and was enough to push the Government into action. The King was forced to agree to Earl Grey's demands, the threat of new peers was enough to stop any further opposition from the House of Lords and the Reform Act finally became law on 7 June 1832.

SOURCE 2 The Bristol riots, October 1831. Twelve people died in the riots and over 100 rioters were arrested. 31 were sentenced to death, four of whom were hanged while the rest were transported

SOURCE 3 An extract from a letter written by the London lawyer Matthew Davenport-Hill to the Whig reformer Lord Brougham, October 1831

❝ I have been these two days in Birmingham and have taken some pains to ascertain [find out] the feelings of the people. Peace will however be preserved I have no doubt, if a speedy prospect can be held out of passing the Bill. I have also been through the West of England and South Wales and the result of my observations is that nothing but a speedy reform can avert revolution. ❞

Reform Committee,

Anxious to preserve as far as may be in their power, the property and peace of this *Town and Neighbourhood* from further violation, and deprecating the scenes of tumult, riot and destruction which have already taken place, earnestly intreat the *Inhabitants of this Town and Neighbourhood* to abstain from those *nightly tumultuous assemblages* which have ed to these breaches of the peace, and to use all their exertions to prevent others from engaging in the same, convinced that such outrages are *disgraceful to Englishmen* and most injurious to the *Cause of Reform.*

Masters and Parents are particularly requested to use their utmost endeavours to keep their children and servants at home.

BLANDFORD, October 19th, 1831.

SOURCE 4 A public notice for Blandford in Dorset

How great were the changes made by the 1832 Reform Act?

THE REFORM ACT made changes in two key areas:

■ it extended the franchise
■ it redistributed seats.

Changes to the franchise

The right to vote still depended upon property but changes were made to both county and borough seats. In the counties only those owning the freehold of land worth more than 40 shillings a year had been eligible to vote. The vote was now also given to all male copyholders (an old-fashioned way of renting land or property) of land worth £10 per annum and to all male leaseholders of land worth more than £50 per annum.

In the boroughs one new qualification replaced all the old ones. The right to vote was given to all male householders occupying property worth at least £10 per annum. The impact of this was not the same everywhere in Britain because of different property values. For example, in the London borough constituencies it produced a large electorate because of high property values, whereas in Leeds, where property values were much lower, far fewer people gained the right to vote.

The redistribution of seats

Some boroughs gained two MPs, others gained one. At the same time some boroughs lost their MPs or were only able to return one Member. Source 1 shows the changes in detail.

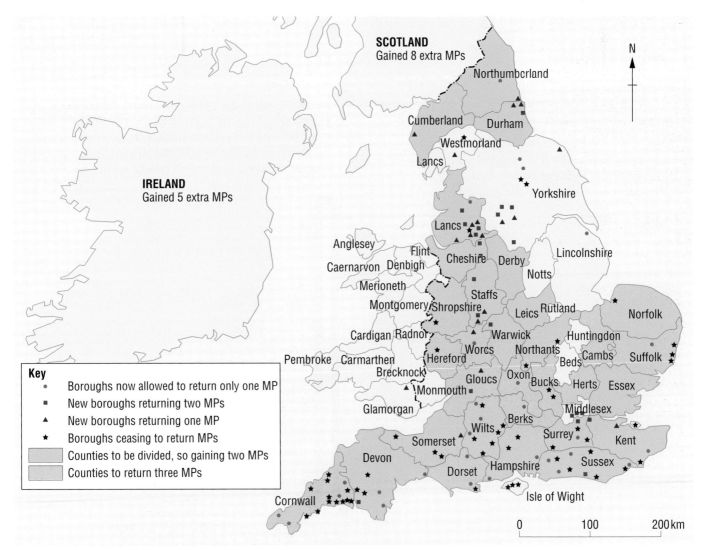

Key
- • Boroughs now allowed to return only one MP
- ■ New boroughs returning two MPs
- ▲ New boroughs returning one MP
- ★ Boroughs ceasing to return MPs
- Counties to be divided, so gaining two MPs
- Counties to return three MPs

SCOTLAND
Gained 8 extra MPs

IRELAND
Gained 5 extra MPs

SOURCE 1 A map of the British Isles showing the redistribution of seats under the 1832 Reform Act

How great was the Reform Act?

This Act used to be called the Great Reform Act by historians but the term is not always used now. Before the Reform Act something like one in ten men in England and Wales had the right to vote; afterwards it was more like one in five. Most of these new voters were prosperous middle-class men. The majority of the working classes still did not have the vote. The reforms did nothing for them.

In the first general election that followed the Reform Act over 70 per cent of the MPs represented the landed interest. In many constituencies the electorate, although bigger than it had been before the Act was passed, might still be quite small in relation to the total population and still be unrepresentative. About 50 seats were still controlled by individuals. So the Act represented no more than a stage in the process of reform. It certainly gave a greater voice to the industrial north of England. To its Whig architects it had achieved its key objectives. It had held off the threat of revolution by satisfying many of the moderate objectors to the old system. But it still maintained the power of the aristocracy and the influence of land. For some reformers, mainly the middle class, it did enough but for many others there was still much to do. The movement that arose from this dissatisfaction was Chartism and you will find out more about this in Chapter 8.

Essentially the Reform Act was Old Britain, the landed interest, allowing New Britain, the middle-class manufacturing interest, a share in power. After 1832 this combination of Old and New Britain moved to tackle some of the major problems facing Britain, problems of poverty and of working and living conditions. Sometimes the two worked together in harmony, sometimes in conflict.

■ REVIEW ACTIVITY

At a number of places in this book you are 'taking the revolutionary temperature' to decide how great the danger of revolution was. This is the second point, May 1832.

1. First look back over the events leading up to the passing of the Reform Bill in June 1832.

2. Now shade in your copy of the thermometer according to how great you think the danger of revolution was in May 1832. If you believe the danger was very great at this time, you'll shade all the way to the top. If you think the danger was not so serious, you won't shade so far.

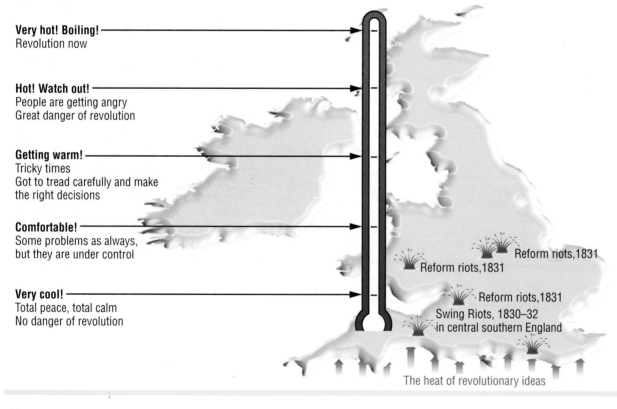

Very hot! Boiling!
Revolution now

Hot! Watch out!
People are getting angry
Great danger of revolution

Getting warm!
Tricky times
Got to tread carefully and make the right decisions

Comfortable!
Some problems as always, but they are under control

Very cool!
Total peace, total calm
No danger of revolution

Reform riots, 1831
Reform riots, 1831
Reform riots, 1831
Swing Riots, 1830–32 in central southern England

The heat of revolutionary ideas

section 2

DEALING WITH THE TORRENT OF SOCIAL PROBLEMS

chapter 3

HOW WERE THE POOR TREATED AND HOW DID THEY RESPOND?

YOU ARE NOW going to look at a particular group of people – the poor and the downtrodden. Their main concern was not getting the right to vote, but rather getting enough food to feed themselves and their children. So what did they do, and how did the Government respond?

Were the Swing rioters a threat to the Government?

THE SWING RIOTS were disturbances that broke out in the autumn of 1830. More than a thousand incidents took place, including machine breaking, arson, wage riots, people being sent threatening letters and money being extorted from farmers. They were known as the Swing Riots because 'Swing' or 'Captain Swing' was the name signed on many of the threatening letters (see Source 1). Although many English counties were affected, the greatest number of incidents took place in the agricultural areas of southern and eastern England.

■ TASK

1. Copy the table below and use it to make notes on the Swing Riots nationally. Read pages 44–47 and use Sources 1–7 to help you.
2. Use Sources 8–17 to help you decide if what happened in Dorset fitted the national pattern.

	England	Dorset
What were the causes of the Swing Riots?		
What did the rioters do?		
Who were the rioters?		
What was the government response?		
Aftermath and punishment		

3. Now use your notes to help you answer the key question: were the Swing rioters a threat to the Government?

SOURCE 1 A threatening letter sent to Mr P. Rumsey, Mere, Wiltshire

We understand you be about to put up your Threshing Machine as you cannot afford to pay men to thresh as you ought although you seem to be such a man of consequence. If you dare put up that cursed Machine you may depend upon it fire shall be the <u>consequence</u> and I hope to god that you will <u>feel the heat.</u> Show this to your drinking companions who have Threshing Machines. It save us the trouble of writing to them as it makes no difference to us whether water or steam powers them. I hope you will take warning by this and not give us the trouble to call on you. Employ the poor to Thresh with the flail as they used to do, do not boast <u>too much</u> of your bravery, as you will come down with your Machine.

Swing

SOURCE 2 A modern illustration of Swing rioters breaking a threshing machine

What were the causes of the Swing Riots?

The poor harvest in 1830, which followed poor harvests in 1828 and 1829, and promised a hard winter of poverty and unemployment

A vague sense of expectation caused by the July 1830 revolution in France and the beginning of the crisis over reform of Parliament in England

The population growth in rural areas. In some areas this was not accompanied by a growth in employment. Often there was a decline in cottage industry and large-scale manufacturing did not develop to replace it. This led to a surplus of labour and a fall in wages.

Higher food prices

The introduction of cheap Irish labour. In some places labourers had a choice of working for lower wages or not working at all.

The introduction of new technology – threshing machines. These replaced labourers. Threshing by hand was the only paid work available in the winter.

The post-war (1815) slump in agriculture. Prices fell and so did the wages paid to labourers.

Rural poverty. Over 10 per cent of the total population of the southern and eastern counties were on Poor Relief. During the 1820s there were increasing attempts to cut the cost of Poor Relief, which made this problem worse.

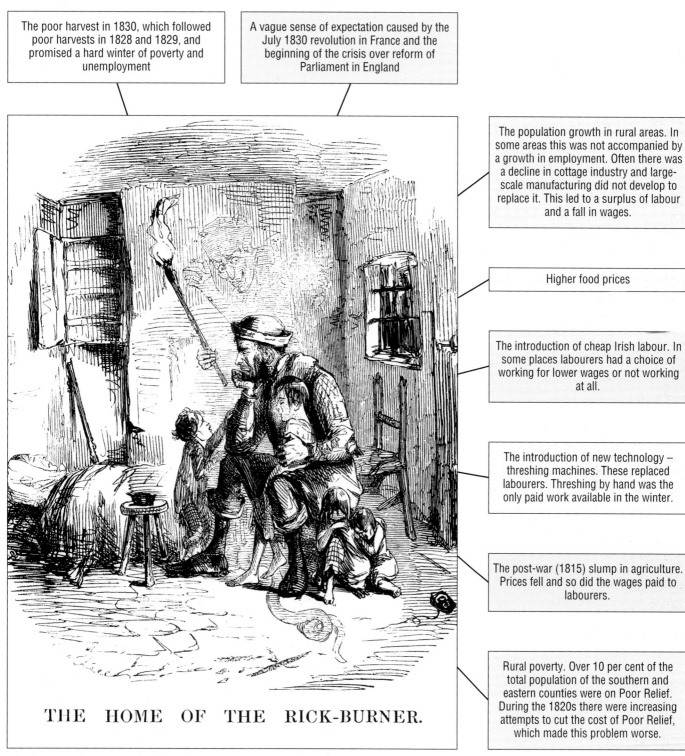

THE HOME OF THE RICK-BURNER.

SOURCE 3 A cartoon of a labourer in his poverty-stricken cottage, published in *Punch* in 1844. *Punch* was a satirical magazine of the time

1. What does the cartoonist in Source 3 identify as the major cause of the disturbances?

SOURCE 4 A graph showing wage levels in rural areas and food prices. The graph shows national trends. Agricultural wages in the south were lower than in the north. In the north people could find alternative employment in the new industrial towns, so farmers there had to pay higher wages to prevent their farm workers from leaving. There were variations in wage levels in the south too. Poor wages was one of the causes of the Swing Riots, but there were others

Key
— Agricultural wages in England
— Food prices

SOURCE 5 An extract from William Cobbett's *Rural Rides*. He is describing rural poverty. Cobbett planned his travels so that he could find out about the real state of the countryside and used the material for articles in his *Political Register*, founded in 1816. This was a cheap newspaper in support of reform, read by the poorer classes

66 Those who do the work are half starved ... What injustice, what a hellish system it must be to make those who raise the food skin and bone and nakedness, while the food and drink are heaped on the rich and undeserving. 99

2. What would Justice Alderson (Source 6) have thought of William Cobbett, the author of Source 5?
3. On what does Justice Alderson blame rural poverty?
4. How does he think Britain compares to other European countries in the treatment of the poor?

SOURCE 6 An extract from the Charge (speech) of Mr Justice Alderson to the jury at the opening of the Special Commission at Dorchester, Dorset, on Tuesday 11 January 1831

66 I do not doubt that distress is one of the causes of the disturbances, distress sufficiently heavy, but yet, I fear, greatly exaggerated by interested and wicked men, for their own bad purposes. Even in this kingdom, in which alone of all others there is a legal provision for the poor, poverty prevails, perhaps increased by the maladministration of those laws which are intended to relieve it. The encouragement which has been given to early and thoughtless marriages and the resulting increase of the population, together with the payment of part of his wages in many parishes from the poor rate have lowered the labourer in the scale of society. At the same time the general spread of education has placed him in a position to feel more acutely his relative inferiority without going far enough for him to fully understand the real causes of the change in his condition. 99

Who were the rioters?

One important characteristic of the disturbances was their orderliness. Despite the strong language of the threatening letters no one was killed. The riots were not an attack on the gentry and aristocracy. The rioters' demands were economic, not political – they wanted work and a living wage, rather than the vote and changes to the political system. They were essentially organised on a local basis. Many groups of rioters even had a treasurer who held the money collected from farmers, at least until the evening when it was spent in the alehouse. The rioters themselves were not the poorest people. Generally they were the respectable elements of rural society, among the better paid and including many village craftsmen. A study of the rioters in Dorset shows that over half of them were aged under 22.

What was the government response?

At first the authorities were slow to act. They feared disturbances in the industrial towns more and that is where many troops were stationed. For example, in 1826 in East Lancashire handloom weavers had smashed 1100 newly installed power looms. The four-day riot left six people dead and 40 were arrested. Ten of these were transported and 30 imprisoned.

Soon, however, the authorities became very frightened by the disturbances in southern England, especially as they spread so rapidly from one area to the next. The disturbances spread from Sussex to Wiltshire in less than a week! The Government response included offering rewards: £50 for each person caught and convicted of destroying machines and £500 for the conviction of those starting fires. Forces of special constables were sworn in, the Yeomanry mobilised and troops sent to the worst-affected areas. In some places farmers and magistrates gave in to the demands of the labourers and stopped using, or even destroyed, their threshing machines. In other places the magistrates set up new agreed wage levels. The Government disapproved of this. They wanted the rioters arrested. They were very aware of the July revolution in France and its effect in provoking revolutions in Holland and Poland and unrest in Germany and Italy. They feared revolution in England.

Aftermath

The disturbances themselves lasted no more than a few weeks and it was then relatively easy for the authorities to arrest suspected rioters. A Special Commission was set up to try the rioters in some of the worst-affected counties – Hampshire, Wiltshire, Berkshire, Dorset and Buckinghamshire. An exceptionally high number of those convicted were sentenced to transportation (see Source 7). This reflected the Government's determination to deal harshly with the rioters. Once people were transported to Australia very few ever managed to return to England. Agitators were blamed for the riots. One, William Cobbett, was tried for starting the revolt but he was acquitted.

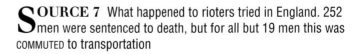

Transported 505

Acquitted 800

Imprisoned 644

19 Executed
7 Fined
1 Whipped

SOURCE 7 What happened to rioters tried in England. 252 men were sentenced to death, but for all but 19 men this was COMMUTED to transportation

Did the Swing Riots in Dorset match the national picture?

■ TASK

1. Sources 8–17 all relate to the Swing Riots in Dorset. Use them to complete the table you began on page 44.
2. Now use your completed table to help you answer this question: did the Swing Riots in Dorset match the national picture?

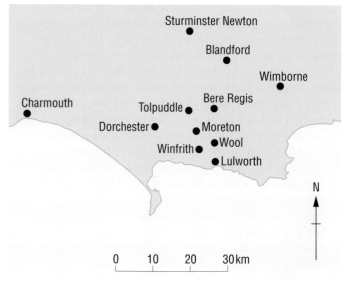

SOURCE 8 A threatening letter sent to Mr Castleman of Wimborne

> *Blandford, 1830*
> *Mr Castleman. Sir, Sunday night your house shall come down to the Ground for you are an inhuman monster and we will dash out your brains – Banks [another landowner] and your set ought to be sent to hell. The Hanley Torches have not forgot you.*

SOURCE 9 A map of Dorset, with all the places mentioned in Sources 9–17 marked

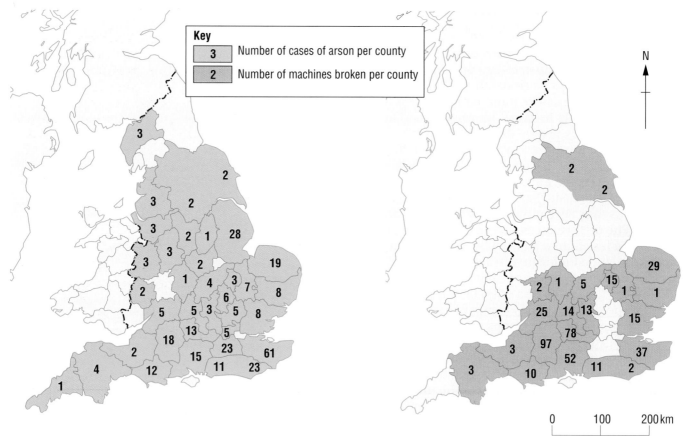

SOURCE 10 Two maps showing the number of cases of arson and machine breaking 1830–32 by county

5. What pattern to the Swing Riots do the maps in Source 10 show? Can you explain this pattern?

SOURCE 11 Extracts from the diary of Mary Frampton (1773–1846) of Moreton in Dorset

❝ November 1830

As the month advanced it became very gloomy. A universal spirit of dissatisfaction pervaded every class. The setting fire to corn stacks and barns which first began in the month of October spread rapidly from Kent. These fires were in general unconnected with the riotous mobs which at the same time assembled, breaking and destroying machinery, surrounding gentlemen's houses, extorting money and demanding an increase in wages. These mobs rose very unexpectedly and spread with alarming rapidity.

22 November 1830

On 22 November the first risings took place in this county. Viscount Portman [of Bryanston in Blandford] immediately promised to raise the wages of his labourers, and by doing this without agreement with other gentlemen, greatly increased their difficulties. My brother, Frampton, harangued [argued angrily with] the people at Bere Regis, and argued with them on the impropriety of their conduct, refusing to concede to their demands whilst asked with menaces. This spirited conduct caused him to be very unpopular, and threats were issued against him and his house.

28 November

Notice was received of an intended rising of the people at the neighbouring villages of Winfrith, Wool and Lulworth, which took place on the 30th. My brother, Mr Frampton, was joined very early on that morning by a large body of farmers from his immediate neighbourhood, as well as from some distance, all special constables, amounting to upwards of 150, armed only with a short staff, the pattern for which had been sent by order of Government to equip what was called the Constabulary Force. The numbers increased as they rode on towards Winfrith, where the clergyman was unpopular, and his premises supposed to be in danger. The mob, urged on from behind hedges by a number of women and children, advanced rather respectfully, and with their hats in their hands, to demand increase of wages, but would not listen to the request that they would disperse. The men were particularly well dressed, as if they had put on their best clothes for the occasion. [On this occasion the Riot Act was read, the protesters were dispersed and the three captured were taken to gaol in Dorchester.]

There were no soldiers in the county, all having been sent towards London, Wiltshire and Hampshire, where riots raged first; and in the beginning of December hourly accounts of the assembling of mobs, for the purpose of breaking threshing machines, rick burning, increase of wages and extorting money arrived. Under these circumstances, it was judged necessary to block up all the lower windows of Moreton House, as well as all the doors. The Mayor of Dorchester ordered the staff of Dorset militia to go to Moreton to defend the house, nightly patrols were established, and Mr Frampton or his son sat up alternately for many nights. My sister-in-law also took her turn in sitting up with another woman, Lady Harriot, saying that they were more watchful than the men. Spies were certainly sent from the rioters to see the state of the house. [The house was never actually attacked, possibly because it was so obviously well prepared.]

A troop of lancers arrived at Dorchester about this time, December 12th, and were joyfully received. Most of the threshing machines in this neighbourhood were, however, either laid aside or destroyed by the farmers themselves and no rising occurred very near Dorchester. The troop of lancers looked very worn down by the fatigues of the riots in Wiltshire. About 70 prisoners were at different times committed to gaol, and mobs and tumults became again rare occurrences. But alas! The fires still continued at intervals and no clue in this county any more than others could be found by which to detect the perpetrators.

10 January 1831

The Special Commission came to Dorchester. The procession, I think, extended a full mile, and the crowd was very great to witness their arrival. The Judges, Baron Vaughan and Mr Justice Alderson, dined with us afterwards, and we had a large party besides, amounting to sixteen. The business at Dorchester was finished in two days, and there were no capital convictions, only death recorded in about six or seven instances which ensured transportation for life. After the heavy offences at sessions in Hampshire and Wiltshire this was deemed very light. ❞

6. What is Mary Frampton's attitude to the rioters?
7. Look back at your work on Peterloo. What similarity can you see between the Swing rioters and the Peterloo marchers?

NOTICE!

Having received Information that the GOVERNMENT of this

Country are taking the most active measures for the *prevention of the Outrages* which have disgraced different parts of England, and that they wish all well disposed persons of *every class*, to have an opportunity of enrolling themselves as

Special Constables

for the protection of the Property of the Country.

We hereby give Notice,

that we are now ready in this Town, and will attend in any Village in our Division, to swear in and enrol any Persons who may be disposed to *defend this County from the wicked attempt of the common Enemy.*

Signed, JOHN WYLDBORE SMITH,
J. J. FARQUHARSON,
E. B. PORTMAN,
JOHN JAMES SMITH.
BLANDFORD, *November 24th,* 1830.

OAKLEY, PRINTER, BLANDFORD.

SOURCE 12 Notice printed in Blandford, 24 November 1830

SOURCE 13 Minutes of the Charmouth VESTRY, 29 November 1830

66 *At a meeting of the Inhabitants of this village to take into consideration the best measures under the present circumstances of the country to be adopted for the protection of private property and the preservation of the public peace.*

Resolved that the inhabitants enrol as special constables and that those present are sworn in forthwith [immediately].
Resolved that staves be delivered to the special constables at the Vestry to be held on Thursday next. Resolved that given all the circumstances a nightly watch be established and that the special constables who wish it do form themselves into such watch, four of their number each night. Resolved that a subscription be entered into to defray any contingent circumstance [pay for any expenses]. 99

SOURCE 14 A letter from Viscount Portman

66 *Bryanston, Nov 27, 1830*

We are all safe in our division, and have organised our matters so well that we can assemble 200 armed and mounted and about 2000 pedestrian special constables ready to resist any mob . . . 99

SOURCE 15 An extract from the editorial in the *Dorset County Chronicle*, Thursday 2 December 1830

66 *Some of those disgraceful disturbances, which have, for some time past, alarmed the Kingdom, have at length taken place in our county. At such a moment as the present when the nation may be said to have arrived at a crisis it is the duty of the authorities to take those coercive and severe measures which alone can preserve the peace of our country . . .*
. . . The readiness with which the gentry, farmers, the tradesmen and the sober portion of the peasantry have come forward and the energy they have displayed have struck the disaffected with a panic, which we trust will prevent their again attempting any serious disturbance. It is to the towns being garrisoned by organised bands of special constables and to the villages and open country being scoured by the mounted and armed patrol that the ease with which the risings have been quelled in their very commencement [stopped almost as soon as they began] is to be attributed. This has succeeded in making the disturbance in this county of a minor character. 99

8. Look at Sources 8, 12 and 13. Did the local authorities think the Dorset rioters were revolutionaries?
9. Do you think they were revolutionaries?
10. Do you think that the authorities in Dorset were slow to react to the disturbances?
11. The minutes in Source 13 were printed and circulated. Why do you think that was done?
12. Does the editor of the *Dorset County Chronicle* (Source 15) believe that there was a danger of revolution in:
    a) Britain
    b) Dorset?

SOURCE 16 A description of one case at the Special Commission, as reported in the *Dorset County Chronicle*, Thursday 20 January 1831

" William Stokes, William Anstey, Samuel Zillwood, Robert Zillwood, John Read and James Thick were charged with destroying a threshing machine belonging to James Dixon. The prosecutor said that on 24 November a mob came to his house armed with sledges [sledge-hammer] and large sticks. Stokes said they were come to break the machine, and that there were some faggots and they would burn it. Read brought a lighted candle in a lantern and the mob then burnt the machine. The witness identified all the prisoners except Anstey as being present during the time the machine was burning. Anstey entered the barn and threw out a box containing tools used for putting the machine up and the mob broke it to pieces.

In his cross-examination he said that the machine had not been taken down before the mob came.

Richard White heard one of the mob say, they were come to break the machines, and that they had authority from King William IV to do so and were to be paid 2 shillings a day for their work. Captain Paton and Captain Blackwood identified all the prisoners except Anstey as being with the mob.

Ann Lucas proved that Samuel Zillwood had been pressed by them and compelled to go. The Learned Judge having summed up, the Jury found Stokes, Robert Zillwood and Read guilty, and acquitted the others.

They were afterwards sentenced – Stokes and Read to one year's imprisonment and Robert Zillwood to six months' imprisonment and to be kept to hard labour.

[On another charge Read was sentenced to death, commuted to transportation for life.] "

SOURCE 17 Minutes of a meeting of volunteers to suppress riot held at Sturminster Newton, 7 December 1830

" That we view, with anxiety and alarm, the state of this once tranquil and loyal county, and are anxious to exert ourselves individually and collectively, for the maintenance of social order, and the preservation and protection of the lives and property of ourselves and neighbours.

That we are anxious to meet the wishes of the Labourers and Mechanics, and pay them a fair remunerating rate of wages ...

That we will form ourselves into a body for mutual protection and support, ...

... we declare our determination not to be intimidated by fear of personal violence, or the destruction of our property, into lavish expenditure, or an extravagant rise of wages. "

What were the effects of the Swing Riots?

The improved wage agreements of 1830 lasted for a few years in some places, and the Poor Law was improved. Threshing machines were slowly reintroduced, but as late as 1843 a writer commented that 'at this moment, in a large part of the agricultural districts of the south, the threshing machines cannot be used, owing to the destructive vengeance with which the labourers resisted its introduction'.

Rural protest continued. There were continuing incidents of arson, poaching, cattle stealing and animal maiming. It was not until the 1870s that agricultural trade unions developed to represent the interests of rural labourers.

The disturbances certainly frightened the Government and must have had some influence on parliamentary reform in 1832 and the new Poor Law of 1834. It is impossible to say how great this influence was. Although many people may have sympathised with the rioters, the numbers actually involved were not huge, considering the size of the rural population. The disturbances were also concentrated in southern and eastern England.

■ **ACTIVITY**

Look back to the map on page 42 where you took the revolutionary temperature for 1832. From what you have learned about the Swing rioters, do you think you need to change the thermometer reading?

Why did George Loveless get sent to Australia?

IN THE EARLY hours of the morning of 24 February 1834 George Loveless said goodbye to his beloved wife and three children and stepped outside his Tolpuddle cottage on the way to work in the fields. Outside was a police constable who arrested him for the crime of taking part in an 'illegal oath' ceremony. George, along with five other labourers who were also arrested, then walked 11 km to Dorchester where he was formally charged and imprisoned in the Bridewell, the cells below the court. Four months later George was on a ship transporting him to seven years' PENAL SERVITUDE in Australia. He would not see his family again for nearly three years.

So why did George Loveless get sent to Australia? Did he and his friends represent a threat to the Government?

■ ACTIVITY

Working in groups of four, read the story of the Tolpuddle Martyrs. The principal actors in this tragic human story were George Loveless, James Frampton and Lord Melbourne.

1. Three of you should each choose one of these men. Talk through the story, explaining at each stage how your character acted and why you think he acted as he did.
2. The fourth member of your group should think about the story from the point of view of Diana Loveless, George's wife. How do you think she might have felt about these events?

SOURCE 1 'The Returned "Convicts"', from *Cleave's Penny Gazette*, 12 May 1838. From left to right the men are: James Brine (aged 20 when he was transported to Australia), Thomas Stanfield (aged 44, married with six children. He is Diana Loveless's brother), John Stanfield (aged 21. He is Thomas's son), James Loveless (aged 25, married with two children. He is George's brother), George Loveless (aged 37, married to Diana with three children). The sixth man, James Hammett, is not included in this illustration. He was 22 and married with one child. Five of these men were METHODISTS and the Loveless brothers were both LAY PREACHERS. Methodists played a strong role in early working-class organisations. They learned organising and speaking skills through their religious activities, and they deliberately set out to minister to the working classes who were often ignored by the established Church of England. As a result, the clergy of the Church of England were often hostile towards them. In Tolpuddle Methodists suffered religious persecution in 1824–25. This persecution took the form of refusing them employment locally

Since the Swing Riots disputes over wages had continued in Dorset. In 1832 the agricultural labourers in Tolpuddle met with local farmers who agreed to pay a wage of ten shillings a week, in line with wages elsewhere in the county. The farmers then went back on the agreement and never paid more than eight shillings a week. In 1833 they cut wages, first to seven and then to six shillings. This was not enough for men and their families to live on.

It was at that point that the Tolpuddle labourers set out to start a union branch. Unions were not illegal and the Grand National Consolidated Trades Union (GNCTU), which had just been set up by Robert Owen, was growing. The authorities were alarmed by the threat posed by a large, national working-class movement. The leader of the Tolpuddle men was the 37-year-old labourer and Methodist lay preacher George Loveless.

The local landowner and Justice of the Peace, James Frampton, worked to gather evidence that he could use to stop the union. This was the same James Frampton whom you have recently met confronting Swing rioters (see page 49). As a young man at the time of the French Revolution, he had developed a hatred of mob rule. He complained to Lord Melbourne, the Home Secretary, that labourers in the village of Tolpuddle had 'combined' to prevent him cutting their wages. The two men were not sure what law, if any, the Tolpuddle labourers were breaking. However, Melbourne pointed out that while belonging to a union was not illegal, swearing secret oaths was. Many branches of the early unions did use rituals and oaths. It was a way of keeping men together in the face of intimidation from employers like James Frampton. Frampton gathered evidence that the Tolpuddle labourers had sworn illegal oaths. He had the Tolpuddle labourers arrested and charged with taking part in an illegal oath ceremony. This was done with the backing of Lord Melbourne. The men were then held in the Bridewell prison in Dorchester until their trial at the Dorchester Assizes on 17 March 1834.

At the trial George and his fellow labourers were found guilty and sentenced to seven years' transportation, the maximum sentence. There was never any doubt that they would be convicted. The severity of the sentences reflected the fears of the authorities both in Dorset and nationally. The families of the men were also treated harshly and prevented from claiming Poor Relief. James Frampton commented that if they could afford union subscriptions then they did not need Poor Relief, completely ignoring the fact that the breadwinners of the family were gone.

SOURCE 2 George Loveless wrote this note and passed it to Judge John Williams at his trial

" *My Lord, if we had violated any law, it was not done intentionally; we have injured no man's reputation, character, person or property; we were uniting together to preserve ourselves, our wives and our children, from utter degradation and starvation. We challenge any man, or number of men, to prove that we have acted, or intended to act, different from the above statement.* "

SOURCE 3 The words of Judge John Williams when passing sentence at Dorchester Assizes, 19 March 1834

" *I am not sentencing you for any crime you have committed, or that could be proved that you were about to commit, but as an example to the working class of this country.* "

1. Read Source 2. Are these the words of a revolutionary?
2. Read Sources 2 and 3. On what point do George Loveless and Judge Williams agree?

Aftermath

The harsh sentences and treatment of the families led to protests across the country, including a march in London on 21 April 1834 which an estimated 30,000 people attended. But the sentences stood. They achieved what the Government wanted. Many labourers were scared into not joining or even leaving the GNCTU. By 1835 it had collapsed.

The protests and pressure on the Government continued. Eventually, in February 1836, the martyrs were fully pardoned and brought home to England. The then Home Secretary, Lord John Russell, son of the Duke of Bedford, arranged this. James Hammett remained in Tolpuddle for the rest of his life but the other five men and their families emigrated to Canada in 1844 and 1846 to start a new life. You will meet them again later (see page 116).

The following year, 1837, a similar series of events took place in Scotland. Five members of the Cotton Spinners Union in Glasgow were each sentenced to seven years' transportation. Just as with the Tolpuddle Martyrs this caused great anger amongst trade unionists and Radicals throughout the country. Their cause was also taken up by the Chartists.

What was wrong with the old Poor Law system?

IN 1815 EACH PARISH was responsible for looking after its own poor people. There were approximately 15,000 parishes. This was the system that had been set up back in 1601 in the reign of Queen Elizabeth I. It had survived for so long because it worked and because those who paid for it were happy with it.

The Elizabethan Poor Law

Under the Elizabethan Poor Law the property owners in each parish paid a Poor Rate, which was collected by an official called the Overseer of the Poor. This Overseer was appointed by the local Justices of the Peace. He had to do the job for one year, unpaid. In larger parishes a paid assistant Overseer might do the work. Having collected the Poor Rate, it was his job to use the money to help the poor, often known as paupers, of the parish. These were people who could not support themselves – the sick, the aged, the orphaned, the widowed and the disabled – and were known as the 'impotent poor'. There were also healthy people who could not find work and therefore needed help, who were known as the 'able-bodied poor'. The Overseer would be particularly keen to find them work so that they could support themselves and not be a burden on the parish. The people who paid the Poor Rate in each parish were always keen to keep costs down. This concern lay behind the concept of 'settlement'. If people moved to another parish to seek work they needed a 'Certificate of Settlement' which stated that the parish of their birth would support them if they ever needed Poor Relief.

One important feature of the system was its flexibility. It allowed parishes to adopt a variety of approaches to the problem of Poor Relief. Some different approaches are explained on this page.

Roundsman system

In some parishes the Overseer would give paupers a ticket to take round to local employers, usually farmers. If they had work to be done they took the ticket and the pauper would be paid what they would have received in Poor Relief. Some parishes actually created work for their paupers, paying them with Poor Relief. This had the twin effect of keeping wage levels low and also discouraging paupers from actually working. Why bother to work if you received Poor Relief anyway? The importance of this system has been exaggerated; it was only used in about five per cent of parishes.

More money for you this week – bread prices have gone up again.

Speenhamland system

This system was intended to prevent revolution as well as to prevent suffering. People recognised that if the poor were starving they would become desperate – after all, that is what had happened in the lead-up to the French Revolution. The system was named after Speenhamland parish in Berkshire. Here, from 1795, the amount of relief a pauper received depended upon the size of his family and the cost of bread, bread being the staple part of the poor's diet. So as food prices rose, so too did the amount of Poor Relief paid to paupers. Many other parishes copied this system, particularly during the Napoleonic Wars, but it was never popular in the industrial north. As the numbers of the poor rose it became increasingly expensive and parishes were unable to control how much they had to spend. By 1834 its use had almost entirely disappeared.

Workhouses

The early workhouses were exactly that, houses where the 'able-bodied poor' were made to work. Gilbert's Act changed that in 1782. It permitted parishes to group together to build a workhouse but these could only be used to house the 'impotent poor'. Few parishes actually did build workhouses.

SOURCE 1 A painting showing the parish workhouse at St James's in London in the early nineteenth century

1. Workhouses were sometimes criticised for being too comfortable. Do you think the artist of Source 1 wanted to show that the workhouse was comfortable or harsh?

Problems with the Elizabethan Poor Law

The system was facing problems in the period after 1815.

A combination of changes in farming and industry, poor harvests, high food prices, trade depressions and unemployment increased the numbers claiming Poor Relief.

Some people at the time argued that the existing system, particularly 'OUTDOOR RELIEF', encouraged the poor to have large families and be idle. Outdoor relief was the money paid to paupers who continued to live in their own homes rather than in a workhouse.

Costs rose. In 1803 the national cost of Poor Relief was £4 million. By 1832 this had risen to over £7 million.

Overseers were criticised as incompetent (see Source 2).

SOURCE 2 An extract from a report presented to the Royal Commission set up in 1832 to investigate the way the Poor Law was working. The report was written by an assistant commissioner whose job was to visit parishes gathering evidence

    As a body I found annual Overseers wholly incompetent to discharge the duties of their office, either from the interference of private occupations, or from a lack of experience and skill, but most frequently from both of these causes. Their object is to get through the year with as little unpopularity and trouble as possible, their successors therefore have frequently to complain of demands left unsettled and rates uncollected . . .

2. What might make Overseers unpopular with the poor? What might make them unpopular with those who paid Poor Rates?

The Royal Commission, 1832

By the 1830s the existing system was close to collapse, both in the large urban centres and in rural areas. The growth of industry and the cycle of trade slumps meant that at times large numbers of people could be unemployed. In industrial areas this swamped the parish system. Of course, in the new towns and cities all the existing forms of government were already struggling to cope with the urban revolution, but the outbreak of the Swing Riots in the rural southern counties made the need for change more urgent. In 1832 a Royal Commission of eight Commissioners was set up to look into the problems arising from the way the Poor Law worked. Twenty-six assistant commissioners were appointed to inspect the parishes and report on their findings. The debate about what should be done was influenced by the ideas of a number of groups and individuals described below.

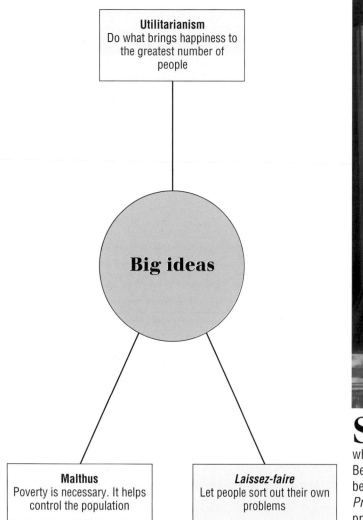

Utilitarianism
Do what brings happiness to the greatest number of people

Big ideas

Malthus
Poverty is necessary. It helps control the population

Laissez-faire
Let people sort out their own problems

SOURCE 3 The preserved body of Jeremy Bentham (1748–1882). Bentham's bones were inserted into a 'sock' which was then stuffed. His real head is between his feet. Bentham spent the early part of his career in law before becoming an author and philosopher. His book *Introduction to Principles of Morals and Legislation* explained many of the principles of Utilitarianism

Utilitarianism

UTILITARIANISM was the name given to the ideas of Jeremy Bentham and others. These ideas were important because they influenced so many people in the period 1815–51. Bentham's aim was to build a scientific and logical foundation for the laws which should govern the lives of people in society. He believed that all actions and laws could be judged against his 'Principle of Utility'. This principle would show if an action or law had 'utility', or was useful, in bringing about the happiness of the greatest number of people.

He firmly believed that his ideas could be of practical use. One man who was greatly influenced by him was Edwin Chadwick, one of the assistant commissioners who was later promoted to Commissioner. He took three key ideas from Bentham's thinking:

- when dealing with any problem you should start with the problem itself and ignore existing solutions; you should look for new solutions to old problems
- government action was essential to solve social problems
- everything should be judged by the 'Principle of Utility'; did it bring happiness to the greatest number of people?

People influenced by these ideas wanted the Government completely to alter the Poor Law system.

The ideas of the Reverend Thomas Malthus

Malthus published an *Essay on the Principle of Population* in 1798. His views on population were influential with men like Chadwick. Malthus believed that population was controlled by certain natural checks such as war, disease and starvation. If the population grew too big, it would outstrip the means to support it, in other words, the food supply. He believed that Poor Relief kept the population too high. This in turn led to a surplus of workers, who were paid low wages, which meant workers needed to claim Poor Relief to survive.

Laissez-faire

LAISSEZ-FAIRE was the name for the ideas of those who believed that the Government should take no action. It should leave people to sort out their own problems, which they would do if left to themselves. The Government should leave the existing Poor Law system alone.

■ ACTIVITY

The year is 1832 and you have been appointed as one of the eight Royal Commissioners to investigate the workings of the Poor Law. The Bishop of London is Chairman of the Commission. The Government is very worried about rising costs and the fact that, despite such high spending, the poor have been restless, notably in the Swing Riots. There is also a growing threat from trade unions. A solution is needed and you and your colleagues are expected to come up with it.

1. Produce a report containing brief summaries of the following issues:

> **What is the historical background to the current system?**

> **How does the current system work?**

> **What are the current problems?**

> **How do the Utilitarians, the supporters of Thomas Malthus and the supporters of *laissez-faire* suggest tackling the problem?**

End your report by recommending what action, if any, the Government should take.

2. Now find out how your recommendations compare with those of the Commissioners in 1834. You can do this by looking at pages 58–61.

THE ROYAL COMMISSION made its report in 1834. It noted that the cost of Poor Relief was rising rapidly; that local administration was inefficient and corrupt in many parishes, not just those where the Roundsman and Speenhamland systems were still used; and that the main problem was outdoor relief. The report, which was heavily influenced by Edwin Chadwick, made a number of recommendations:

- end outdoor relief for the able-bodied poor
- establish one system of Poor Relief for the whole country, run by a central board (this was known as the principle of uniformity)
- make parishes join together to build and run large workhouses
- give Poor Relief only to those living in a workhouse
- make sure that life in the workhouse would always seem a worse option than the life of even the poorest-paid worker living outside it (this was known as the principle of less eligibility)
- separate men, women and children inside the workhouse.

Interestingly enough the Commission did not look into the causes of poverty. That was not part of its brief. It also exaggerated the importance of the Roundsman and Speenhamland systems, which perhaps explains why so many textbooks still make this mistake.

1. Why might the Commissioners have chosen to exaggerate the importance of the Roundsman and Speenhamland systems?

The Poor Law of 1834

The new Poor Law was set up by Act of Parliament in response to the report of the Royal Commission in August 1834. Some of the credit for the Act must go to the Bishop of London, C.J. Blomfield, who helped to get it passed by the House of Lords. There were two underlying principles:

- uniformity
- less eligibility.

It was intended to solve the problems caused by the growing population of the urban areas. A central Poor Law Commission was set up, based in London, with three paid Commissioners appointed to bring in the changes and run the system. Edwin Chadwick was bitterly disappointed not to become a Commissioner. Instead he was appointed as Secretary to the Commission, an enormously influential position. He was responsible for much of the early direction of the new Poor Law. A key point to remember, however, is that although the new system was a national one, it had to be put into practice at a local level.

SOURCE 1 Two extracts from the Royal Commission report, 1834

" Uniformity in the administration of relief we deem as [consider] essential ...

The first and most essential of all conditions, a principle which we find universally admitted [everyone agrees upon], is that the pauper's situation on the whole shall not be made really or apparently so eligible [desirable] as the situation of the independent labourer of the lowest class. "

Unions and Guardians

Parishes were to be grouped into unions. By 1838 there were 573 unions, although there were some parts of Yorkshire and Lancashire where no unions were set up. In each union all those who paid the Poor Rate elected a Board of Guardians. Just as with parliamentary elections this was not a secret ballot, but far more people were entitled to vote. The Guardians were usually drawn from the local élite and were responsible for running the Poor Law in their union.

The workhouses

Workhouses were the centrepiece of the new system. Each union had to use its funds to either build a workhouse or adapt an existing one, in which the paupers would live. In the workhouse families would be split up, as the sexes had to be separated and children were separated from adults. All had to live under strict discipline and work as ordered. The diet was deliberately plain and sparse. The intention was to make the workhouse such an unpleasant place that the poor would only enter it as a last resort. The principle of less eligibility meant that the worst-off labourer outside the workhouse was still better off than any pauper living inside it.

2. What attitude towards the poor was reflected in the new Poor Law?
3. Whose fault was poverty assumed to be?
4. Who was going to run the new system?
5. Look at Source 2. What impression would this workhouse building have had on a poor person?

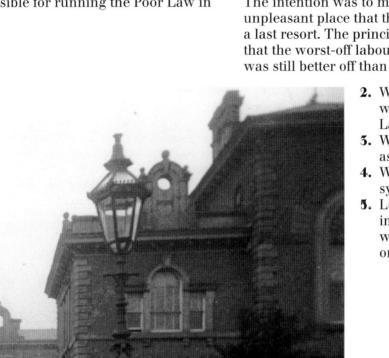

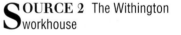

SOURCE 2 The Withington workhouse

SOURCE 3 A timeline of the Poor Law:

1832	Royal Commission set up
1834	Poor Law Act Chadwick appointed Secretary to the Poor Law Commission
1841	Removal of Chadwick as Secretary
1845	Andover scandal
1847	Replacement of Poor Law Commission by the Poor Law Board
1871	Poor Law Board replaced by the Local Government Board.

The officials

Each Board of Guardians appointed a number of officials.

- The Clerk to the Guardians ensured that the wishes of the Guardians were carried out; his was, therefore, a very important job. He was usually a local solicitor working part-time for the Guardians.
- The Master and Mistress were expected to live in the workhouse and take responsibility for its day-to-day running.
- The Medical Officer, a local doctor, was paid to look after the health of the paupers in the workhouse. In many parishes there were two Medical Officers, one for the workhouse and the other for the district.
- Eventually in every union a schoolmaster or schoolmistress was appointed to run the workhouse school.
- The local Church of England clergyman, who was a very influential person in the community, acted as the workhouse chaplain.
- Finally, there was the Relieving Officer, the man responsible for organising outdoor relief. This continued to be given during the winter in rural areas; in urban areas it remained the main method of providing Poor Relief.

SOURCE 4 An extract from the 1834 Poor Law Act

“ It shall be lawful for the Commissioners, by such rules, orders or regulations as they think fit, to declare to what extent and for what period the relief to be given to able-bodied persons and their families in any particular union may be administered out of the workhouse. ”

6. Which important recommendation of the Royal Commission was not implemented in 1834?

The quality of the people involved in running workhouses varied from union to union and it is very difficult to make generalisations about them. What can be said is that some were honest and concerned for the welfare of the paupers in their charge while others were corrupt and abused their power. You can make your own judgement about some of the officials in the Worcestershire unions in the next enquiry, on pages 62–65.

The rules

SOURCE 5 An extract from the Seventh Annual Report of the Poor Law Commissioners, 1841. The rules in every individual workhouse would have been based upon these

“ WORKHOUSE (Rules of Conduct)
Any Pauper who shall neglect to observe any of the regulations therein contained as are applicable and binding on him;
Or who shall make any noise when silence is ordered to be kept;
Or shall use obscene or profane language;
Or shall refuse or neglect to work, after having been required to do so;
Or shall play at cards, or other games of chance;
Shall be deemed DISORDERLY.

Any pauper who shall within seven days, repeat any one or commit more than one of the offences specified;
Or shall by word or deed insult or revile the master or matron, or any other officer of the workhouse, or any of the Guardians;
Or shall be drunk;
Or shall wilfully disturb the other inmates during prayers or divine worship;
Shall be deemed REFRACTORY.

It shall be lawful for the master of the workhouse ... to punish any disorderly pauper by substituting, during a time not greater than 48 hours, for his or her dinner a meal consisting of eight ounces of bread, or one pound of cooked potatoes and also by withholding from him during the same period, all butter, cheese, tea, sugar, or broth.

And it shall be lawful for the Board of Guardians to order any refractory pauper to be punished by confinement to a separate room [known as a refractory ward], with or without an alteration to the diet for no longer than 24 hours. ”

7. What do the rules in Source 5 tell you about the behaviour of paupers in workhouses?

You can find out more about conditions in the workhouses – the diet, the work and education – in the case studies on pages 62–65.

The buildings

SOURCE 6 A plan of a workhouse published by the Poor Law Commission as an example of how other workhouses might be built

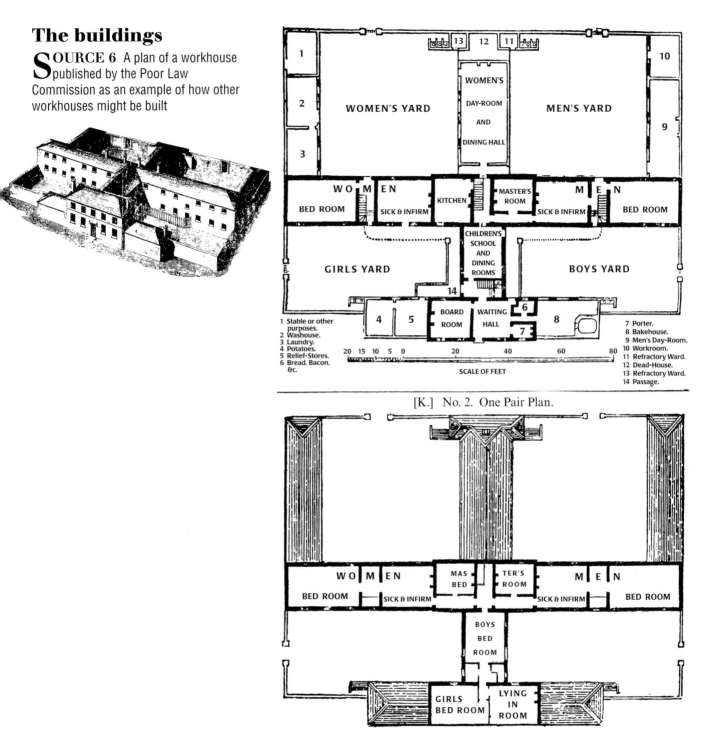

1 Stable or other purposes.
2 Washouse.
3 Laundry.
4 Potatoes.
5 Relief-Stores.
6 Bread, Bacon, &c.

7 Porter.
8 Bakehouse.
9 Men's Day-Room.
10 Workroom.
11 Refractory Ward.
12 Dead-House.
13 Refractory Ward.
14 Passage.

SCALE OF FEET

[K.] No. 2. One Pair Plan.

8. What information about the treatment of paupers in the workhouse can you take from Source 6?

■ TASK

Discuss the following questions with your neighbour.

1. How did the new Poor Law try to save money?

2. How did it try to force the poor to solve their own problems?

3. Why don't we have this system any more? Do you think we *should* still have this system?

The evening arrived; the boys took their places. The master, in his cook's uniform, stationed himself at the copper; his pauper assistants ranged themselves behind him; the gruel was served out; and a long grace was said over the short commons. The gruel disappeared; the boys whispered to each other, and winked at Oliver; while his next neighbours nudged him. Child as he was, he was desperate with hunger, and reckless with misery. He rose from the table; and advancing to the master, basin and spoon in hand, said: somewhat alarmed at his own temerity; 'Please sir, I want some more.' The master was a fat, healthy man; but he turned very pale. He gazed in stupefied astonishment on the small rebel for some seconds; and then clung for support to the copper. The assistants were paralysed with wonder; the boys with fear.

'What!' said the master at length, in a faint voice.

'Please sir,' replied Oliver, 'I want some more.'

The master aimed a blow at Oliver's head with the ladle; pinioned him in his arms; and shrieked aloud for the beadle.

The board [of Guardians] were sitting in solemn conclave, when Mr Bumble rushed into the room in great excitement, and addressing the gentleman in the high chair, said, 'Mr Limbkins, I beg your pardon sir! Oliver Twist has asked for more!' There was a general start. Horror was depicted on every countenance.

'For more!' said Mr Limbkins. 'Compose yourself, Bumble, and answer me distinctly. Do I understand that he asked for more, after he had eaten the supper allotted by the dietary?'

George Cruikshank

SOURCE 1 An extract from *Oliver Twist* by Charles Dickens, published in instalments between 1837 and 1839. George Cruikshank drew the original illustrations

SOURCE 2 A still of the same incident from the film musical *Oliver!*, made in 1968

Under the old Poor Law children were likely to receive outdoor relief. After 1834 they were more likely to be in the workhouse. In 1836 there were over 42,000 children under sixteen in workhouses. By 1840 this number had risen to over 68,000. The numbers fluctuated with the seasons. Numbers rose in autumn and winter and fell in spring and summer.

The types of children found in the workhouse fell into two main categories:

■ those who had been orphaned or deserted, who might spend all their childhood years in the workhouse until they were apprenticed

■ 'ins and outs', who were in the workhouse with their destitute parents and might stay a night, several nights or sometimes even longer.

Whilst the authorities could plan for the education and training of the first group they could do little about the children who stayed for only short periods. In the Tenbury Wells workhouse, for example, 61.1 per cent of child inmates were 'ins and outs' in 1851. This was the largest proportion nationally.

■ TASK

Sources 1 and 2 give a stereotypical view of the workhouse – poor, hungry Oliver asking for more food! This is a popularly held STEREOTYPE, but is it accurate?

Study Sources 3–10 on the following pages to help you decide.

Copy the table below, or use one that your teacher gives you, to record examples of good and bad aspects of workhouse life.

Now write your answer to this question: Is *Oliver Twist* accurate? Was the life of children in the workhouse as bad as the stereotype suggests?

Remember that these extracts from the records of thirteen Worcestershire workhouses represent a moment in time for that union only.

Aspect of workhouse life	Good	Bad
Diet		
Housing		
Separation of sexes and ages		
Education and training		
Punishments		
Work/occupations		
Medical treatment		
Moral well-being		

The Worcestershire workhouses

In the Midland county of Worcestershire there were thirteen Poor Law union workhouses. These varied in size and location, some being in industrial towns like Stourbridge and Kidderminster and others being in rural areas like Pershore or Martley. As with any national legislation, the law was interpreted in varying ways at local level. Those who drew up the new Poor Law did not expect this and keeping the local unions in line became an important role for the assistant Poor Law commissioners. It is safe to argue, therefore, that the principle of uniformity never entirely applied. Some historians argue that because the children in the workhouse were in many ways no worse off than those outside it, the principle of less eligibility did not apply either (see Source 10).

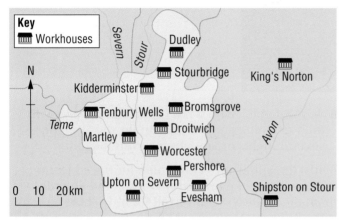

Key
🏚 Workhouses

Severn · Stour · Dudley · Stourbridge · King's Norton · Kidderminster · Bromsgrove · Tenbury Wells · Teme · Droitwich · Martley · Avon · Worcester · Pershore · Upton on Severn · Shipston on Stour · Evesham

0 10 20km

SOURCE 3 A map showing the locations of workhouses in Worcestershire. These workhouses did not all open in 1834. Some unions were more willing to act than others, because the need for workhouses was greater in urban areas than in rural areas. In rural areas with few paupers, building a workhouse was a very expensive way of tackling the problem of poverty

SOURCE 4 Occupations recorded in Worcestershire workhouses

66 *Stone breaking.*
Road building.
Flour grinding.
Street cleaning.
Grating rotten potatoes to obtain potato starch or farina, which was then made into soup for the paupers – this practice was abandoned after the Andover scandal (see page 68) as it was believed to be bad for paupers' health.
Training in trades such as shoe-making, tailoring.
Cleaning the workhouse – this was done by girls but they were not allowed into the men's wards, nor those wards containing 'immoral women'. 99

DIETARY for Able-bodied Men and Women

	BREAKFAST		DINNER				SUPPER		
	Bread	Gruel	Cooked Meat	Potatoes	Soup	Suet or Rice Pudding	Bread	Cheese	Broth
	oz.	Pints	oz.	lb.	Pints	oz.	oz.	oz.	Pints
Sunday Men	6	1½	5	½	—	—	6	—	1½
Women	5	1½	5	½	—	—	5	—	1½
Monday Men	6	1½	—	—	1⅓	—	6	1½	—
Women	5	1⅓	—	—	1⅓	—	5	1½	—
Tuesday Men	6	1½	5	½	—	—	6	—	1½
Women	5	1½	5	½	—	—	5	—	1½
Wednesday Men	6	1½	—	—	1⅓	—	6	1½	—
Women	5	1½	—	—	1⅓	—	5	1½	—
Thursday Men	6	1½	5	½	—	—	6	—	1½
Women	5	1½	5	½	—	—	5	—	1½
Friday Men	6	1½	—	—	—	1½	6	1½	—
Women	5	1½	—	—	—	1½	5	1½	—
Saturday Men	6	1½	—	—	1⅓	—	6	1½	—
Women	5	1½	—	—	1⅓	—	5	1½	—

OLD PEOPLE, of 60 Years of Age and upwards, may be allowed 1oz. of tea, 3oz. of Butter, and 7oz. of Sugar per week in lieu of Gruel for Breakfast, if deemed expedient to make this change.
CHILDREN, under 9 Years of Age, to be Dieted at discretion;—above 9 to be allowed the same quantities as Women.
SICK.......... To be Dieted as directed by the Medical Officer.

SOURCE 5 The weekly food allowances or 'dietary' used in all Worcestershire workhouses. The historian M.A. Crowther had made the judgement that 'The workhouse diet was stripped of everything that made similar food acceptable to the poor; sometimes even salt was not offered at the table.' The national diet adopted by all Worcestershire unions in 1853 has been computer analysed. This analysis showed it to have a 56 per cent shortfall in energy, a 50 per cent deficiency in vitamin C, almost no vitamin D and a serious deficiency in calcium. It is worth remembering that this sort of computer analysis was not available in 1853

SOURCE 6 Extracts from documents relating to punishments. The most common forms of punishment were the removal of privileges such as loss of free time, hard labour and corporal punishment. The most common crimes were disobedience, bad language, damage to workhouse property and running away.

66 *An extract from the Clerk to the Guardian's report, Kidderminster, 1840*
In consequence of the porter John Stokes putting a boy named – Perks aged 6 years in a sack, tying him up, and hanging him up in one of the rooms of the workhouse for nearly an hour, he [the Clerk] had taken a summons against Stokes, who had been fined by the magistrates for assault.

Punishment regulation, 1841
No corporal punishment 'shall be inflicted on any boy except by the school master or master of the workhouse ... to be inflicted with a rod or other instrument such as shall be approved by the Board of Guardians or visiting committee.' 99

BROMSGROVE UNION.

APPOINTMENT OF SCHOOLMISTRESS.

THE BOARD of GUARDIANS of this UNION, at their Meeting on TUESDAY, the 9th day of May next, intend to elect a SCHOOLMISTRESS for the WORKHOUSE. The person appointed will be required to instruct both boys and girls, and to perform such duties as are set forth in the General Consolidated Orders of the Poor Law Board. The salary will be £20 per annum, subject to such increase as may be awarded by the Committee of Council on Education, with Rations, Lodging, and Washing in the Workhouse.

Applications in the handwriting of the candidates, with testimonials as to character and ability, to be sent to me on or before Monday, the 8th of May next, and the applicants will be expected to attend at the Board Room on the following day (Tuesday), at Eleven o'clock in the Forenoon. No travelling expenses will be allowed.

By order of the Board,

THOMAS DAY, Clerk.

Board Room, Bromsgrove, 25th April, 1865.

SOURCE 7 An advertisement for a schoolmistress for Bromsgrove workhouse, 1865. Workhouse schools found it difficult to recruit high-quality schoolteachers because of the low social status attached to the job in the workhouse

SOURCE 8 Extracts from the Minute Book of the Proceedings of the Bromsgrove Union, 1842. A coroner's inquest had found Mr Fletcher, the workhouse surgeon, negligent in his treatment of a three-year-old boy, Henry Cartwright. Henry had been suffering from a skin complaint, the 'itch', which was common in workhouses. He died as a result of being immersed in a solution of sulphuret of potassium. The Board of Guardians had met to decide what action to take against the surgeon.

66 The Board having taken into consideration the circumstances attending the death of Henry Cartwright are of the opinion that Mr Fletcher is to blame for having delegated the application of a powerful remedy for the cure of the itch, which existed among a portion of the children in the workhouse, to nurse Sarah Chambers. But in consideration of his previous zeal [hard work] in the performance of his duties of his office, of his kind attention to his pauper patients and his to date unblemished professional character, it is resolved [agreed] that he be retained in his present office subject to the approval of the Poor Law Commissioners. 99

The Poor Law Commissioners agreed with this decision. Sarah Chambers, however, was found guilty of neglect and dismissed

SOURCE 9 Comments on the education provided in workhouse schools. For the children of the poor outside the workhouse there would probably be no education

66 Board of Guardians for Pershore workhouse in 1839
It is quite unnecessary to teach the children in the union workhouse the accomplishment of writing.

Chaplain to Kidderminster workhouse in 1839
The children have made considerable progress in reading and most often can say the catechism [a summary of Christian beliefs] and can answer questions from it. They are learning the parables, and can answer questions from those they know tolerably well … suitable prayers are read at the commencement [start] and termination [end] of school hours.

Comments of the government education inspectors who inspected Droitwich workhouse school in 1853
The elder children are already improving and I expect will make further advance this year under Miss Smith who has excellent methods of imparting knowledge and I think will train the children morally and industrially and exercises a kindly influence over them. Separation must be entire and absolute between the sexes, who are to live, sleep and take their meals in totally separate parts of the building, with an enclosed yard for each. 99

SOURCE 10 An extract from *Workhouse Children* by the historian Frank Crompton, published in 1997

66 To the casual observer a more, rather than less, eligible treatment of pauper inmates in workhouses was apparent. They lived in adequate workhouse accommodation, which was regularly cleaned, although sometimes overcrowded. They were given plentiful but uninteresting food, which was cooked in sanitary [hygienic] conditions and their health was regularly monitored, with illness and injuries promptly treated by trained medical staff. This more eligible treatment may have appeared particularly so for child paupers, who were also provided with an intellectual, moral and industrial training superior to that offered to most of their non-pauper contemporaries, at least for the first couple of decades after 1834. 99

Was the new Poor Law a success?

■ **TASK**

Was the new Poor Law a success or a failure? Did it fulfil the aims of those who had set up the Act? Use the information on the following pages to construct two spider diagrams, one showing successes, the other showing failures.

Between 1834 and 1836 the new Poor Law was set up in southern England. As this was a time of good harvests and low unemployment there was not too much opposition, certainly little organised opposition. The two key groups affected were those who paid the Poor Rate, who welcomed any system designed to save them money; and the poor, who were fewer in number due to the favourable economic conditions. In many unions the cost of Poor Relief decreased.

Why was there opposition in the north of England?

In 1836 the Poor Law Commissioners moved to introduce the system in the north of England. Here, there was significant resistance to the new Poor Law. There were even some parts of Yorkshire and Lancashire where it was not implemented at all. There were several reasons for this.

Employment patterns
The more industrial north had a more fluid type of unemployment than the south; trade slumps could put large numbers of workers out of work for relatively short periods of time. It was cheaper to give outdoor relief while people were out of work than to set up a workhouse system. In 1837, at the very time when the Poor Law Commissioners were trying to introduce the new system, there was an economic depression. Chadwick was viewed as the person responsible for trying to abolish outdoor relief and during the 1837 general election there were demonstrations against him.

Opposition from the poor and the middle classes
The poor of the industrial areas were in a more powerful position than those in the south, because there were so many of them living together in the growing towns – their opposition to the changes presented more of a threat.

Many of the northern factory owners, magistrates and newly elected Poor Law Guardians were opposed to the new system, too. Tory magistrates such as Richard Oastler saw it as striking at the traditional roots of society. Factory reformers like John Fielden were against it. One of the most prominent opponents was Joseph Rayner Stephens, a Methodist minister.

SOURCE 1 Evidence given by Langham Rokesby, Chairman of the Market Harborough Poor Law Union, printed in the Second Annual Report of the Poor Law Commissioners, 1836

66 Persons who never could be made to work before have become good labourers, and do not express any dissatisfaction with the measure. In most parishes the moral character of the poor is improving. There is a disposition [willingness] to be more orderly and well behaved. So far as I can judge, from the enquiries I have made from time to time, and from conversations with respectable farmers and others, who hold no offices, I may venture to say that the measure is working very satisfactorily. That the great body of the labouring poor throughout the Union has become reconciled to it. That the workhouse is held in great dread. That there is a greater disposition to seek employment, very few complaints of misbehaviour, and that cases of bastardy are on the decline. 99

SOURCE 2 The costs of Poor Relief, 1818 and 1837 (note that the population figure given is for the nearest year in which a census return was made)

Population 1821	*11,978,875*
Costs for year ending 25 March 1818	*£7,870,801*
Population 1831	*13,897,187*
Costs for year ending 25 March 1837	*£4,044,741*

SOURCE 3 An extract from the Chartist newspaper, the *Northern Star*, 10 March 1838, on the forthcoming Poor Law elections in Huddersfield

66 Fellow Rate Payers
The time is come for you to give a practical demonstration of your hatred to the new Starvation Law.
Recollect! That the 25th March is the day which is set apart for the election of new Guardians for the ensuing year; therefore it will depend upon your efforts, whether you allow men to be elected as Guardians, who are the mere tools of the three Commissioners in carrying out their diabolical schemes for starving the poor, reducing the labourer's wages and robbing you ratepayers of that salutary control you have previously had over your own money and your town's affairs ... 99

1. What are the two strands of the Chartist writer's argument in Source 3?

Well-organised opposition

Opponents of the new Poor Law used public meetings and pamphlets to stir up public feeling. The workhouses were labelled as Bastilles, after the infamous Paris prison stormed during the French Revolution. In 1838 John Fielden introduced a motion in the House of Commons demanding the repeal of the new Poor Law. He was backed by a petition with more than 100,000 signatures but his motion was heavily defeated.

Bradford in 1837

On 30 October 1837 Alfred Power, an assistant Poor Law commissioner, went to Bradford to advise the local Poor Law Guardians on the introduction of the new Poor Law. The local people heard of his visit and insisted on attending the meeting. The Guardians were forced to meet in public and tried unsuccessfully to answer the questions of the hostile crowd. Their meeting was then adjourned until 10 November. As Alfred Power left he was pelted with stones and mud and forced to make a run for safety.

The meeting fixed for 10 November was postponed until 13 November because the Guardians still feared trouble. Alfred Power took the precaution of arranging for soldiers to be sent to the town. The building in which the meeting took place was soon surrounded by a hostile crowd several thousand strong. The local magistrate sent for the soldiers and a full-scale riot broke out. The soldiers were pelted with stones and in retaliation charged the crowd, hitting out with the flats of their swords. It was not until nightfall that order was restored. The Guardians went ahead with their plans and brought in the new Poor Law in 1838. Needless to say, they still faced a great deal of opposition from the local people.

2. Does the fact that there was opposition to the Poor Law Act mean that it was a failure?

SOURCE 4 A drawing from the *Illustrated London News* showing an attack on the workhouse during the Stockport riots, August 1842

The weaknesses of the Poor Law Commission

The resistance in the north of England highlighted some of the problems with the new Poor Law. For areas with fluctuations in employment the workhouse by itself was not the best solution. In fact, the workhouse could be a very costly solution, being expensive both to build and run. There were other problems too. Disagreements between Edwin Chadwick and the three Commissioners on how the system should be run led to him being forced out of his job as Secretary in 1841. Some sections of society and, importantly, the press felt that the Commissioners had too much power. Finally, in 1842 the number of assistant commissioners was cut from twelve to nine, increasing the workload of those remaining and hampering the efficiency of the Commission.

> **SOURCE 5** Numbers of able-bodied adults receiving outdoor relief in 1841
>
> 66 Able-bodied adults receiving poor relief 345,656
> Able-bodied adults in workhouses 65,467 99

3. Look at Source 5. How many able-bodied adults were still receiving outdoor relief in 1841? What do you conclude from this?

The Andover workhouse scandal

In 1845 a parliamentary select committee investigated the running of the notorious Andover workhouse. It emerged that the paupers there were employed in breaking and grinding bones, which was bad for their health, and that some of them were so hungry that they were eating the marrow from the bones. This was seen as mismanagement at a local level, which had not been properly dealt with by the Poor Law Commission. It was acknowledged that the local Board of Guardians was disobeying the regulations issued by the Commissioners, but the Commissioners should not have allowed it to happen.

The Commissioners' position was already weak and the bad publicity that resulted from the Andover scandal was the final blow. In 1847 the Commission was replaced by the Poor Law Board. This was to be headed by a President who would be an MP, a member of the Government, which in theory would ensure that the system was properly supervised.

> **SOURCE 6** Evidence from the Report of the Select Committee on the Andover Union, 1846
>
> 66 **Mr Wakeley:** *What work were you employed about when you were in the workhouse?*
> **Charles Lewis:** *I was employed breaking bones.*
> **Wakeley:** *Were other men engaged in the same work?*
> **Lewis:** *Yes.*
> **Wakeley:** *During the time you were so employed, did you ever see any men gnaw anything or eat anything from these bones?*
> **Lewis:** *I have seen them eat marrow out of these bones.*
> **Wakeley:** *Have you often seen them eat the marrow?*
> **Lewis:** *I have.*
> **Wakeley:** *Did they state why they did it?*
> **Lewis:** *I really believe they were hungry.*
> **Wakeley:** *Did you yourself feel extremely hungry at this time?*
> **Lewis:** *I did but my stomach would not take it.*
> **Wakeley:** *You could not swallow the marrow?*
> **Lewis:** *No.* 99

■ TASK

Most historians agree that the workhouse was the most feared and despised institution in Victorian England. Certainly those who went there were seen as social failures.

1. Look at the spider diagrams you have produced (see page 66).
   a) Is it possible to make a comparison between the two?
   b) Can you draw any conclusions from them about the success of the new Poor Law?
2. How do our attitudes to the treatment of the poor compare with those of the Victorians?

■ REVIEW ACTIVITY

At a number of places in this book you are 'taking the revolutionary temperature' of Britain to decide how great the danger of revolution was. This is the third point, 1842.

1. First look back over the events since 1832 to remind you of the changes that have been made to the Poor Law.
2. Now either sketch the map below or use the copy your teacher gives you and shade in the thermometer.

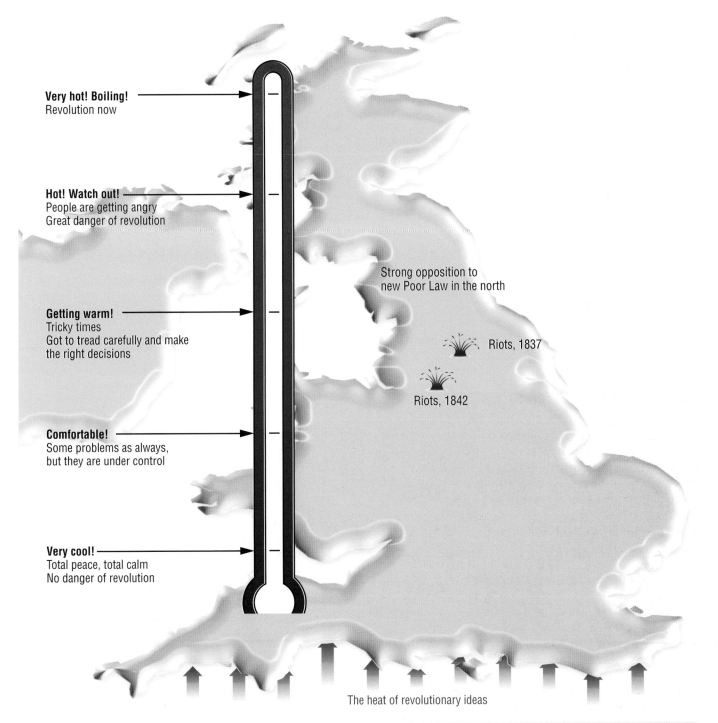

Very hot! Boiling!
Revolution now

Hot! Watch out!
People are getting angry
Great danger of revolution

Getting warm!
Tricky times
Got to tread carefully and make
the right decisions

Comfortable!
Some problems as always,
but they are under control

Very cool!
Total peace, total calm
No danger of revolution

Strong opposition to
new Poor Law in the north

Riots, 1837

Riots, 1842

The heat of revolutionary ideas

chapter 4

HOW DID PEOPLE ATTEMPT TO IMPROVE LIVING CONDITIONS IN THE TOWNS?

AS YOU SAW earlier in the book there was a great growth of towns in the period we are studying. This was partly because the population was increasing rapidly among people already living in the towns and partly because more people were moving to the towns from the English and Welsh countryside, Ireland and the western Highlands of Scotland. You are now going to look at the problems caused by this rapid growth and at the attempts people made to tackle them.

What was it like to live in an industrial town?

■ TASK

As you read Sources 1–8, make a list of the problems you would expect to find in the growing towns.

1. Look at Source 1. During which decade were towns growing fastest?
2. Which towns grew the most?

3. What criticisms of the growing towns was Cruikshank making in Source 2?

SOURCE 2 *London going out of Town or the March of Bricks and Mortar*, a cartoon by George Cruikshank on the growth of towns, published in 1829

SOURCE 1 Population figures (in thousands) for selected towns

	1801	1811	1821	1831	1841	1851
Birmingham	71	83	102	144	183	233
Bradford	13	16	26	44	67	104
Bristol	61	71	85	104	124	137
Cardiff	2	2	4	6	10	18
Glasgow	77	101	147	202	275	357
Kidderminster	6	8	10	15	17	21
Leeds	53	63	84	123	152	172
Liverpool	82	104	138	202	286	376
London	1,088	1,259	1,504	1,778	2,073	2,491
Manchester	75	89	126	182	235	303

SOURCE 3 'I Can't find Brummagem', a song written by the entertainer James Dobbs and sung for the first time by him at the Theatre Royal, Birmingham in 1828. It was issued on broadsides and remained popular for many years. Similar songs were written for other towns

66 *Full twenty years and more have passed*
Since I left Brummagem
But I set out for home at last
To good old Brummagem;
But every place is altered so,
There's hardly a single place I know
Which fills my heart with grief and woe,
For I can't find Brummagem.

As I was walking down our street
As used to be in Brummagem,
I knowed nobody as I did meet:
They change their faces in Brummagem.
Poor old Spiceal Street's half gone
And the poor old Church stands all alone;
And poor old I stands here to groan
For I can't find Brummagem.

Amongst the changes we have got
In good old Brummagem,
They've made a market on the moat
To sell the pigs in Brummagem.
But that has brought us more ill luck:
They've filled up poor old Pudding Brook,
Where in the mud I've often stuck,
Catching jack-bannils [sticklebacks] near
        Brummagem.

But what's more melancholy still
For poor old Brummagem,
They've taken away all Newhall Hill,
From poor old Brummagem.
At Easter time, girls fair and brown
Used to come roly-poly down,
And show their legs to half the town,
Oh, the good old sights of Brummagem.

[One verse omitted]

I remember one John Growse,
A buckle-maker in Brummagem,
He built himself a country house
To be out of the smoke of Brummagem.
But though John's country house stands still,
The town itself has walked up hill;
Now he lives besides a smokey mill
In the middle of the streets of Brummagem.

[Last verse omitted] 99

Broadside ballads

Broadsides cover a wide range of subjects, including famous events, battles, disasters, crime, fashion and politics. One printer, J. Catnach of London, is said to have sold 2.5 million copies each of two broadsides about sensational murders in 1848 and 1849. Historians have sometimes dismissed broadside ballads (the oral tradition) as unreliable sources, and in some ways they may be. But, as Roy Palmer has written, 'There are few more reliable ways of finding out about the past: here after all is the real voice of the people who lived in the past.'

4. After reading 'I Can't find Brummagem' (Source 3) do you agree with Roy Palmer's view of broadside ballads?

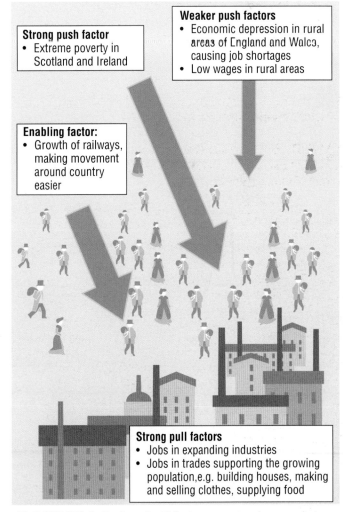

Strong push factor
• Extreme poverty in Scotland and Ireland

Weaker push factors
• Economic depression in rural areas of England and Wales, causing job shortages
• Low wages in rural areas

Enabling factor:
• Growth of railways, making movement around country easier

Strong pull factors
• Jobs in expanding industries
• Jobs in trades supporting the growing population, e.g. building houses, making and selling clothes, supplying food

SOURCE 4 Push and pull factors encouraging people to move into the towns

Why were people so horrified by the growth of towns?

At the time people at all levels of society were becoming aware of the growth of towns and the problems that then developed. These were new problems and Britain was the first European country to experience them.

SOURCE 5 George Weerth, a young German on holiday in England, described Bradford in an article that he wrote for a German newspaper in 1846

  Every other factory town in England is a paradise in comparison to this hole. In Manchester the air lies like lead upon you; in Birmingham it is just as if you were sitting with your nose in a stove pipe; in Leeds you have to cough with the dust and the stink as if you had swallowed a pound of cayenne pepper in one go – but you can put up with all that. In Bradford, however, you think you have been lodged with the devil incarnate. If anyone wants to feel how a poor sinner is tormented in Purgatory let him travel to Bradford.

SOURCE 6 A painting of an early industrial scene, *c.* 1825

SOURCE 7 A description of the imaginary town of Milton from the novel *North and South* by Elizabeth Gaskell. Gaskell (1810–65) was married to a Unitarian minister with a Manchester parish. She was shocked by the poverty she witnessed among the textile workers. Her novel was published in instalments in Charles Dickens' weekly journal *Household Words* between 1854 and 1855

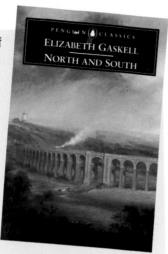

SOURCE 8 A description of the imaginary town of Coketown from the novel *Hard Times* by Charles Dickens, also published in *Household Words*, in 1854. In 1851 this journal had a circulation of 40,000 copies a week, so the ideas of novelists like Dickens and Gaskell reached a large audience

❝ *For several miles before they reached Milton, they saw a deep lead-covered cloud hanging over the horizon in the direction in which it lay. It was all darker from contrast with the pale grey-blue of the wintry sky, for in Heston there had been the earliest signs of frost. Nearer to the town, the air had a faint taste and smell of smoke; perhaps, after all, more a loss of fragrance of grass and herbage than any positive taste or smell. Quick they were whirled over long, straight, hopeless streets of regularly-built houses, all small and of brick. Here and there a great, oblong, many-windowed factory stood up, like a hen attending her chickens, puffing out black 'unparliamentary' smoke, and sufficiently accounting for the cloud which Margaret had taken to foretell rain. As they drove through the larger and wider streets, from the station to the hotel, they had to stop constantly; great loaded lurries blocked up the not over-wide thoroughfares. (Margaret had now and then been into the city in her drives with her aunt. But there the heavy lumbering vehicles seemed various in their purposes and intent; here every van, every wagon and truck, bore cotton, either in the raw shape in bags, or the woven shape in bales of calico. People thronged the footpaths, most of them well dressed as regarding the material, but with a slovenly looseness which struck Margaret as different from the shabby, threadbare smartness of a similar class in London.)* ❞

❝ *It was a town of red brick, or of brick that would have been red if the smoke and ashes had allowed it; but as matters stood it was a town of unnatural red and black like the painted face of a savage. It was a town of machinery and tall chimneys, out of which interminable serpents of smoke trailed themselves for ever and ever, and never got uncoiled. It had a black canal in it, and a river that ran purple with ill-smelling dye, and vast piles of buildings full of windows where there was a rattling and a trembling all day long, and where the piston of the steam-engine worked monotonously up and down like the head of an elephant in a state of melancholy madness. It contained several large streets all very like one another, and many small streets still more like one another, inhabited by people equally like one another, who all went in and out at the same hours, with the same sound upon the same pavements, to do the same work, and to whom every day was the same as yesterday and tomorrow, and every year the counterpart [the same] of the last and the next.* ❞

5. Look at Sources 7 and 8. Both novelists based their descriptions on the new industrial towns they had visited themselves. Compare their two imaginary towns of Milton and Coketown. How are they similar?

6. Do these two novelists like the new industrial towns? What words or phrases give you a clue to their attitude?

7. What social class do you think these novelists and their readers belong to?

8. How useful to our study of the urban revolution (growth of towns) are their descriptions?

The problems of working-class housing in the new towns

The growth of towns led to a housing shortage and the working classes were forced to live in poor-quality housing in the worst parts of towns. Thousands of new houses were built by builders and landlords keen to make large profits. As many houses as possible were crowded on to each building plot and often the cheapest materials were used. In many towns the houses were back-to-backs, often arranged around courts. Even the cellars would be used to house families. This gave rise to a number of problems.

Overcrowding
The demand for housing led directly to overcrowding. Landlords realised there was more money to be made from overcrowding than from building adequate accommodation. Whole families were forced to live in a single room and for financial reasons might even take in lodgers. (See the example of Knaresborough in 1851, page 133.) Apart from the problems of lack of privacy, it became easy for infectious diseases to spread through the crowded slums.

Damp and poor ventilation
Housing for the poor was often badly built. With earth floors, walls only the thickness of a single brick and poor roofing materials, many houses were damp. They were built so close together that it was difficult to get either fresh air or light into the rooms. The health of the inhabitants suffered as a result.

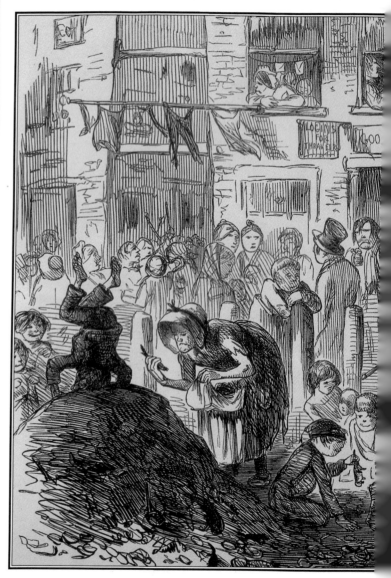

SOURCE 9 *A Court for King Cholera*, a cartoon published in *Punch* magazine in 1852

Drinking water
Most houses did not have piped water but instead had to rely on stand-pipes, wells, streams and rivers. All of these were at risk of being polluted by waste from the town. This meant that waterborne diseases like cholera could spread. The link between cholera and polluted water was not proved until 1854.

Rural housing
All these problems were often equally true of rural housing but at least in the country there was less air pollution. Although individual dwellings might be overcrowded there were not the huge numbers of people living crowded together that there were in the towns.

Threats to public order

The point about the large numbers of people crowded together in towns is crucial. It increased the problems associated with poor housing. It also aroused the fears of the ruling classes. The massing of people together created a public order problem. One reason for the Government's slow response to the Swing Riots in southern England was their fear of disorder in the industrial towns of the north. That is where many of the troops later used to suppress the disorders in the southern counties were stationed in 1830.

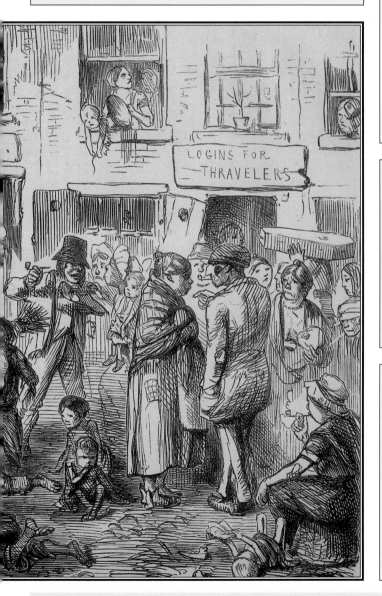

Hygiene

The lack of clean water made it difficult for people to wash themselves, their clothes and their bedding. Many people had body lice, which helped to spread typhus. There were epidemics of this disease in 1837 and 1839. Food storage was also a problem. Diseases like typhus, typhoid and diarrhoea flourished. Diarrhoea was a great killer, the number of its victims incalculable according to one historian. Prince Albert, Queen Victoria's husband, died from typhoid in 1861 at the age of 42. Even the rich were not immune from disease.

Rubbish

In many towns there was no effective system for collecting rubbish. Rotting rubbish in courts and streets provided yet another breeding ground for disease.

Sewage

Most houses were built without sewers or toilets. The houses in a court usually shared a privy. This might be built over a cesspit or a stream. Since many cesspits were not lined the sewage could seep into the water supply. They were not regularly emptied and often overflowed, particularly in wet weather. They were a major problem because they were a breeding ground for disease and they stank.

■ ACTIVITY

As a researcher for Radio 4 you are asked to prepare a short item for a programme on towns in the first half of the nineteenth century. Your brief is to:

■ examine their growth
■ look at the problems this led to
■ and explain why, despite the problems, so many people moved into them.

The broadcast will be no longer than ten minutes. It should also include an actor reading some source material to maintain audience interest.

Case study: how effective were the Kidderminster Improvement Commissioners?

AS YOU HAVE just seen on pages 74–75, the urban revolution led to many problems for the people living in the towns. Towns were run by CORPORATIONS or by the parish vestry. These forms of local government were not equal to the task of dealing with the problems of overcrowding, poor sanitation, poverty and rising crime. The response in many towns was to obtain an Improvement Act. Between 1800 and 1845 roughly 400 Improvement Acts were passed for towns and cities in England and Wales.

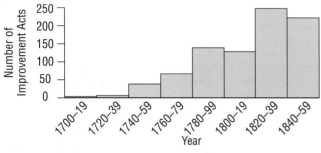

SOURCE 1 A bar graph showing the distribution of Improvement Acts in England and Wales, 1700–1840

1. Study the bar graph in Source 1. When, in your opinion, did people's concern about the problems of the growing towns become most serious?

What was an Improvement Act?

Each Improvement Act passed by Parliament gave to a group of local men, usually the more public-spirited inhabitants, the power to tackle the problems in their town. One such town was Kidderminster in Worcestershire, a small industrial town on the River Stour with the Staffordshire and Worcestershire Canal passing through it. The major industry was carpet making. The Kidderminster Improvement Act was passed on 21 May 1813 and the Kidderminster Improvement Commissioners met to begin work on 9 June 1813. They were to have an important influence on the growing town until their powers were transferred to the corporation under the Municipal Corporation Act on 8 October 1856. The Commissioners were given powers to borrow money, collect rates and undertake a number of tasks. These included the repair of the banks of the River Stour to prevent flooding, paving, lighting and sweeping the streets, building a new bridge, and setting up a system of night-watchmen. They were also given powers to fine those who broke the terms of the Act and created nuisances. This was a problem that the Commissioners were forced to deal with continually throughout their existence.

SOURCE 2 Extracts from An Act for Paving, Cleansing, Lighting, Watching & otherwise improving the Streets, & other public Passages & Places in Kidderminster, in the County of Worcester, 21 May 1813, listing the nuisances that would lead to fines

66 Any slaughterhouse, hogstye, necessary-house [toilet], or other noisome or offensive building deemed to be a nuisance to be removed.

All spouts and gutters which convey water from the tops of houses, warehouses, shops or other buildings directly into any of the streets to be removed or covered, and the water or other material conveyed by pipes into some underground sewer or cistern.

Any encroachments set up in or upon the River Stour, Back Brook or Daddle Brook to be removed.

All owners of steam engines to ensure that [the engines] consume their own smoke to prevent it becoming a nuisance.

No person to cause or allow the chimney of any house, workshop, outhouse or other building to be on fire.

No new buildings within the town to be covered with thatch.

No person to run, draw, drive, carry or place on the footpaths and pavements any coach, wagon, dray, wheel, sledge, wheelbarrow, handbarrow, truck or other carriage.

No person to roll any tub, cask, or wheel, or ride, drive or lead any horse, or other beast or cattle on any of the pavements.

No person to kill, slaughter, singe, scald, dress or cut up any cattle, swine or other beast in any of the streets.

No person to cause or permit blood to run from any slaughterhouse, butcher's shop or shambles [slaughterhouse] or any annoyance from the drain of any stye, cot, court or yard where swine are kept to run into the streets.

No person to hoop, cleanse, wash, fire, scald or burn any cask; or cut or saw any stone, wood or timber; or bind, make or repair the wheel of any carriage; or shoe, bleed or farry any horse in the streets.

No person to set, place or expose to sale any goods, merchandise on or overhanging the pavements.

No person to leave open any cellar door or grate in any of the streets; or to make or assist in making any bonfires or let off any gun, pistol or firework in the streets.

No person to allow ashes, cinders, dust, dirt, filth, soil, dung or rubbish to be left on the streets for any longer than it takes to load and carry them away. 99

■ ACTIVITY

It is October 1814 and you are Joseph Ward, the newly appointed surveyor to the Kidderminster Improvement Commissioners. Source 3 shows the area you have to look after. Your first job is to tour the area and make a list of all the nuisances, obstructions and annoyances, as defined by the Act (see Source 2), that you find. You should then prepare a brief report for the Commissioners to discuss at their next meeting on 19 October 1814 at the Guild Hall. Remember, you want to make a good impression on your new employers so your report must be clear, concise and complete.

SOURCE 3 A modern illustration of Kidderminster in 1813 based on careful research by the author

■ TASK

Use Sources 4–11 to answer these questions.

1. How effective were the Kidderminster Improvement Commissioners in dealing with the problems of the growing town?
2. Do you think their work helped make revolution less likely?

2. Look back at Source 1 on page 70. Did the population growth in Kidderminster (Source 4) match the national pattern?

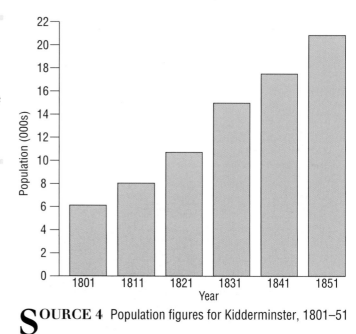

SOURCE 4 Population figures for Kidderminster, 1801–51

SOURCE 5 Selected extracts from the Kidderminster Paving Act Order Book. This was the book in which the decisions of the Commissioners were recorded. Much of what was discussed was routine, matters about street width and new buildings. The extracts below give a flavour of some of the other work of the Commission in its first ten years

9 June 1813	*Clerk appointed.*
25 June	*Rate collector appointed.*
26 July	*Six night-watchmen appointed.*
28 July	*Work on the River Stour to prevent flooding approved.*
20 August	*Night constable appointed.*
14 December	*350 oil lamps to be set up and lit nightly.*
6 September 1814	*Street-sweeping contract awarded.*
6 October	*Surveyor appointed.*
19 October	*List of nuisances discussed.*
14 April 1815	*Further improvements to the River Stour approved.*
28 April 1818	*Surveyor to report annually all nuisances erected in the River Stour, Daddle Brook or Town.*
31 August 1819	*Proposal of the Gas Company to light the town with gas accepted.*
15 August 1821	*New footpaths on both sides of Barn and Fish Street to be made. Drain in Vicar Street to be altered to remove smell.*
10 June 1822	*New drains to be built from new buildings on Bird Lane and from opposite the Dispensary to Daddle Brook.*
28 June	*New drain in Barn Street to be deepened.*
11 June 1823	*New drain to be built in Mill Street.*
10 September	*Night watch reorganised with two night constables and eight watchmen appointed.*
16 June 1824	*New drains from National School to Mill Street and from the Square to Mill Street.*
16 August	*Agreement to help fund the new bridge over the River Stour.*

SOURCE 6 Extracts relating to Kidderminster from the 'Report on the State of Birmingham and other Large Towns' by Robert A. Slaney, part of the Second Report of the Health of Towns Commission, 1845

66 *The streets where the richer classes live are open and well drained; but the small streets, alleys and courts inhabited by the working classes are much neglected, and are in want of drainage and cleansing.*

Some very bad places, narrow courts up close entrances, bad surface drains, stagnant filthy cesspools in gardens in Queen Street back and front. Jerusalem, Mouth of Nile – bad. Pantile Row – very bad cesspool. New Street – fever. Courts on West side of Mill Street – very bad courts, obliged to stoop to enter; damp and trickling with foul drain the only outlet; open privy. The square, Bewdley Road – open privy, heaps of filth, muck holes full, well of water between two muck holes.

The powers of the Paving Act are inefficient and defective and not sufficiently acted upon. 99

SOURCE 7 An extract from a report in the *London Daily News* on Kidderminster, 19 December 1849

66 *In all England it would be difficult to find a more thoroughly disagreeable town. It is close, confined, dirty and dingy. Its streets are irregular, badly paved and indifferently lighted. Judging from the offensive nuisances which meet your eye and nose at every corner, there is neither drainage nor decency. And the character of the town is only a reflex [reflection] of the character of its people.* 99

SOURCE 8 Total expenditure of the Improvement Commission 1828–56

Lighting	£14,208
Watching (up to 1837 when the watch became the responsibility of the new Council)	£2,197
Salaries and costs including sweeping	£8,330
Major works	£2,040
Interest on loans	£5,433

SOURCE 9 A comment made by the Earl of Dudley, the major local landowner, in the 1860s

66 *Kidderminster stank from end to end.* 99

SOURCE 10 Incidence of disease in Kidderminster

1832 August–October	*First major cholera epidemic (119 cases, 64 deaths)*
1844	*Typhus epidemic*
1847	*Smallpox epidemic*
1848	*Influenza epidemic*
1849 October	*Second major cholera epidemic (18 cases, 10 deaths)*

SOURCE 11 A table to show the occupations of the 165 men who served as Kidderminster Paving Commissioners between 1813 and 1856

Accountant	*1*
Baker	*3*
Banker	*2*
Butcher	*2*
Builder	*2*
Carpet manufacturer	*67*
Chemist	*3*
Clergy	*1*
Commercial traveller	*1*
Commission agent	*4*
Currier/Tanner	*3*
Draper	*5*
Farmer/Gentry	*4*
General merchant	*1*
Grocer	*5*
Iron founder	*4*
Ironmonger	*2*
Maltster	*9*
Miller	*5*
Painter	*1*
Poor Rate collector	*1*
Shopkeeper	*2*
Solicitor	*6*
Surgeon	*9*
Tax collector	*1*
Victualler	*4*
Wine & spirit merchant	*5*
Wool & yarn merchant	*4*
Unknown	*8*

3. Which class did the men in Source 11 come from?

Case study: was the Duke of Bedford a 'five-per-cent philanthropist'?

THE RUSSELL FAMILY were the Dukes of Bedford. Amongst their lands they held estates in west Devon and owned much of the land and housing in Tavistock. Until the mid-nineteenth century they had used their influence to limit the growth of housing and control the development of the town. This had resulted in serious overcrowding. In 1839 Francis, seventh Duke of Bedford, inherited the estates. He lived in London or at Woburn in Bedfordshire, and his Devon estates were managed by a steward.

A rich duke!

In 1844 the Duke was persuaded to allow prospecting for copper on his land in the Tamar valley. A very rich vein of copper ore was quickly discovered, so rich that by the mid-1850s the Tamar valley was the richest copper-mining district in the world. As landowner the Duke's estate was entitled to 8.5 per cent of the value of the copper ore mined. This provided him with an annual income of £10,000. By 1865 the cumulative value had reached more than £200,000. At the same time the annual profit from his west Devon farm properties was close to £25,000.

Housing crisis

The development of copper mining led to a rapid growth in the population of Tavistock as people came in search of work. Between 1811 and 1851 the town's population nearly doubled and it reached a peak in 1861. The existing shortage of accommodation in the town became a housing crisis. The problem was two-fold:

- overcrowding became worse as more people tried to fit into the existing housing
- the housing that was available was of poor quality; much of it was owned by the Duke.

Improvements

From 1845 onwards the Duke's estate began to build cottages. The Duke was involved in the planning and decision making but his steward, John Benson, and the architect-surveyor, Theophilus Jones, did much of the work on the ground. Jones was always anxious to build more cottages to improve living conditions. He often grew impatient with estate policy and his written reports were sometimes edited by Benson before being shown to the Duke.

Five-per-cent philanthropist?

In 1973 the historian J.N. Tarn coined the phrase 'five-per-cent philanthropist' to describe those men and women whose good works on behalf of the working classes were also planned to benefit themselves financially. In other words, these men and women were primarily motivated by selfish intentions, and only secondly by their concern for the working classes.

■ SOURCE INVESTIGATION

1. Study Sources 1–14 on the following pages.
2. List the sources on your copy of the table below.
3. In the second and third columns make a note of any information you can use to help you answer the questions.

Source	What was the housing problem in Tavistock?	How did the Duke try to improve housing?

4. Was the seventh Duke of Bedford a 'five-per-cent philanthropist'? Use your notes and the writing frame below to help you with your answer.

Start with an introductory paragraph describing the growth of the copper industry and how this affected Tavistock.
The discovery of large deposits of copper on the Duke of Bedford's west Devon estates led to problems in Tavistock. The . . .

Your second paragraph should describe what the Duke did to improve housing.
As the major landowner the Duke of Bedford had great influence in Tavistock. His estate . . .

Your third paragraph should describe what else the Duke did for Tavistock.
The Duke also . . .

Your fourth paragraph should explain what the Duke got out of all this.
The Duke's estate benefited from these good works in a number of ways. For instance . . .

Your fifth paragraph should outline what problems still remained and what else the Duke could have done.
Despite the building of model cottages there was still a problem with housing in Tavistock because . . .

Your conclusion should be your judgement on whether the seventh Duke of Bedford was a 'five-per-cent philanthropist'.
In conclusion I would argue that the Duke of Bedford was . . .

SOURCE 1 Population figures and housing stock for Tavistock, 1811–71

Census year	Population	No of houses	No of houses vacant	% vacant
1811	4,723	506	11	2.2
1821	5,483	703	23	3.3
1831	5,502	*	*	*
1841	6,272	856	34	4.0
1851	8,147	1,037	18	1.7
1861	8,965	1,182	30	2.5
1871	7,781	1,194	50	4.2

*No figures available

1. Do these figures fit with the pattern of population growth in England and Wales? Look back at Source 1 on page 70.

SOURCE 3 An extract from a report by John Benson, the Duke's west Devon steward, on taking up his post, 30 April 1836

66 *Many parts of the town are so old and decayed and, at the same time, so very shamefully dirty, as to be hardly worth repairing and the outlay on them is almost thrown away.* 99

SOURCE 4 An extract from the Sanitary Report of the Town of Tavistock. This was prepared by a group of the leading townsmen, including clergymen and shopkeepers. They submitted their report to the Duke's estate office in 1846. Knowledge of its imminent publication encouraged the Duke to start his building programme

66 *Very many of the houses inhabited by the poorer classes are in a most dilapidated and disgraceful state, in some cases neither wind- nor watertight. Many of them are dark, damp, and otherwise unsuited for human habitation.... There are 453 families each living in a single room.* 99

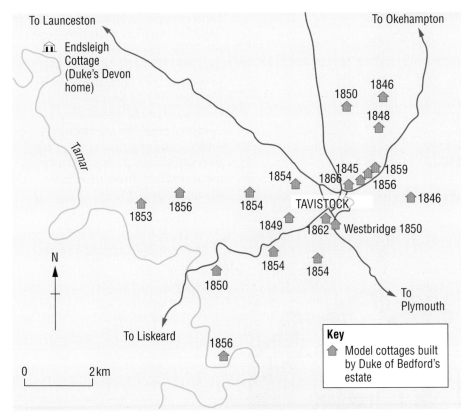

SOURCE 2 A map of west Devon showing where the Bedford estate built model cottages in the Tavistock area. Although the mining district was the Tamar valley the cottages were built in places where the estate thought there would be continuing demand even after the copper mines closed down. As part of their long-term strategy they did not want property in isolated places standing empty and not earning rent

SOURCE 5 The seventh Duke of Bedford who died in 1862. This statue was erected in the Duke's honour and stands in Tavistock today. The Duke financed the redevelopment of Tavistock town centre, the building of a new school and the improvement of the town's water supply and sewage system. Despite these developments the town still suffered cholera epidemics in 1849 and 1866. The Duke also improved the housing of agricultural labourers on his Bedfordshire estates

SOURCE 6 New cottages built in Tavistock by the Duke of Bedford, 1845–62

Date	Location	Number	Cost to the Duke			Cost per Dwelling			Weekly Rent[1]	
			£	s	d	£	s	d	s	d
1845	Dolvin Road	18	2,110	4	8	117	4	8	2	0
1846	Mana Butts	4	408	0	8	102	0	2	1	0
1846	Taviton	4	339	11	3	84	17	9	1	6
1848	Wilminstone	2	149	2	3	74	11	1		–
1849	Bowrish	4	288	1	11	72	0	5	1	6
1850	Westbridge	64	5,529	10	7	86	7	10	1	6
1850	Gulworthy	6	560	10	8	93	8	5	1	6
1850	Kilworthy	4	404	15	2	101	3	9		–
1853	Wheal Maria	20	1,397	1	3	69	17	0	2	0
1854	Church Park	4	368	3	2	92	0	9	1	6
1854	Crowndale	4	355	16	11	88	19	2	1	6
1854	Millhill	24	1,993	5	4	83	1	0	1	6
1856	Morwellham	20	1,813	11	9	90	13	7	2	0
1856	Woodovis	4	374	2	7	93	10	7		–
1856	Vigo Bridge	4	695	7	8	173	16	11		–
1859	Guildhall[2]	2	226	3	5	113	1	8		–
1859	Parkwood	24	2,251	7	5	93	16	1	1	9
1862	Fitzford	36	3,487	10	1	96	17	6	1	9
1864	Lumburn	4	493	5	1	123	6	3		–
1865	Week	2	241	13	5	120	16	8		–
1866	Kilworthy Road	40	5,386	16	8	133	16	8		–
	Totals	**294**	**28,874**	**2**	**4**	**98**	**4**	**2**		

[1] Weekly rents where known.
[2] Cottages built for the town's police.

Cornish slate roofs

Cast-iron guttering and downpipes

Rubble stone walls

Duke's crest

Window frames, porches, sills, quoins and lintels made from Dartmoor granite

2. Compare the total cost of the Duke's programme of cottage building with the annual income he received just from his Devon estates. What conclusion do you reach?

3. Do Sources 5 and 7 suggest that there was opposition to the Duke's estate policy in Tavistock?

SOURCE 7 An extract from the editorial in the *Tavistock Monthly Advertiser*, 4 June 1847

❝ Members of the Sanitary Committee did at one time indulge the hope that energetic measures would at once be taken to build at least a large proportion of the cottages which were proved absolutely necessary to the health, the comfort, and the intellectual and moral improvement of the population of the town. Thus far the expectation has been disappointed. ❞

SOURCE 8 A modern photograph of the Westbridge Cottages, Tavistock, built in 1850

4. The cottages in Source 8 are still lived in today. What does that tell you about the quality of the original building work?

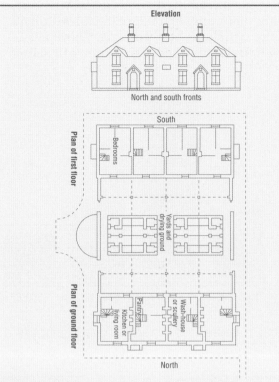

Design specification

Accommodation:

Kitchen, Living room, Scullery/wash-house

Parent's bedroom (grate)

Boy's bedroom (cupboard), Girl's bedroom

Outside: Pigsty, Ashpit, Drying ground, Garden

Construction: Rubble stone walls

Dressed granite step, sills, lintel

Duchess slate roof

Lead-lined eaves and gutters

Cast-iron rainwater pipes

Granite drying posts

Flint tile (9 inch) floors

Cast-iron oven and grate (in living room)

Mains water: each pair of cottages to be served by a brass standpipe and small granite reservoir

Cost: Total 64 cottages: £5,719 18s 9d

Each cottage: £89 7s 5d

SOURCE 9 The plans and specifications for Westbridge Cottages, Tavistock, drawn up in 1849. These cottages were of a far higher quality than other working-class housing in the town

SOURCE 10 A table showing the benefits to tenants living in the Westbridge Model Cottages. This table is based upon information in the papers of the Bedford estate. The estate was concerned with recording the effects of its building programme

	Westbridge	Previous home
Number of families	64	64
Number of people	379	368
Total number of rooms occupied	320	108
Average number of people per room	1.18	3.41
Average annual rent	£3.18.0d.	£4.1s.9d.

5. Study Sources 8–10. What would you say were the main benefits for the people living in the Westbridge cottages?

SOURCE 11 The Duke of Bedford, writing in the Journal of the Royal Agricultural Society in 1849

" To improve the dwellings of the labouring class, and afford them the means of greater cleanliness, health and comfort in their own homes, to extend education, and thus raise the social and moral habits of those most valuable members of the community, are among the first duties and ought to be among the truest pleasures of any landlord. "

SOURCE 12 A description of the model cottages published in the *Tavistock Gazette*, 18 November 1859. By moral the writer meant that the three bedrooms ensured that children did not have to sleep in the same room as their parents and that older children of either sex could sleep separately

" I think these are not only model, but moral cottages for they enable a family to live together without entailing the violation of the commonest proprieties. These are great times, my dear fellow, when a poor man can get a good house, a garden, and a stye for the porker for eighteen pence a week. "

SOURCE 13 An extract from the annual report of John Benson, the west Devon steward, in 1864

" I find every hole and corner in the town so overcrowded and we have no place to remove anyone into who comes out of the houses that require to be taken down. "

SOURCE 14 The historical geographer Mark Brayshay, writing in 1996

" There can be little doubt that the estate could have provided many more cottages, but the Duke was content to build just enough to 'stop the outcry' and no more. Even so, the seventh Duke appears to have enjoyed his reputation as a philanthropic landowner, as well as the epithet the 'Good Duke', and he not only published an article on his cottage-building activities in a popular journal, but even sanctioned the supply of lithographed plans to those who wished to follow his example. "

Why did the Government pass the Public Health Act of 1848?

BY THE 1830s there was increasing criticism of the efforts of local government, town corporations and Improvement Commissions to deal with the problems of towns. They were seen as inefficient and, in some cases, corrupt. This criticism combined with three other factors to prompt a response from the Government:

■ the increasingly rapid growth of the towns (look back at Source 1 on page 70)
■ the changed attitude of the ruling Whig party; they had already taken action to reform Parliament and the Poor Law system and were prepared to act again
■ the impact of cholera.

Cholera 1831–32

This disease was particularly shocking to Victorian society for a number of reasons. The most significant was that it struck at all classes of society, not just the poorer working classes. Secondly, its victims died so quickly and horribly. Victims suffered stomach cramps, diarrhoea and vomiting, turned blue-black and died in great pain within 36 hours of the symptoms first showing. Thirdly, it spread with frightening speed from place to place.

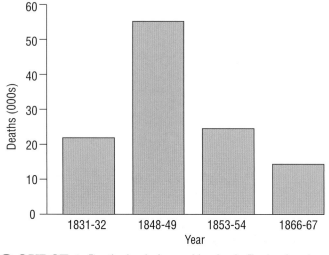

SOURCE 1 Deaths in cholera epidemics in England and Wales, 1831–67

■ **TASK**

1. Use the headings below or the sheet your teacher gives you to make a set of factor cards.

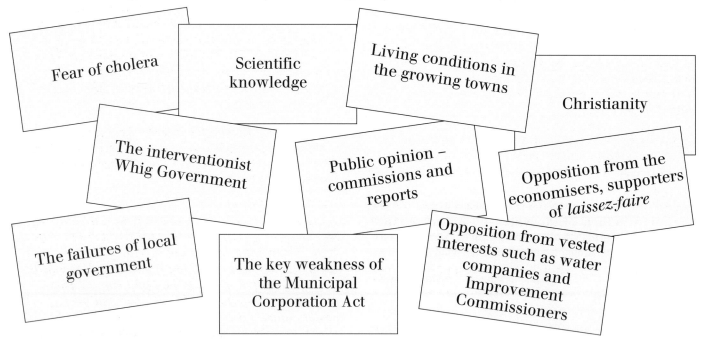

2. On each card note the key points that explain/support each factor. You should look back to the work of the Kidderminster Improvement Commissioners on pages 76–79 and you could also look ahead to Chapter 5.

3. Arrange your completed card set in a diagram that helps you to answer this question: why did the Government pass the Public Health Act in 1848?

SOURCE 2 An extract from a Methodist magazine in 1832

66 To see the number of our fellow creatures, in a good state of health, in full possession of their wonted [normal] strength, and in the midst of their years, suddenly seized with the most violent spasms, and in a few hours cast into the tomb, is calculated to shake the firmest nerves, and to inspire dread in the strongest heart. 99

The Municipal Corporation Act, 1835

In July 1833 the Government set up a Royal Commission to investigate local government. The Commissioners visited nearly 300 towns and examined the work of nearly 250 corporations. Their report, in March 1835, concluded that reform was needed, although they did not make suggestions as to how this should be done. The Government responded with the Municipal Corporation Act in 1835.

Towns were to be run by elected corporations headed by a mayor. All members of town corporations were to be elected by the ratepayers. Those elected then elected from among themselves a group of aldermen who served for a longer term of office to give continuity. These corporations had to publish their accounts. All men over 21 who had been owners or tenants of property for two-and-a-half years and who had paid rates were entitled to vote in local elections.

This created the framework for a standard system of local government but towns had to apply to Parliament for permission to set up a corporation, and this was an expensive process. Some chose not to apply; others did not apply straight away. Also the Act did not say what these corporations had to do: it was up to them to decide whether they wanted to make improvements to the housing, sanitation, paving and roads in their town. However, all corporations were required to set up a police force.

1. Why do you think the Act specified that corporations had to publish their accounts?

Enquiries into living conditions

After the cholera epidemic of 1831–32 a number of groups and individuals began systematically to investigate living conditions. The Government set up its own enquiries too. Flu and typhoid epidemics in 1837 and 1838 gave extra urgency to their work. The four most influential reports produced were:

■ the report of the Select Committee on the Health of Towns in 1840
■ the report from the Poor Law Commissioners on an Enquiry into the Sanitary Conditions of the Labouring Population of Great Britain in 1842
■ two reports by the Health of Towns Commission in 1844 and 1845.

The people who carried out the enquiries and those who read them were shocked by what they discovered.

SOURCE 3 An extract from the Report of the Select Committee on the Health of Towns, 1840

66 Sewerage, drainage and cleaning is greatly neglected ... the most necessary precautions to preserve their health in many cases appears to be forgotten ... in consequence fevers and other disorders of a contagious and fatal nature are shown to prevail to a very alarming extent, causing widespread misery among the families of the sufferers, often entailing weakness and prostration [loss of strength] among the survivors, and becoming the source of great expense to the parishes and more opulent classes ... 99

SOURCE 4 An extract from the Bradford Woolcombers Protective Society Sanatory [sic] Committee Report, May 1845. This was one of a number of reports produced by concerned local groups

66 Nelson Court
A great many woolcombers reside in this court. It is a perfect nuisance. There are a number of cellars in it utterly unfit for human dwellings. No drainage whatever. The visitors cannot find words to express their horror of the filth, stench and misery that abounds in this locality, and were unable to bear the overpowering effluvia which emanates from a common sewer which runs from the Unitarian Chapel beneath the houses. Were this to be fully described the Committee might subject themselves to the charge of exaggeration. We trust that some of those in affluent circumstances will visit these abodes of misery and disease. 99

The Poor Law Commissioners' Report, 1842

This report was the work of Edwin Chadwick. He believed in the 'miasmic' theory that disease was caused by bad smells and filth. He recommended that streets should be cleaned and drained, and that houses should be well ventilated. He also recommended the building of adequate sewage systems and the provision of a clean water supply. He believed that a national body was needed to do this. His report also made the significant point that the bad conditions in which the poor lived were not always the fault of the poor themselves.

One technique Chadwick used to secure support for his recommendations was to highlight the financial savings that could be made if they were taken up. His report included chapter headings such as 'Cost of Disease as compared with the Cost of Prevention' and 'Cost of Remedies for Sickness and of Mortality which is Preventable'. Like other report writers he appreciated the need for careful presentation or even propaganda.

2. Chadwick's idea of how cholera was caused was wrong. If you have studied Medicine and Health Through Time you will already know that it was caused by polluted drinking water. Does this mean that Chadwick's recommendations would have done no good?

Opposition to improvements

There was significant opposition from two groups to the demand for improvements. Firstly, there were those with a vested interest, such as Improvement Commissioners who didn't want to lose their powers, or water companies that didn't want to lose their profits.

Secondly, there were the 'economisers'. The economisers argued that ratepayers' money should not be spent on sanitary reform for the benefit of the poor who could not vote and did not pay rates. The doctrine of liberalism and self-help lay behind their argument. They questioned whether the poor died of cholera because they were poor or because of their moral failings. If it was because of their moral failings then sanitary reform was not needed. This is another example of *laissez-faire*. It would morally weaken people if they were helped; they should learn to look after themselves and then they would grow strong and independent. The poor were poor because they were sinful; nothing could or should be done about this.

As well as the opposition from these groups, there was also considerable scepticism about the efficiency of local and national administration and their ability to put such improvements into practice.

S OURCE 5 Statistics quoted by Chadwick to support his argument that where a person lived and what they did for a living affected how long they would live. He felt improvements could add as much as thirteen years to some people's lives. His report sold 20,000 copies and a further 10,000 were given away

Key

- Professional people, gentry and their families
- Tradesmen, farmers and their families
- Labourers and their families

3. Look at Source 5. Where did Chadwick get his figure of thirteen years?

The Public Health Act, 1848

Eventually the arguments of the improvers led to an attempt to pass an Act of Parliament in 1847. Its opponents, who became known as the 'Dirty Party', defeated this. However, in 1848 there was a new and even more devastating outbreak of cholera. Opposition disappeared and the Public Health Act was passed in 1848.

SOURCE 6 An extract from a speech by Titus Salt, at that time Mayor of Bradford, after the cholera epidemic of 1848. As mayor he had already tried to make improvements but had been opposed by many councillors

> 66 *The cholera most forcibly teaches us our mutual connection. Nothing shows more powerfully the duty of every man to look after the needs of others. Cholera is God's voice to his people.* 99

The major weakness of this Act was that it was not compulsory. Towns only had to set up a Board of Health if one-tenth of all ratepayers wanted it or if conditions were so bad that the death rate in the town was greater than the national average of 23 deaths per 1,000 people each year. By 1854, when the national Board of Health was disbanded, there were only 182 local Boards of Health in towns. Of these, 71 had plans for water and sewage systems but only thirteen had put their plans into action. The major improvements were to come outside our period.

4. Do you think the 1848 Public Health Act was a success? What evidence could you use to support your answer?

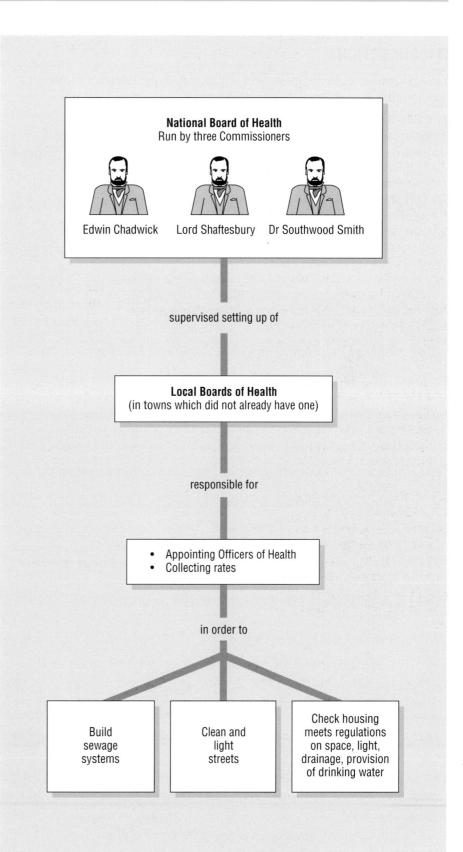

National Board of Health
Run by three Commissioners

Edwin Chadwick   Lord Shaftesbury   Dr Southwood Smith

supervised setting up of

Local Boards of Health
(in towns which did not already have one)

responsible for

- Appointing Officers of Health
- Collecting rates

in order to

| Build sewage systems | Clean and light streets | Check housing meets regulations on space, light, drainage, provision of drinking water |

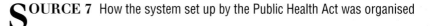

SOURCE 7 How the system set up by the Public Health Act was organised

Edwin Chadwick: the people's enemy or the people's friend?

■ CONNECTIONS

You are going to write an answer to the question: Edwin Chadwick –
the people's enemy or the people's friend?

1. Look back at pages 54–69 and 84–87 and use the sources and
information on this page and page 89. For each of the social
problems make notes on what Chadwick did and decide whether it
helped the poor or not. Remember that those helped by a
government measure do not always recognise it at the time.
2. You should also look at the opposition he faced from vested
interests such as water companies and undertakers.
3. Use your notes to write your answer to the question.

SOURCE 1 Biographical details of Edwin Chadwick

1800	Born at Longsight near Manchester on 24 January.
1823	Began his law studies in London.
1830	Worked as secretary to the Utilitarian thinker Jeremy Bentham.
1832	Appointed assistant commissioner for the Royal Commission on the Poor Laws.
1833	Appointed Commissioner for the Royal Commission on the Poor Laws. Appointed Commissioner for the Royal Commission into Child Labour in Factories.
1834	Appointed Secretary to the Poor Law Commission.
1837	During the general election there were public demonstrations against him.
1838	Asked by the Government to conduct an enquiry into sanitation.
1839	Married Rachel Kennedy.
1841	Excluded from his Poor Law Commission post.
1842	Published his Report on the Sanitary Conditions of the Labouring Population. Asked to investigate the problem of burial in towns.
1845	Published a paper on the working and living conditions of navvies.
1847	Dismissed from Poor Law Commission.
1848	Appointed Commissioner to the Board of Health.
1854	Agreed to resign from the Board of Health as he was so unpopular. Given a pension of £1000 per annum
1889	Knighted.
1890	Died 6 July.

SOURCE 2 His daughter Marion
on her father, written in 1928

*Whatever may have been his
faults, harsh, gloomy and severe
he certainly was not. To
understand him one must
remember that he belonged to a
generation which was working
its way out of the barbarism of
former ages. The Reformers of
those days were so much
absorbed in the tasks they had
undertaken that they had
hardly any thoughts for the
minor details of social and
domestic life, and my father was
an extreme example of that type.
Being somewhat passionate and
fanatical he looked on those
who disagreed with him as
enemies of humanity. This made
him many enemies but also
many warm friends amongst
those who respected the
genuineness of his convictions.*

SOURCE 3 John Simon,
Chadwick's successor, writing in
September 1890

*In the earlier stages of Mr
Chadwick's career, when the
essence of his work was to force
public attention to the broad
facts and consequences of a
great public neglect, it mattered
little whether he possessed the
quality of judicial patience; but
in his subsequent position of
authority demands for the
exercise of that virtue were great
and constant ... To those services
of Mr Chadwick's – to the ten
years' arduous labour which he
had given the cause before the
General Board of Health was
called into being – we of this
nation unquestionably owe that
our statesmen of those times
were first awakened to the duty
of caring for the Public
Health...*

Poor Law reform
After his appointment in 1832 as an assistant commissioner for the Royal Commission on the Poor Laws Chadwick became enormously influential. He directed the early development of the new Poor Law system. The importance of his role can be seen in the demonstrations against him in 1837. He was personally blamed for the reforms by the strong opposition groups. As a Benthamite Chadwick saw the poor as being to blame for their poverty.

Public health
Chadwick believed that the problems caused by poor living conditions were the fault of landlords, water companies and the failures of local government. This did not make him very popular with those influential groups, especially as his ideas would cost them money. This helps to explain his removal from the Board of Health in 1854.

Navvies
At the time of the second railway boom of 1845 Chadwick investigated the working and living conditions of the NAVVIES (see pages 132–35). To Chadwick their poor moral behaviour was a result of the conditions in which they were forced to live and work. He made a number of recommendations in a paper, 2000 copies of which were printed and distributed at his own expense to newspapers and Members of Parliament.

He wanted contractors to provide accommodation at low rents in portable weatherproof houses, food from temporary kitchens, savings bank facilities and temporary schools and hospitals. He also wanted them to improve safety standards. While his ideas drew opposition from many of the railway companies he did influence others. In April 1846 a parliamentary committee was set up to investigate the issue although no legislation was passed.

Factory reform
In 1833 Chadwick was asked to chair a Royal Commission on factory conditions. He believed that the poor working conditions were the fault of the employers and his report showed that government action was necessary. The result was the 1833 Factory Act.

Burial in towns
As towns grew in size pressure on space in the burial grounds of churches increased. Overcrowded churchyards were a health hazard. Decomposing bodies contaminated water supplies and spread disease. Chadwick produced a report calling for an end to burials in town churchyards and the creation of a system of public cemeteries outside towns. He also recommended that medical officers should be appointed to check the cause of death and to act to safeguard the others in the house in the case of infectious diseases.

SOURCE 4 An extract from *Edwin Chadwick: Poor Law and Public Health*, by Roger Watson, published in 1969

66 *Edwin Chadwick probably did more to affect the daily life of working people in the nineteenth century than any other man. We owe a great deal to him, but in his time he was known as the most hated man in England. He was hated by the working classes for the new Poor Law under which they suffered. He was hated by many of the wealthier classes for the Public Health Act because they had to pay for the improvements which were made under it.* 99

SOURCE 5 The historian Norman McCord's judgement on Chadwick, 1991

66 *Chadwick was an influential writer on public health and other social problems, though his tendency to alienate others limited his influence in practice.* 99

chapter 5

HAD WORKING CONDITIONS IMPROVED BY 1851?

YOU ARE NOW going to look at working conditions in the industrial towns and mining areas. Dramatic changes took place in the way many people worked as a result of the Industrial Revolution.

What were working conditions like in the textile factories?

THE INDUSTRY THAT changed fastest in our period was the textile industry. New machines powered by water and, later, by steam were introduced; in the worsted industry, which produced woollen fabrics, the number of power looms increased from 2768 in 1836 to 29,539 in 1850, an enormous leap. The use of new machinery led to the development of factories (or mills) to house them. The changes in the textile industry are well documented and so historians focus upon the question of what working conditions were like in these factories. However, it is important to realise that many people did not work in factories. Instead, they worked in their own homes or in small businesses employing only a few workers, such as nail making.

It is not only historians who are interested in working conditions in the textile factories. People at the time were concerned about them, too. Cotton, for example, had to be spun at a certain temperature, 27–29°C, and the air kept damp to stop the cotton breaking. Unfortunately this affected the health of factory workers, many of whom suffered from diseases of the throat and lungs. Men, women and children worked very long hours and accidents were frequent. The factory rules (see Source 1) seem very harsh to us today.

RULES TO BE OBSERVED By the Hands Employed in THIS MILL.

RULE 1. All the Overlookers shall be on the premises first and last.

2. Any Person coming too late shall be fined as follows:—for 5 minutes 2d, 10 minutes 4d, and 15 minutes 6d, &c.

3. For any Bobbins found on the floor 1d for each Bobbin.

4. For single Drawing, Slubbing, or Roving 2d for each single end.

5. For Waste on the floor 2d.

6. For any Oil wasted or spilled on the floor 2d each offence, besides paying for the value of the Oil.

7. For any broken Bobbins, they shall be paid for according to their value, and if there is any difficulty in ascertaining the guilty party, the same shall be paid for by the whole using such Bobbins.

8. Any person neglecting to Oil at the proper times shall be fined 2d.

9. Any person leaving their Work and found Talking with any of the other workpeople shall be fined 2d for each offence.

10. For every Oath or insolent language, 3d for the first offence, and if repeated they shall be dismissed.

11. The Machinery shall be swept and cleaned down every meal time.

12. All persons in our employ shall serve Four Weeks' Notice before leaving their employ; but L.WHITAKER & SONS, shall and will turn any person off without notice being given.

13. If two persons are known to be in one Necessary together they shall be fined 3d each; and if any Man or Boy go into the Women's Necessary he shall be instantly dismissed.

14. Any person wilfully or negligently breaking the Machinery, damaging the Brushes, making too much Waste, &c., they shall pay for the same to its full value.

15. Any person hanging anything on the Gas Pendants will be fined 2d.

16. The Masters would recommend that all their workpeople Wash themselves every morning, but they shall Wash themselves at least twice every week, Monday Morning and Thursday morning; and any found not washed will be fined 3d for each offence.

17. The Grinders, Drawers, Slubbers and Rovers shall sweep at least eight times in the day as follows, in the Morning at 7$\frac{1}{2}$, 9$\frac{1}{2}$, 11 and 12; and in the Afternoon at 1$\frac{1}{2}$, 2$\frac{1}{2}$, 3$\frac{1}{2}$, 4$\frac{1}{2}$ and 5$\frac{1}{2}$ o'clock; and to notice the Board hung up, when the black side is turned that is the time to sweep, and only quarter of an hour will be allowed for sweeping. The Spinners shall sweep as follows, in the Morning at 7$\frac{1}{2}$, 10 and 12; in the Afternoon at 3 and 5$\frac{1}{2}$ o'clock. Any neglecting to sweep at the time will be fined 2d for each offence.

18. Any persons found Smoking on the premises will be instantly dismissed.

19. Any person found away from their usual place of work, except for necessary purposes, or Talking with any one out of their own Alley will be fined 2d for each offence.

20. Any person bringing dirty Bobbins will be fined 1d for each Bobbin.

21. Any person wilfully damaging this Notice will be dismissed.

The Overlookers are strictly enjoined to attend to these Rules, and they will be responsible to the Masters for the Workpeople observing them.

WATER-FOOT MILL, NEAR HASLINGDEN,
SEPTEMBER, 1851.

J. Read, Printer, and Bookbinder, Haslingden

SOURCE 1 Rules from Water-Foot Mill near Haslingden in Lancashire, 1851

It is important to remember, however, that managing a large number of people working together in one place was something new to the factory owners. It was new to the workers too; in some parts of the country it was not unusual for people to take 'St Monday' off after having a good time over the weekend. It took time to get used to the discipline forced on them by the factory system, in which everyone had to be working at the same time, not when they wanted. Working hours were the same for men, women and children because the different tasks they performed were all needed to keep the machines running. Employers believed that the longer their workers were working, the more would be produced and the more money they would receive. They frequently put forward the idea that all their profits were earned in the last hour.

SOURCE 3 *English Factory Slaves*, a cartoon by George Cruikshank, published in 1835

1. Sources 2 and 3 are examples of the propaganda produced to highlight conditions in cotton factories. Apart from the obvious reference to slavery, how do the artists try to manipulate our feelings?

SOURCE 2 An engraving supposedly showing the treatment of children in cotton mills. This is the title page of a book called *The White Slaves of England*, which was published in 1853

Tommy shops

Some employers exploited their workers by running 'Tommy shops'. These were found in many industries, not just in cotton. The employer paid his workers in tokens instead of money. The workers could only spend these tokens in the employer's shop where he could charge higher prices. So he made a further profit. One railway contractor in the 1840s supposedly made a loss on his building contract but made £7000 from the Tommy shop his navvies had to buy from. In some places this was known as the truck system.

SOURCE 4 A token paid to workers, which could only be spent in the employer's shop

■ TASK

Produce a spider diagram to summarise what was wrong with working conditions in cotton factories.

Robert Owen

Not all factory owners ran their businesses in the same way. One who was particularly concerned for the well-being of his workforce was Robert Owen (1771–1858). You could say he was another representative of New Britain. He believed that people would work their best if their working and living conditions were good. At his New Lanark Mills in Scotland working hours were limited to ten-and-a-half hours a day. No children below the age of ten were employed. He also provided sick pay, good housing and a school for his workers. He ran a store that sold goods on to his workers at cost price. He was the man behind the early trade unions that you looked at briefly in your work on the Tolpuddle Martyrs in Chapter 3.

Owen hoped that the way he treated workers at his New Lanark Mills would encourage other factory owners to follow his example. It was therefore important for him to publicise his methods. He wrote several books, including *The Formation of Character* (1813) and *A New View of Society* (1814). Between 1815 and 1825 an estimated 10,000 people visited his factories to see his methods. Despite criticism from other employers he continued with his ideas and continued to make a profit!

The Ten Hours Movement

One idea Owen tried to promote was a shorter working day. He was not alone in this. Its most famous advocate was Richard Oastler (1789–1861) who founded what became known as the Ten Hours Movement. Oastler was a supporter of the Tory party, as were many supporters of factory reform. He could be seen as a representative of Old Britain, so the Ten Hours Movement saw Old and New Britain working together. He was against universal suffrage (everyone having the right to vote) and trade unions but believed it was the responsibility of the ruling classes to protect the weak and vulnerable. For example, he thought the 1834 Poor Law was too harsh and campaigned against it.

Oastler thought the best way to protect children was to obtain a maximum ten-hour working day. On 29 September 1830 Oastler wrote a letter to the *Leeds Mercury* attacking the employment of young children in textile factories. He compared it to the treatment of slaves, a powerful argument at the time as the anti-slavery movement was so influential. (Slavery was abolished in the British Empire in 1833.) John Hobhouse, a Radical Member of Parliament, read Oastler's letter and

SOURCE 5 Robert Owen's factory at New Lanark

decided to introduce a Bill restricting child labour. After details of this were published, workers began forming what became known as Short Time Committees to support efforts to reduce working hours. Short Time Committees were first formed in Huddersfield and Leeds but within months they were set up in most of the major textile towns. While Hobhouse's Bill was eventually passed, it did not go far enough for Oastler and his supporters. It only applied to cotton mills and there were difficulties in enforcing it.

Oastler continued his campaign aided by two MPs, John Fielden and Michael Sadler, who continually raised the matter in Parliament. Fielden was a millionaire factory owner and his Todmorden factory employed more than 3000 workers. Lord Shaftesbury also gave his support. The Ten Hours Movement used the wealth and connections of its supporters and the skills of Oastler as a public speaker to argue their case. Their focus on the treatment of children showed their skill in public relations. Their campaign led to the setting up of a parliamentary select committee in 1831.

The parliamentary select committee

The committee spoke to hundreds of witnesses involved in the textile industry – employers, overseers and workers, both adults and children. The report the committee published presented a shocking view of conditions but people saw it as being manipulated by Michael Sadler. Historians today share this view. The witnesses rehearsed their answers in advance and their expenses were paid by unions. The employers felt they had not been able to present their case properly. The immediate response was the setting up of a Royal Commission in 1833 under the chairmanship of Edwin Chadwick. Whilst less sensational, its report also showed that government action was necessary.

■ TASK

Examine the selection of evidence in Source 6. Do you think the person asking the questions intended to give the worst possible view of factory conditions? You should focus on the language used and the questions asked.

SOURCE 6 Evidence given to Michael Sadler's House of Commons Committee

66 James Turner, 17 April 1832
The work of the children, in many instances, is reaching over to piece the threads that break; they have so many that they have to mind and they have only so much time to piece these threads because they have to reach while the wheel is coming out.

Matthew Crabtree, 18 May 1832
I began work at Cook's of Dewsbury when I was eight years old. We had to eat our food in the mill. It was frequently covered by flues from the wool; and in that case they had to be blown off with the mouth, and picked off with the fingers, before it could be eaten.

Eliza Marshall, 26 May 1832
Q: What was your hours of work?
A: When I first went to the mill we worked from six in the morning till seven in the evening. After a time we began at five in the morning, and worked till ten at night.
Q: Were you very much fatigued by that length of labour?

A: Yes.
Q: Did they beat you?
A: When I was younger they used to do it often.
Q: Did the labour affect your limbs?
A: Yes, when we worked over-hours I was worse by a great deal; I had stuff to rub my knees; and I used to rub my joints a quarter of an hour, and sometimes an hour or two.
Q: Were you straight before that?
A: Yes, I was; my master knows that well enough; and when I have asked for my wages, he said that I could not run about as I had been used to do.
Q: Are you crooked now?
A: Yes, I have an iron on my leg; my knee is contracted.
Q: Have the surgeons in the Infirmary told you by what your deformity was [caused]?
A: Yes, one of them said it was by standing; the marrow is dried out of the bone, so that there is no natural strength in it.
Q: You were quite straight till you had to labour so long in those mills?
A: Yes, I was as straight as any one.

Source 6 continues

Joseph Hebergram, 1 June 1832

Q: What were your hours of labour?

A: From five in the morning till eight at night.

Q: You had fourteen-and-a-half hours of actual labour, at seven years of age?

A: Yes.

Q: Did you become very drowsy and sleepy towards the end of the day?

A: Yes: that began about three o'clock; and grew worse and worse, and it came to be very bad towards six and seven.

Q: How long was it before the labour took effect on your health?

A: Half a year.

Q: How did it affect your limbs?

A: When I worked about half a year a weakness fell into my knees and ankles: it continued, and it got worse and worse.

Q: How far did you live from the mill?

A: A good mile.

Q: Was it painful for you to move?

A: Yes, in the morning I could scarcely walk, and my brother and sister used, out of kindness, to take me under each arm, and run with me to the mill, and my legs dragged on the ground; in consequence of the pain I could not walk.

Q: Were you sometimes late?

A: Yes, and if we were five minutes too late, the overlooker would take a strap, and beat us till we were black and blue.

Jonathan Downe, 6 June 1832

When I was seven years old I went to work at Mr Marshall's factory at Shrewsbury. If a child was drowsy, the overlooker touches the child on the shoulder and says, 'Come here'. In a corner of the room there is an iron cistern filled with water. He takes the boy by the legs and dips him in the cistern, and sends him back to work.

David Rowland, 10 July 1832

Q: At what age did you commence working in a cotton mill?

A: Just when I had turned six.

Q: What employment had you in a mill in the first instance?

A: That of a scavenger.

Q: Will you explain the nature of the work that a scavenger has to do?

A: The scavenger has to take the brush and sweep under the wheels, and to be under the direction of the spinners and the piecers generally. I frequently had to be under the wheels, and in consequence of the perpetual motion of the machinery, I was liable to accidents constantly. I was very frequently obliged to lie flat, to avoid being run over or caught.

Dr Samuel Smith, a Leeds doctor, 16 July 1832

Q: Is not the labour in mills and factories 'light and easy'?

A: It is often described as such, but I do not agree at all with that definition. The exertion required from them is considerable, and, in all the instances with which I am acquainted, the whole of their labour is performed in a standing position.

Q: What are the effects of this on the children?

A: Up to twelve or thirteen years of age, the bones are so soft that they will bend in any direction. The foot is formed of an arch of bones of a wedge-like shape. These arches have to sustain the whole weight of the body. I am now frequently in the habit of seeing cases in which this arch has given way. Long-continued standing has also a very injurious effect upon the ankles. But the principal effects which I have seen produced in this way have been upon the knees. By long-continued standing the knees become so weak that they turn inwards, producing that deformity which is called 'knock-knees' and I have sometimes seen it so striking, that the individual has actually lost twelve inches of his height by it.

John Hall, Overseer

Q: Do you live at Bradford?

A: Yes.

Q: Are you the overseer of Mr John Wood?

A: I am.

Q: Will you have the goodness to state the present hours of working in your factory?

A: Our present hours are from six till seven.

Q: With what intervals for rest and refreshment?

A: Half an hour for breakfast and 40 minutes for dinner.

Q: Do you believe that the children can endure the labour you have been describing without injury?

A: No, I do not.

Q: When your hands [workers] have been employed for some time do you see any alteration in their appearance?

A: In the course of a few weeks I see a paleness in their faces, and they grow spiritless and tired.

Q: Have you remarked [noticed] that cases of deformity are very common in Bradford?

A: They are very common. I have the names of, I think, about 200 families I have visited myself that have deformed children, and I have taken particular care not to put down one single case where it might have happened by accident, but only those whom I judge to have been thrown crooked by the practice of piecing. **"**

What were working conditions like in the mines?

ONE INDUSTRY THAT saw a massive growth in the period 1815–51 was the coal industry, as you can see in Source 1. There was an increased demand for coal to heat the furnaces of the new iron industry, to power the new machines with steam engines and to run the railway locomotives. There was also the continuing demand for coal as a domestic fuel. Increased demand led to the opening of new mines and made it profitable for mines to be made deeper. Yet there had been no real developments in the technology of mining. The coal was cut by men using picks and hauled to the bottom of the mine shaft by women and children. As demand for coal increased, more people were needed to do the work. Conditions in mines had always been dangerous; the new, deeper mines made them more dangerous still.

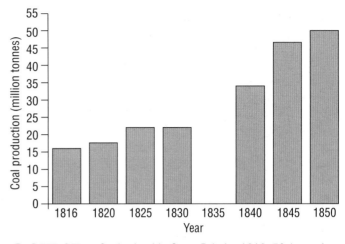

SOURCE 1 Coal mined in Great Britain, 1816–50 (note that no figures are available for 1835)

What were the most common dangers in coal-mines?

SOURCE 2 An engraving of Ardsley Main Colliery, near Barnsley in Yorkshire

Rock falls
These tended to happen when miners were blasting with gunpowder to get at the coal, or when the roof collapsed because the pit props supporting it were rotten or too far apart.

Falls down mine shafts
People were lowered down mine shafts on ropes. Sometimes they fell or the ropes snapped. There were also accidents in which miners were killed or injured by objects being dropped down mine shafts.

Ill health
The miners worked in poor conditions, breathing in coal dust, and so fell victim to lung diseases.

Explosive and suffocating gases
Miners needed light to work underground and to begin with they used candles. However, the naked flame could ignite explosive gases, most commonly methane. Two men, Sir Humphrey Davy and George Stephenson, invented safety lamps at about the same time in 1815. The other part of the solution to this problem was to ensure that the air circulated, to prevent pockets of explosive gases (firedamp) or poisonous gases (chokedamp) from building up. Children were employed to open and close doors in the tunnels to keep the air moving.

SOURCE 3 Casualty figures for coal mining in Great Britain, 1838 and 1864

Cause of death	1838	1864
Explosion of firedamp	80	94
Roof falls	97	396
Falls of objects down mine shafts	4	51
People falling down mine shafts	66	64
Explosions of gunpowder	4	15
Suffocation	8	8
Drowning	22	11
Crushed by tram wagons	21	56

1. Which man usually gets the credit for the invention of the miner's safety lamp? Try asking members of your family.
2. Suggest possible reasons why the number of deaths was higher in 1864 than in 1838.

The Royal Commission on the Employment of Women and Children in Mines and Collieries, 1842

After the factory reforms of the 1830s the reformers turned their attention to working conditions in the mining industry. In 1840 Parliament set up a Royal Commission headed by Lord Shaftesbury. There were four Commissioners and twenty assistant commissioners. They visited some coal-mines, interviewed men, women and children and sent questionnaires to all mine owners. Their report was published in 1842.

SOURCE 4 A man and a woman are winched up the mine shaft in a basket

SOURCE 5 Two boys push a truckload of coal from the face to the bottom of the mine shaft

SOURCE 6 Two girls carry sacks or baskets of coal up a ladder

SOURCE 7 A miner lies on his back to hew coal from the coal-face

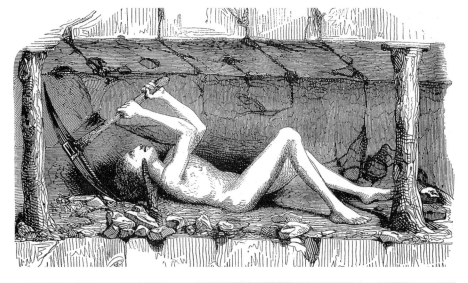

SOURCE 8 A woman bent double as she carries a sack of coal. This is reproduced approximately as it appeared in the 1842 report

Janet Cumming, eleven years old, bears coals, and says:

"I gang with the women at five and come up at five at night; work *all night* on Fridays, and come away at twelve in the day. I carry the large bits of coal from the wall-face to the pit-bottom, and the small pieces, called chows, in a creel. The weight is usually a hundred-weight; does not know how many pounds there are in a hundred-weight, but it is some weight to carry; it takes three journeys to fill a tub of four hundred-weight. The distance varies, as the work is not always on the same wall; sometimes 150 fathoms, whiles 250 fathoms. The roof is very low; I have to bend my back and legs, and the water comes frequently up to the calves of my legs. Has no liking for the work; father makes me like it. Never got hurt, but often obliged to scramble out of the pit when bad air was in." (Ibid, p. 436.)

The following represents an older girl carrying coals.

Isabella Read, twelve years old:

"I am wrought with sister and brother; it is very sore work. Cannot say how many rakes, or journeys, I make from pit-bottom to wall-face and back, thinks about 30 or 25 on the average; distance varies from 100 to 250 fathoms. I carry a hundred-weight and a quarter on my back, and am frequently in water up to the calves of my legs. When first down, fell frequently asleep while waiting for coal, from heat and fatigue. I do not like the work, nor do the lassies, but they are made to like it. When the weather is warm, there is difficulty in breathing, and frequently the lights go out." (Ibid., p. 439.)

Agnes Kerr, fifteen years old, coal-bearer, Dryden Colliery:

"Was nine years old when commenced carrying coals; carry father's coal; make eighteen to twenty journeys a day; a journey to and fro is about 200 to 250 fathoms; have to ascend and descend many ladders: can carry one-and-a-half hundred-weight." (Ibid., p. 448.)

What were the arguments for and against government legislation on working conditions?

■ ACTIVITY

Prepare for a class debate on the question: is government legislation on working conditions necessary? Your teacher will tell you if you need to prepare the argument for or against legislation. You should use the evidence that the Commission heard and the reports that they produced to help you to support your case.

Arguments over government action

No one should be working twelve hours a day and more! The way to get the best out of the workers is to treat them well. If my fellow factory owners will not take action by themselves then the Government must force them to it.

The views of Robert Owen and fellow reformers

The way I run my factory is my business! How am I expected to keep people in work if I cannot make a profit? Besides, if my workers did not want to work so many hours they would not do it.

A factory owner

You cannot expect us to take the Commission's report seriously! The way they collected their evidence was a disgrace. Everyone knows the witnesses were told what to say.

A mine owner

I need my job in the mine – how else can I afford to feed my children?

A woman mine worker

SOURCE 1 An extract from a speech against women working by Lord Shaftesbury, 1842

66 *Everything runs to waste; the house and children are deserted; the wife can do nothing for her husband and family; she can neither cook, wash, repair clothes, or take charge of infants.*

Dirt and ignorance are to be found in such households. Females are forming clubs and gradually gaining all those privileges of the male sex. They meet together to drink, sing and smoke, they use disgusting language. 99

SOURCE 2 An extract from a speech by John Bright in favour of women working

66 *You forbid them to work, as if working less would give them more food. Give them liberty to work, give them the market of the world for their produce, give them the power to live comfortably; increasing wealth, and increasing intelligence, will quickly make them wise enough to limit their work so they can enjoy life.* 99

SOURCE 3 The comments of another mine owner on the methods used by the Royal Commission on Mines to gather its evidence

66 *The men professing to be Methodists are the spokesmen on these occasions, and the most difficult to deal with. These men may be superior to the rest in intelligence, and generally show great skill, and cunning and circumvention [ability to catch people out] . . .* 99

SOURCE 4 The comments of the MP George Hudson in 1847. You will meet George Hudson again later in Chapter 7 (see page 129). You might then have a clue to his attitude towards Parliament looking into people's business.

66 *The country is sick of centralisation, of commissions, of inquiries. The people want to be left alone to manage their affairs. They do not want Parliament to be so fatherly as it wishes to be . . . interfering in everybody's business.* 99

SOURCE 5 Comments on the 1842 Mines Report by Lord Londonderry, a mine owner

66 *The way in which the Commissioners collected the evidence talking to artful [crafty] boys and ignorant young girls – and putting answers into their mouths – was most unfair. The manner in which the report was accompanied by pictures of a disgusting and obscene character was designed to excite people's feelings, not help them form a reasoned judgement. The trapper's job is not dull and boring. He is not kept in darkness all the time in the pit. The trapper is usually happy and cheerful and passes his time cutting sticks, making models of windmills and drawing figures in chalk on his door.* 99

■ CONNECTIONS

In the 1830s and 1840s a number of major social problems were investigated.

1. Use the table below to summarise the main points relating to each one.
2. Then use your table to explain the similarities and differences in the way the Government tackled each problem.

Problem	Commission set up and individuals involved	Reports	Government action
Poor Law			
Public health			
Conditions in textile factories			
Conditions in coal-mines			

1833 (Ten Hour) Factory Act

This Act was passed by Parliament on 29 August 1833. It made it illegal for children under nine to work in textile factories. Children aged between nine and thirteen could not be employed for more than eight hours a day. The reformers were disappointed with this Act for a number of reasons:

- children over thirteen were still allowed to work for up to twelve hours a day
- only four inspectors were employed to monitor the legislation; the reformers argued that with thousands of mills for the inspectors to visit factory owners would still get away with employing very young children
- with no accurate registration of births it was possible for both factory owners and parents to lie about children's ages
- the fines for breaking the law were so small that some employers were prepared to pay them to keep their mills running.

The reformers had hoped that if children could only work for ten hours other workers' hours would also be limited because production would have to stop when the children went home. Employers got round this by the use of a shift or relay system.

SOURCE 1 An illustration from Frances Trollope's book

Later factory reforms

After 1833 the reformers continued to argue for more changes. In 1836 Oastler began encouraging workers to use strikes and sabotage in their campaign for factory legislation and changes in the Poor Law. When his employer, Thomas Thornhill, heard about this he sacked Oastler from his job as steward of Fixby estate and took legal action against

him for unpaid debts. As Oastler was unable to pay the money back he was jailed in Fleet Prison for debt in December 1840.

His friends started to raise money to help him but it was not until February 1844 that the debt was paid and he was released. He then went back to campaigning for the ten-hour day.

Frances Trollope

Frances Trollope (1780–1863), the daughter of a clergymen, became involved in the campaign against the employment of children in factories. In 1840 after visiting several factories in Manchester and Bradford she wrote *Michael Armstrong, the Factory Boy.* It was supposedly based around the real-life experiences of a boy called Robert Blincoe but historians now agree that the story was made up. Trollope was criticised for writing about such a subject. One critic claimed that her novel would encourage people to hate factory owners and burn factories. The book could be bought in parts, making it affordable to the working classes. This led another critic to say that Frances Trollope should be sent to prison for writing such a dangerous book.

1. What significance do you think Frances Trollope's gender had for her critics?
2. Look at Source 1. How does the artist try to win our sympathy for the child workers? Does this illustration look familiar?

"*A serious gentleman as owns a factory.*"

SOURCE 2 The illustration on the title page of *Michael Armstrong, the Factory Boy*

The final stages in the long campaign were:

■ **1837 Civil Registration Act** This made it compulsory to record details of births, marriages and deaths.
■ **1844 Factory Act** Children aged eight to thirteen could work for no more than six-and-a-half hours a day. Young people aged fourteen to eighteen and women could work no more than twelve hours. This Act also included some safety requirements for machinery to be fenced in.
■ **1847 Factory Act** Young people aged fourteen to eighteen and women could work no more than ten hours a day. The campaign had finally succeeded.
■ **1850 Factory Act** This prohibited the use of shifts or relays of women and children. It raised permitted hours to ten-and-a-half hours but limited the working day to twelve hours with one-and-a-half hours of breaks. Now all textile workers had a ten-and-a-half hour day.

1842 Mines and Collieries Act

This Act was passed in 1842 after Shaftesbury's Royal Commission had published its report. Under its terms no children under the age of ten and no women could be employed underground. The Act also allowed the employment of inspectors who could visit a mine at any time. In fact, only one inspector was employed. The payment of miners' wages in public houses was banned.

Just as with the textile industry there were mine owners who ignored the law and workers who lied about their age. A later act in 1850 strengthened the powers of inspectors by allowing them to go underground and men with mining expertise were appointed.

These acts applied to coal-mines and textile factories. In 1851 just six per cent of the workforce in England and Wales worked in factories. These acts did not cover other industries or agriculture, in which most of the rest of the population worked. This effectively meant that by the end of the period 1815–51 most people in Britain still worked in unregulated working conditions.

■ TASK

1. List the weaknesses in the 1833 Factory Act. Now study the Acts of Parliament which followed it and explain how they corrected the weaknesses.
2. How effective were the Factory and Mines Acts?

Case study: what were conditions like for the nailers of Bromsgrove?

■ ACTIVITY

You are making a radio programme about working and living conditions in the nineteenth century, using the nail-making trade as a case study. You want to challenge the stereotypical view that government legislation improved things for everybody by the 1840s. Use Sources 1–5 and the information on these pages to help you.

In 1812 a crisis hit the nail-making trade in the Midlands. War with the USA meant that one of the major markets for nails was closed. Many firms in Birmingham and the Black Country went out of business or began making other items. Bromsgrove in Worcestershire, however, carried on making nails and so became the centre of the trade. The nailers made a decent living until the 1830s. At that time they faced competition from machine-made nails. This drove prices down, resulting in longer hours and lower pay.

The trade was organised by nail masters who bought the iron rod and gave it out to the nailers, who made an agreed quantity of nails for a set price. The nail master then sold the finished nails.

SOURCE 1 A letter published in the *Bromsgrove and Droitwich Weekly Messenger*, 4 April 1862

THE TRUCK SYSTEM
To the editor
SIR,
You will much oblige by publishing the accompanying statements, which I am prepared to prove correct.
I am, Sir,
Yours truly,
WM. LAUGHER

A Master's Price.			A Fogger's Price.		
2 lb. Hobs 7.25d per thousand.			2 lb. Hobs 6d per thousand.		
20 oz best Flemish 8.5d.			20 oz best Flemish 6d.		
20 oz best Battin 7d.			20 oz best Battin 6d.		
2 lb. best Clout 9.5d.			2 lb. best Clout 7d.		

A Grocer's Shop.			A Truck Shop.		
4 lbs. bacon 6d per lb.		2s 0d	4 lbs. bacon 10d per lb.		3s 4d
3 lbs. cheese 6d per lb.		1s 6d	3 lbs. cheese 9d per lb.		2s 3d
2 lbs. butter 12d per lb.		2s 0d	2 lbs. butter 14d per lb.		2s 4d
1 lb. soap 3d per lb.		0s 3d	1 lb. soap 6d per lb.		0s 6d
2 lbs. lard 7d per lb.		1s 2d	2 lbs. lard 10d per lb.		1s 8d
2 lbs. sugar 5d per lb.		0s 10d	2 lbs. sugar 6d per lb.		1s 0d
		7s 9d	Total		11s 0d

Nailers, assisted by their families, made the nails in nail shops at the back of their houses. The nail shops were small, approximately 3 m square. Each was fitted with a forge, a bellows and a workbench with a small anvil. There was also an oliver, a heavy hammer operated by a treadle, to shape the nail head. The room was poorly lit and, because of the forge, filthy.

The nailers worked for 70–80 hours a week but they were still their own masters, in that they decided when they worked and for how long. In 1860 it was estimated that the average nailer was making 2500 nails a day. One was quoted as saying, 'I have this day made 3000 nails and struck 64,000 blows with my hammer.'

The foggers

In our period a middleman emerged, the fogger. He would buy iron, give it out to nailers on a small scale and sell the finished nails to a nail master. However, many foggers paid in tokens (this was also known as the truck system, see page 91), others paid low wages and still others cheated with the weighing of nails. They gained a very bad reputation but in the hard times from the 1830s onwards nailers were sometimes forced to work for them.

1. The author of Source 1 is clearly hostile to both foggers and the truck system. How does he make his point?
2. Does the fact that the letter was printed in the local paper make it likely to be reliable?
3. Does it prove that foggers deserved their bad reputation?

Children as nail makers

Children were employed from an early age as a matter of financial necessity. Their earnings helped to feed the family. Very young children were used to pump the bellows, often standing in the roof, with their backs to a beam and using their feet to pump. As soon as they were big enough to reach the nail block they began making nails. According to local legend children reluctant to become nailers were nailed, through the lobe of their ear, to the door-post until they agreed to start work! The nail shop could be a dangerous place. In 1838, in nearby Sedgley, ten children were recorded as burned to death in nail-shop accidents.

SOURCE 2 Detailed figures taken from the 1861 census showing the age of nailers in Worcestershire

	under 5	5	10	15	20	25	35	45	55	65	75
Male	95	710	662	590	908	732	618	437	211	70	7
Female	69	712	767	614	825	540	362	195	108	28	1

4. Look at Source 2. How many children under the age of ten were employed as nailers?

SOURCE 3 An extract from the statements made to the Children's Employment Commission in 1862/3

66 *Richard Nock aged 10*
Works at nailing with his father, mother, sisters and brothers, not all in same shop; his sisters work in nail shops in Wales; gets up to work in the morning about 4 o'clock and leaves off at 8 at night, with half an hour for breakfast, an hour for dinner, and half an hour for tea. They get enough to eat; they all work Monday; can read in the Testament; went to day school when he was three years old, and was taken away at four years old to work at nails. 99

SOURCE 4 A strangely sanitized illustration of a girl nailer in Bromsgrove, an illustration taken from 'The White Slaves of England', an article in *Pearson's Magazine*, 1896

5. Bearing in mind what you have learned of the campaigns to improve conditions in the factories and mines, how reliable do you think Source 4 is likely to be?

Nailers' cottages

Nailers' cottages were essentially one up, one down buildings. The front door opened into a small living room with a pantry under the stairs. Upstairs there was a little landing with one bedroom. The living-room floor was beaten earth. It contained a fire and hob and furniture, usually a sofa, a table and chairs (if they had not been pawned). In the pantry there was a sink with tap and shelves. The lavatory was in the yard or garden. Upstairs the landing was big enough for a single mattress and the bedroom was big enough for one-and-a-half beds.

6. Would the Duke of Bedford have seen these as 'moral cottages'?

SOURCE 5 Extracts from the 1851 census returns for Bromsgrove of two typical nailers' cottages

49 St John Street

Name	Relationship	Age Male	Age Female	Occupation
Elizabeth Eades	Head – widow		not given	Nailer
Mary Eades	Daughter – unmarried		25	Nailer
Edith Eades	Daughter – unmarried		18	Nailer
Thomas Eades	Son – unmarried	16		Nailer
Josh Eades	Son – unmarried	12		Nailer
Oliver Eades	Grandson	5		
Josh Eades	Grandson	4 months		
William Tedstone	Lodger	17		Nailer

43 John Street

Name	Relationship	Age Male	Age Female	Occupation
Sarah Kimberley	Head – unmarried		46	Nailer
Katharine Kimberley	Daughter – unmarried		not given	Nailer
Ann Kimberley	Daughter – unmarried		not given	Nailer
Emma Kimberley	Daughter – unmarried		not given	Nailer
Elizabeth Kimberley	Granddaughter		4	
Edwin Kimberley	Grandson	2		
Henry Carter	Lodger	24		Nailer

How did the Churches and social reformers try to improve the lives of the working classes?

■ TASK

1. As you read this section, use a copy of the table below to make notes on what the Church of England and the Methodists did to help the working classes.

Group	What they did for the working classes
Church of England	
Methodists	

2. Which of the two organisations provided most help, do you think?

The Church of England

The Church of England or Anglican Church was the Established or official Church. Before 1828, only Anglicans could become Members of Parliament or hold other positions of authority in public life. (In 1828 NONCONFORMISTS also gained this right and Roman Catholics did so in 1829.) The Anglican Church had great influence on politics. Its bishops sat in the House of Lords and its Oxbridge-educated clergy were well connected and well regarded.

The Religious Census of England and Wales in 1851 showed that, although the Church of England had great influence in public life, its dominant position was not reflected in church attendance. Slightly more people were attending Nonconformist services than those of the Church of England, and 65 per cent of the population did not attend any service on the day the census was taken.

To many people, the Church of England seemed to be concerned with the rich and middle classes while ignoring the problems of the working classes. Certainly there was a lack of churches in the new industrial towns. In the countryside clergymen were often landowners and magistrates.

Attitudes to the poor

For the middle classes a visit to church was a social event; many paid rent for their pews. They did not go there expecting to rub shoulders with the poor. The views of many churchmen added to this problem. To these men the poor were poor because they were sinful. Any charity work they might do, such as giving food, clothing, shelter or money, would only help the poor in the short term, and it could not save them from their sin.

SOURCE 1 *The Clerical Magistrate*, a cartoon produced by George Cruikshank in 1819. The two-faced figure represents the two roles of the clergyman – preacher on the left, magistrate on the right; representative of the Church and enforcer of law and order

SOURCE 2 An extract from a sermon by Richard Watson, Bishop of Llandaff

> 66 *God never meant that the idle should live upon the labour of the industrious ... He hath therefore permitted a state of property to be everywhere introduced; that the industrious might enjoy the rewards of their diligence [hard work]; and that those who would not work, might feel the punishment of their laziness.* 99

Attempts at reform

Of course not all Anglicans thought this way. C. J. Blomfield, Bishop of London, argued that it was the duty of those in authority to 'increase the comforts and improve the moral character of the masses'. In 1818 the Church Building Society was founded and from 1836 new parishes were organised. Some clergymen chose to work in poorer parishes. These individuals worked for the good of their parishioners and became active in movements such as the Ten Hour Movement. Others felt it was their responsibility to take the Christian message to the working classes and the poor. They became known as Evangelicals. Amongst their number was Lord Shaftesbury, whom you have already met a couple of times.

SOURCE 3 The entry for Kidderminster in the 1851 Religious Census of England and Wales. All those present in church or chapel on 30 March, Mothering Sunday, were counted. The religious census was never repeated as its results were so controversial

Religious denomination	Number of Places of Worship	Number of Sittings			Number of Attendants at Public Worship on March 30, 1851 including Sunday Scholars		
		Free	Appro-priated	Total	Morning	After-noon	Evening
TOTAL	15	3,756	5,629	9,685	5,027	801	4,066
PROTESTANT CHURCHES							
Church of England	5	2,556	2,689	5,545	2,780	484	2,212
Independents	1	100	1,000	1,100	533	–	300
Particular Baptists	1	120	280	400	224	–	181
Society of Friends	–	–	–	–	–	–	–
Unitarians	1	50	500	550	311	–	157
Wesleyan Methodists	3	340	550	800	400	167	683
Primitive Methodists	2	110	140	250	210	–	233
Wesleyan Association	–	–	–	–	–	–	–
Wesleyan Reformers	–	–	–	–	–	–	–
Lᵞ Huntingdon's Connex.	1	230	470	700	200	–	300
OTHER CHRISTIAN CHURCHES							
Roman Catholics	1	250	–	250	300	150	–
Latter Day Saints	–	–	–	–	–	–	–

sitting = pew or seat   appropriated = reserved for someone, so probably rented

SOURCE 4

Date	Number of Anglican Churches
1811	11,444
1821	11,558
1831	11,883

1. On the basis of the figures in Source 4, was the Church Building Society successful in its work?
2. The population of Kidderminster at this time was 18,462. If everyone wanted to attend church at the same time could they? How many sittings were there?
3. a) Compare the numbers attending Church of England services with those attending Nonconformist services.
   b) Compare the number of sittings to the numbers attending the morning and evening sessions.
4. What conclusions can you draw from your findings?

SOURCE 5 Horace Mann's report based on the 1851 Religious Census

❝ *The most important fact that this investigation as to attendance brings before us is, unquestionably, the alarming number of the non-attendants. Even in the least unfavourable aspect of the figures just presented, and assuming (as no doubt is right) that the 5,288,294 absent every Sunday are not always the same individuals, it must be apparent that a sadly formidable portion of the English people are habitual neglectors of the public ordinances of religion. Nor is it difficult to indicate to what particular class of the community this portion in the main belongs...* ❞

5. Which class does Horace Mann refer to in the last line of Source 5?

SOURCE 6 Sweeping up the poor: a picture published in 1869

■ ACTIVITY

Source 6 is a cartoon that gives one view of the attitude of the Church of England to the poor. Draw a cartoon to show your view of the attitude of the Church of England to the poor.

The growth of Methodism

Whilst the 1851 census showed that over half the population did not attend church at all, religion was still one of the most important influences in society. People dissatisfied with the Church of England turned to other Christian Churches which had a different style of worship – the Nonconformist Churches. In particular, they turned to Methodism. Founded by John Wesley in the eighteenth century, the Methodist Church took its message to the poor and the working classes. Where there was no chapel, the Methodists preached in the open air.

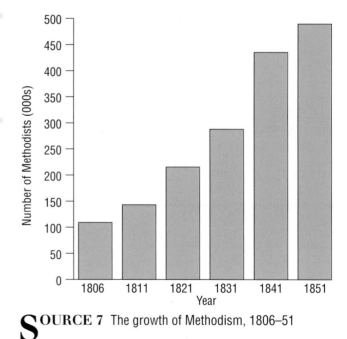

SOURCE 7 The growth of Methodism, 1806–51

They encouraged ordinary people to preach and held regular Bible classes. Their successful tactic of sending out lecturers was later copied by the Chartists (see pages 142–56).

> **S**OURCE 8 An extract from John Glyde's *Condition of Ipswich*, 1850
>
> 66 *The disciples of John Wesley gained a footing, and threw open the doors of Christ's kingdom to all. They moved among the poor; and by their earnestness and self-sacrifice, gained the love and reverence of the care-worn and the prostrate. The extent and nature of Wesleyan influence among the neglected classes were soon manifest [made clear], and not the least of the benefits it conferred, was the partial awakening of the members of other churches to some sense of their neglect in reference to their poor brethren. The very fact of the people flocking eagerly to hear the stirring appeals of the disciples of Wesley, is conclusive that the Establishment, and other religious bodies in the town at that period, failed in supplying the religious wants of the masses.* 99

The strong working-class element within Methodism enabled its members to achieve a number of important things.

■ They gave good example to their fellow workers; many Methodists, for example, were TEETOTAL and strong supporters of the Temperance Movement.
■ Their experience as lay preachers and as church organisers gave these working men the organisational experience and public-speaking skills required to argue for improvements in pay and working conditions. The Tolpuddle Martyrs were Methodists, and if you look back to Source 3 on page 99 you will see an example of their influence in the movement to improve conditions in the mines. Many historians argue that the Methodists had an enormous influence on our period.

6. One historian, Elie Halevy, writing in 1924, argued that Methodism actually prevented revolution. What do you think? Use the index to find every reference to Methodism in this book and then discuss the Methodists with your partner.

Temperance Movement

Drink was seen as one of the major evils affecting the poor in the period. In 1830 the Beerhouse Act made matters worse. Any householder who paid the Poor Rate could open his house as a beershop with no need for a licence. Something like 31,000 new beer sellers were set up. At the same time the tax on beer was removed. These measures were intended to reduce the problems caused by drinking spirits, particularly gin. Also, as the water was boiled in the brewing process beer was a healthier drink than much of the urban drinking water. In fact, the two measures led to an increase in drunkenness and associated social problems. To make matters worse, many employers at the time paid their workers in beer or paid wages in public houses.

This led to the development of the Temperance Movement. Temperance societies sprang up in towns and cities across the country and in 1842 a National Temperance Society was founded. Their members worked to cut down drinking. Although alcohol was never completely banned the Movement did exert a positive influence.

Co-operative Societies

In Rochdale in 1844 Chartist flannel weavers joined together to form a CO-OPERATIVE. Members each paid 2d a week to buy goods which they could then sell on in their shop. These goods were cheaper and of better quality than many of those existing shopkeepers offered. The Rochdale co-operative was very successful and copied elsewhere. By 1851 there were 130 Co-operative Societies and total membership had reached 150,000.

It is important to remember that working-class men and women worked to help themselves through organised religions and also through groups like the Temperance Societies, political groups like the Chartists and economic groups like the Co-operative Societies and trade unions. The nature of the source materials left behind means that this work is often not well documented.

Education

The industrial changes affecting Britain created a demand for skilled and educated workers. They also created the towns where the massing together of workers led to fears of lawlessness, crime and even revolution. There was little government involvement in education for a number of reasons:

- some people argued that to educate the workers would make revolution more likely
- the *laissez-faire* argument said that it would extend government power over people's lives – parents should decide whether their children were to be educated.

From 1833 a government grant was paid to voluntary societies providing education but it was not until after our period that the Government became directly involved in education.

Sunday schools

Robert Raikes set up the first Sunday school in 1780, to teach children reading, Christianity, obedience and good manners. He saw this as the best way to keep noisy children off the streets and out of mischief. They would learn proper respect for authority and have their immortal souls saved. By 1818 there were half a million children attending Sunday school, a figure which had risen in 1833 to one-and-a-half million.

Voluntary schools

The Nonconformist Churches set up the British and Foreign Schools Society in 1801 and the Church of England set up the National Society for Promoting the Education of the Poor in the Principles of the Established Church in 1811. These day schools were voluntary; parents had to pay 1d per child per week.

Not only did they have to pay but their children were not earning while they were at school, so a double cost was involved. Religious studies formed a major part of the curriculum in these schools.

SOURCE 9 Numbers of pupils attending British and National schools, 1815–51

	British schools	Pupils	National schools	Pupils
1815	*	*	564	98,000
1830	*	*	3,670	346,000
1851	1,500	225,000	17,015	956,000

*No figures available.

Ragged schools

John Pound set up the Ragged Schools Union in 1844 and Lord Shaftesbury became its leader. The schools run by this organisation were free and concentrated on teaching reading, writing and arithmetic to the children of the poorest workers.

Poor Law schools

Poor Law unions set up schools which the workhouse children attended as you saw in Chapter 3.

Factory schools

Factory owners were required to set up schools for the children they employed under the Factory Acts of 1802 and 1833. The children of their workers were also educated. Of course the quality of these schools varied widely. In 1857 Factory Inspector Horner reported that of the 427 factory schools in Lancashire 76 were 'good', 26 'tolerably good', 146 'inferior', 112 'worse than that' and 66 'a fraud upon the poor ignorant parents who pay the school fees'.

SOURCE 10 The factory school set up by Robert Owen at New Lanark

What was the contribution of individuals?

It was not just the Churches but also individuals who worked to improve the lives of the working classes. Two individuals strongly motivated by their religion were Elizabeth Fry and Lord Shaftesbury.

Elizabeth Fry (1750–1845)

Elizabeth Fry was the daughter of a banker, the mother of ten children and a devout Quaker. She spent much of her life working to improve prison conditions. She first visited Newgate Prison in 1817 and was shocked by the conditions there for prisoners, particularly the women and children. She organised a school for the children, provided more clothing and persuaded the governor and the women prisoners to accept a set of rules. She saw her work as spreading the word of God, and by doing this believed she would improve or reform the lives of the women. She also organised a night shelter for the homeless in London in the winter of 1819–20. Following her work at Newgate, she spent the rest of her life writing and travelling to promote prison reform. She became a European authority on the subject and influenced prison systems elsewhere in Britain and in other countries. She died in Ramsgate on 12 October 1845.

SOURCE 11 A portrait of Elizabeth Fry. After visiting Newgate she described the scene to committee of the House of Commons: 'The begging, swearing, gaming, fighting, singing, dancing, dressing up in men's clothes were too bad to be described, so that we did not think it suitable to admit young persons with us.'

SOURCE 12 A portrait of Lord Shaftesbury. He wrote in his diary, on 17 December 1827, 'Where can I be so useful as in public service? . . . I am bound to try what God has put into me for the benefit of old England! . . . for the advancement of religion and the increase of human happiness . . .'

Anthony Ashley Cooper, Lord Shaftesbury (1805–85)

SOURCE 13 Biographical details of Lord Shaftesbury

1826 *MP for Woodstock until 1830.*

1830 *MP for Dorchester until 1831.*

1831 *Main supporter of the newly formed Lord's Day Observance Society, an Evangelical group.*

1833 *Became MP for Dorset until 1846. Supported Ten Hours Movement, introduced a Bill in Parliament.*

1840 *Chairman of the Royal Commission on the Employment of Women and Children in Mines and Collieries.*

1844 *Organised Ragged Schools Union to give free education to poor children. Leading member of the Health of Towns Association pressing for reform.*

1848 *Member of the General Board of Health.*

1853 *Resigned from the General Board of Health.*

1863 *Published a report showing children as young as four or five still working in factories.*

SOURCE 14 An illustration of Shaftesbury visiting the slums of London in 1840

7. If you were publishing a biography of Shaftesbury which of these two images of him would you use for the book cover and why?

Was life for the working classes getting any better?

AS YOU KNOW well by now historians do not always agree on what happened in the past. The 'standard of living' debate is a good example of a historical controversy. It concerns the impact of the Industrial Revolution on the lives of the working classes. There are two sides to this controversy, the 'optimists' who argue that the standard of living of the working classes got better and the 'pessimists' who argue that it got worse. In order to talk about standards of living these historians have tried to consider a number of aspects of working people's lives.

These are:

- wages
- prices and what people bought
- health
- housing
- working conditions.

■ TASK

1. With a partner read the views of the four historians in Sources 1–4.
2. For each historian decide if she or he is an **optimist**, a **pessimist** or neither.
3. Can you explain why they differ in their conclusions?
4. Does it matter what happened to standards of living in the period 1815–51? Why?

SOURCE 1 An extract from *The Making of the English Working Class* by E. P. Thompson, published in 1963

66 *In fifty years of the Industrial Revolution, the working-class share of the national wealth had almost certainly fallen as compared to the share of the property-owning and professional classes. The 'average' working man remained very close to subsistence level at a time when he was surrounded by evidence of the increase of national wealth, much of it produced by his labour and passing into the hands of his employers. In psychological terms this felt very much like a decline in standards. His own share in the 'benefits of economic progress' consisted of more potatoes, a few items of cotton clothing for his family, soap, candles, some tea and sugar, and a great many articles in the Economic History Review.* 99

OPTIMISTS

SOURCE 2 An extract from *The First Industrial Revolution* by Phyllis Deane, published in 1980

66 *In effect the sustained growth of national product [the total wealth that the country produced] to which industrialisation gave rise tended to exert an upward pressure on working-class standards of living in three main ways, none of which implied a rise in the price of labour: by creating more employment opportunities for all members of the family . . . , by creating more opportunities for labour specialisation and hence for the higher earnings that a semi-skilled or skilled labourer can command . . . the upward pressure on the workers' standard of living also operated through the reductions in the prices of consumer goods and the widening of the range of commodities which came within the budget of the working classes.* 99

SOURCE 3 An extract from 'A Tall Story', an article by Roderick Floud in *History Today* (Vol 33, 1983)

" One can study separately changes in wage rates, the changing cost of food, rent and clothing, the changing impact of disease, the impact of new work processes, or the environmental costs of urbanisation and the rise of the factory. But it is extremely difficult to weigh up one change against another, or to gather enough information about changes as they affect one or other sub-group within the population. One needs a summary measure of as many as possible of the factors which we think of when we talk about changes in the standard of living of a population. One such summary measure is human height...

The Marine Society made 50,000 measurements of naval recruits between 1770 and 1870. There was a substantial increase in heights. The data suggests that there was a very substantial improvement in the nutritional state of the working classes during the first half of the nineteenth century...

Thus we can conclusively answer the question of the standard of living of the working class during the Industrial Revolution: it did improve. "

OR PESSIMISTS?

SOURCE 4 An extract from *British History, 1815–1906* by Norman McCord, published in 1991

" Even if it is accepted, as now seems likely, that there was on average a slow improvement [in the standard of living] in these years [1815–1830], this will be an average of limited significance because of the variations which it conceals. There can be no simple or uniform answer to questions about the standard of living. We know that there were marked fluctuations in prices, and that temporary depressions could hit employment and earnings hard in some parts of the country. Even if we had more reliable indications of movements in wages, earnings and prices, there are other variables to take into account in considering the condition of the people – housing, health, diet, levels of education and opportunity. "

WHY DID PEOPLE EMIGRATE?

SOURCE 1 *Emigrant Ship* by
Charles Joseph Staniland

SOURCE 2 A letter from Vere Foster to the social reformer Lord Hobart,
describing the conditions on board the purpose-built emigrant ship *Washington*
on the crossing from Liverpool to New York

66 *17 November 1850*
*The doctor this evening heaved overboard a great many of the
chamber pots belonging to the female passengers, saying that
henceforth he would allow no women to do their business below, but
that they should come to the privies on deck. I heard him say, 'There
are a hundred cases of dysentery in the ship, which will all turn to
cholera, and I swear to God that I will not go amongst them. If they
want medicines they must come to me.'*

21 November 1850
A violent gale commenced this evening.

22 November 1850
*The gale became perfectly terrific. For a few minutes we all expected
momentarily to go to the bottom, for the sea which was foaming and
rolling extremely high, burst upon the deck with a great crash, which
made us all believe that some part of the vessel was stove in. The wave
rushed down into the lower deck and I certainly expected every
moment to go down. Some of the passengers set to praying.* **99**

IN OUR PERIOD thousands of
men, women and their children
chose to undertake the hazardous
journey half-way round the world
to start a new life in the British
COLONIES of Australia, Canada,
New Zealand and South Africa, or
in the rapidly growing United
States of America. What
motivated these people to take
such a huge step?

■ TASK

1. Study Sources 3–10 on the following pages. Then prepare a short written report that explains why people emigrated. You should consider both the push and the pull factors outlined below.

2. What do you think were the most important motives of these emigrants? You should consider all their motives before reaching your conclusion.

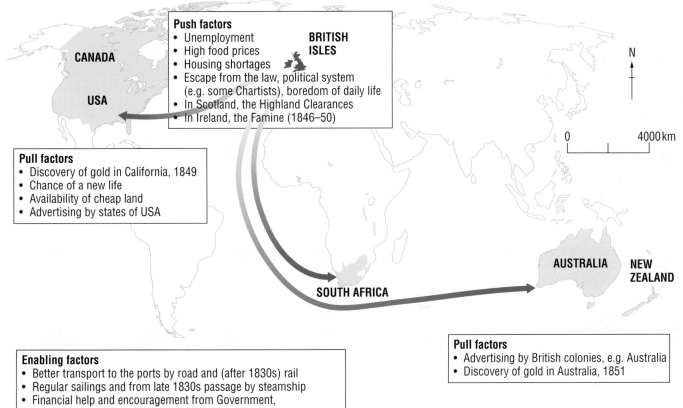

Push factors
- Unemployment
- High food prices
- Housing shortages
- Escape from the law, political system (e.g. some Chartists), boredom of daily life
- In Scotland, the Highland Clearances
- In Ireland, the Famine (1846–50)

Pull factors
- Discovery of gold in California, 1849
- Chance of a new life
- Availability of cheap land
- Advertising by states of USA

Pull factors
- Advertising by British colonies, e.g. Australia
- Discovery of gold in Australia, 1851

Enabling factors
- Better transport to the ports by road and (after 1830s) rail
- Regular sailings and from late 1830s passage by steamship
- Financial help and encouragement from Government, Poor Law Guardians, some landowners and emigration committees

England and Wales

Emigration from England and Wales was not very high until the 1840s. Where rural unemployment was a problem people tended to migrate to the towns and cities. After 1840 people who decided to emigrate were strongly influenced by government incentives and advertising (see page 115).

The Highland Clearances

These began in Sutherland between 1811 and 1821 and carried on throughout our period, reaching their peak in 1846. The new Scottish landlords, anxious to make profits from their lands,

systematically drove the Highland clans from their homes in order to introduce sheep farming. The Highlanders had little choice. They could starve, go to the cities in search of jobs or emigrate. Many chose the third option.

SOURCE 3 Evidence given by George Macaulay of Bernera to the Napier Commission into the Highland Clearances, 1884

❝ Our places were crowded at first when the neighbouring township of Mealista was cleared. Six families were thrown in among us; the rest were hounded away to America and Australia, and I think I hear the cry of the children to this day... ❞

The Irish Famine

In the early part of our period the introduction of the potato to Ireland allowed its population to grow from 5.9 million in 1811 to 8.2 million in 1841. The potato became the mainstay of the Irish diet. In 1845 potato blight destroyed the potato crops in Ireland and the same thing happened again in 1846, 1847, 1848 and 1849. Over those years roughly one million Irish people died of disease, hunger and fever as a direct consequence of the Famine. Thousands, unable to pay their rents, were evicted.

In 1847 what is often described as 'the infamous Gregory clause' formed part of the Poor Law legislation for Ireland passed by the House of Commons. Any family holding as tenants more than a quarter of an acre could not be given Poor Relief either in or out of the workhouse. Not even children could enter the workhouse if the family held land. So if the Irish tenants wanted to eat, they had to give up their land. This was an opportunity for landowners to clear tenants off the land so that they could move from arable to livestock or dairy farming.

Who was to blame for the Irish Famine is still a matter of historical debate. Some argue that the disaster would have been worse if some landowners had not tried to help their tenants and if the British Government had not sent cheap food to Ireland. They point out that in the years 1846–50 food imports to Ireland exceeded food exports. The writer of Source 4, among others, takes a different view. What is not in doubt is that, as Source 8 shows, two-and-a-half million Irish people emigrated in this period, some to Britain but many to the USA and Canada.

SOURCE 4 An extract from the Jail Journal of the Irish Nationalist John Mitchell published in New York, 1854

66 *In every one of those years, '46, '47, '48, Ireland was exporting to England food to the value of £15 million, and had on her own soil at each harvest good and ample provision for double her own population, notwithstanding the potato blight.* 99

SOURCE 5 An extract from *Ireland Before and after the Famine: Explorations in Economic History, 1800–1925* by Cormac O'Gráidà, published in 1988

66 *The current orthodoxy [the view most people take at the moment] ... tends to view the Great Famine as both unavoidable and inevitable. I see it instead as the tragic outcome of three factors: an ecological accident that could not have been predicted, an ideology ill-geared to saving lives and, of course, mass poverty. The role of sheer bad luck is important: Ireland's ability to cope with a potato failure would have been far greater a few decades later, and the political will – and the political pressure – to spend more money to save lives greater too.* 99

SOURCE 6 An extract from *The Irish Famine* by Colm Tóibín, published in 1999

66 *In fact, nobody is suggesting that the administration [British Government and Irish landowners] caused the famine. The suggestion is rather that, impelled [driven] by its contempt for Ireland and their interest in land reform, the administration caused many people to die. This is the possibility some historians are afraid to approach and that others, who come to wildly different conclusions, are too ready to entertain.* 99

SOURCE 7 Miss Kennedy distributing clothing at Kilrush. This contemporary engraving shows the daughter of Captain Kennedy, Poor Law Inspector of the Kilrush Union, giving clothing to evicted tenants in 1849

1. How could Source 7 be used as propaganda for either side in the famine controversy?

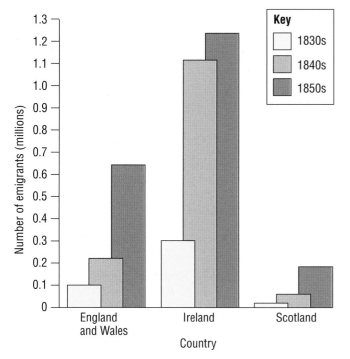

SOURCE 9 Destinations of the emigrants. After 1840 transportation to Australia as a punishment was replaced by imprisonment. From this point onwards the government in Australia was willing to pay for 'suitable emigrants', approved by their agents in Britain, to travel to the colony

Year	Australia and New Zealand	Canada	USA	Other*
1821	320	12,995	4,958	384
1831	1,561	58,067	23,418	114
1841	32,625	38,164	45,017	2,786
1851	21,532	42,605	267,357	4,472

*Excluding South Africa (no figures available)

2. Look at Source 9. What pattern can you see in these figures?
3. How do you think the Australian agents would have defined 'suitable emigrants'?

Government incentives

As early as 1826 a parliamentary select committee reported that in some areas of Britain there were more people than were needed for the work and land available, and also that there was unused land in the colonies. In order to help the poor to emigrate the Government was prepared to provide money to cover the cost of the emigrants' passage. Most of the early emigrants went to Canada but by the 1840s the pattern had changed, as Source 9 shows. Individual American states employed agents and advertised for emigrants, as did the Governments of Australia and New Zealand. Since the latter two were British colonies the British Government often encouraged people to go there. For example, in 1835 a bounty of £20 was given to young married mechanics and agricultural labourers who wanted to emigrate to Australia. Similarly there were financial incentives for young single women to emigrate to the colonies.

In some areas the local Poor Law Guardians paid the passage of emigrants. This was a way to save money in the long run – the poor would no longer have to be supported in Britain but could support themselves in their new homes. In other areas local emigration committees were set up, sometimes funded by local landowners, to help people to emigrate.

SOURCE 10 Advertisement from the Northampton Herald, 1846

“ *FREE EMIGRATION TO SOUTH AUSTRALIA, via Southampton. First class SHIPS of large tonnage, with the best arrangements and equipment, will embark passengers in the Docks, at Southampton, on 28th May, for Adelaide, South Australia; subsequently on fixed days each month. The undersigned are authorised by Her Majesty's Colonial Land and Emigration Commissioners, to grant a free passage by these ships to this healthy and eminently prosperous colony, to agricultural labourers, shepherds, male and female domestic and farm servants, miners, and mechanics of various trades, of good character. The demand for labour in the colony is urgent, with remuneration ensuring the comfort of every well-conducted man and his family.* ”

The gold rush

In 1849 gold was discovered in California. Thousands of young men travelled to the gold diggings in the hope of making a fortune. In fact, when they got there they found most of the best sites already owned by other people. Only a lucky few made their fortune. This pattern was repeated in Australia, where gold was discovered in 1851. Of course, the emigrants from Britain were unlikely to return home. They stayed on to make new lives in the USA and in Australia.

Postscript: did the emigrants have better lives in their new homes?

The emigrants hoped to make better lives for themselves overseas but first they had to survive the journey. Conditions on the ships varied widely. On the worst ships the main problems were over-crowding, poor food, lack of sanitation and disease.

There was also the danger of shipwreck. Between 1847 and 1853, 49 emigrant ships were lost at sea.

The experiences of the emigrants varied once they reached their new homes too. Some found success but for others their new lives were a failure.

SOURCE 11 A letter from William Green, who emigrated in 1834

❝ *Relating to my family and myself we are all well, and doing very well just now. Have got my order for 200 acres of land that I intend to go to in spring. People can say what they like about America. It is one of the finest countries for a poor man that is industrious for he has to want for nothing.* ❞

SOURCE 12 An extract from *Roughing it in the Bush* by Susanna Moodie, published in 1852

❝ *Canada became the great landmark for the rich in hope and the poor in purse. Public newspapers and private letters teemed with the unheard-of advantages to be derived from settlement in the region... They talked of log houses to be raised in a single day by the generous exertions of friends and neighbours. But they never ventured on a picture of the disgusting scenes of riot and low debauchery exhibited during the raising, or upon a description of the dwelling when raised – dens of dirt and misery which would in many instances be shamed by an English pigsty.* ❞

The Tolpuddle Martyrs

One group of emigrants whom we have previously met is George Loveless and his fellow Tolpuddle Martyrs (see pages 52–53). In 1844 they decided to emigrate to Canada. George's youngest daughter Sina died on the journey. After landing in New York the family travelled overland to London in Ontario. By 1847 George was able to buy a 100-acre property with a deposit of £25 and a mortgage of £125. He then built a log farmstead. All the other Tolpuddle men, except James Loveless, also bought land in the same area. John Standfield owned a store and was for a time Mayor of East London.

In Canada the men stayed out of politics. However, Ontario was a strongly Methodist province and they all remained active Methodists. They deliberately kept their past a secret and lived quietly. They believed that their transportation and penal servitude would be a stigma for their children. Only after their deaths was their past revealed. Now there is an annual commemorative service held in their honour in London, Ontario, on Labour Day and their many descendants are proud of their heritage. They were clearly successful emigrants.

SOURCE 13 A cartoon from *Punch*, 1840

HERE AND THERE;
OR, EMIGRATION A REMEDY.

section **3**

THE RAILWAYS

IN 1815 THERE were no railways. By 1851 railways had transformed many aspects of life in Britain. New towns had sprung up; the diet of the urban working classes had improved and it was now possible for them to take day trips to the seaside or travel to a political meeting. For the first time clocks all over the country kept to the same time. Some historians think the railways changed life in Britain so much that the development of railways was the real revolution in our period. In this chapter you will be exploring how and why this great change occurred.

Why was the Liverpool and Manchester Railway built?

The early railways

The first railways were wooden tracks along which horses pulled wagons loaded with coal. In the early nineteenth century iron rails replaced the wooden rails and engineers like Richard Trevithick experimented with steam locomotives that pulled the wagons along the tracks. The pressure for development was felt most strongly in the coal-mining area of north-east England. Here a number of mining engineers built steam locomotives. Amongst these early pioneers were John Blenkinsop, William Hedley and George Stephenson.

The Stockton to Darlington Railway, 1825

In 1821 George Stephenson was appointed engineer in charge of the new Stockton to Darlington Railway. It was intended to carry coal from the coal-mines around Darlington to the port of Stockton, 43 km away. The owners had originally planned to use horses to pull the wagons but George Stephenson and his son Robert built a steam locomotive called *Locomotion*. When the railway opened in 1825 this locomotive was used to move the wagons part of the way; for the rest of the journey they were moved by stationary steam engines and horses. The significance of this railway was that it demonstrated the potential of steam power.

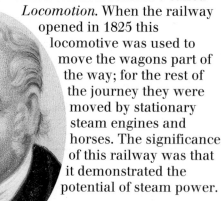

SOURCE 1 A portrait of George Stephenson

Why was the Liverpool and Manchester Railway built?

In 1824 merchants formed the Liverpool and Manchester Railway Company. They wanted to establish good communications between one of the greatest ports in the world and one of the greatest cities. At that time goods could be moved from the port of Liverpool to Manchester by road or canal. By road the cost of moving cotton was 40 shillings (s) per ton. By canal the cost of moving cotton varied from 9s 2d to 20s per ton. As well as being expensive, transport by road and canal was slow and bad weather or heavy traffic caused delays. According to the Railway Company prospectus, there was also a problem with pilfering. Merchants wanted a quicker and cheaper form of transport between the two cities. The answer appeared to be a railway and the success of the Stockton to Darlington Railway seemed to confirm this.

■ ACTIVITY

You are employed at a Railway Centre and Museum and you have been asked to prepare a display panel on the Liverpool and Manchester Railway, suitable for families with children of primary-school age. The four key questions you must answer are:

■ why was the Railway necessary?
■ what problems did the Railway Company encounter?
■ how did they overcome the problems?
■ what impact did the Railway have?

As you read through pages 119–25 make notes under each of these headings. Finally, use your notes to create your panel. Make sure it is visually attractive to engage their interest, otherwise they will just walk by.

The first problem facing the merchants was to raise the estimated building costs of £300,000. Three thousand shares valued at £100 each were sold. The merchants then began a campaign to win parliamentary approval for the railway.

Opposition to the railway was led by two powerful landowners, the Earls of Derby and Sefton, who owned the land the railway would cross. When George Stephenson and his men tried to survey the route, they were attacked. Canal and turnpike companies also sent petitions to Parliament opposing the new railway.

Some people objected to the route Stephenson planned.

Other objectors were worried about the dangers of using steam locomotives. The objectors' campaign was successful and in 1825 the Company's Bill was rejected by Parliament.

The Company decided to change the proposed route, build a tunnel to take the line into Liverpool and offer canal company owners the chance to buy shares in the new railway. They were deliberately vague about whether steam locomotives would be used. This time they were successful. The Bill was passed and in 1826 work could begin.

SOURCE 2 The problems faced by the Liverpool and Manchester Railway
SCompany and how they were overcome

Engineering triumphs

Sources 3, 4, 6 and 7 show the problems George Stephenson had to overcome in building the line. Each of his solutions represented a considerable engineering achievement at the time.

Edgehill tunnel

This tunnel had to be bored through about 2 km of solid rock. It was designed to take the railway down the incline (slope) into the city of Liverpool without disrupting road traffic. The railway wagons were hauled up and lowered down the incline by stationary engines. On the instructions of the company directors Stephenson built his Moorish Arch to conceal these stationary engines. This notion of grand architecture was copied by many of the later railway companies.

SOURCE 3 An engraving of the Moorish Arch by John Forster, published in 1832

Olive Mount cutting

This cutting, 24 m deep at one point, was needed to bring the line into Liverpool. It was the first extensive stone cutting on any railway. The artist shows navvies still working on the cutting's sides while trains were running.

SOURCE 4 A painting of the Olive Mount cutting, published 1831

SOURCE 5 An extract from a letter from George Stephenson to his son Robert, 23 February 1827. The grammar, spelling and punctuation are his

66 We are getting rapitly on with the tunnal under Liverpool it is 22 feet width & 16 feet high we have 6 shafts and driving right & left we have also got a great deal done on chat moss and on the same plans that I prepared before parlament 2 years a go which plans was condemed by almost all the Engineers in England. These plans is by cuting & imbanking with the moss some of the laths 12 feet high and stand remarkably well.

We have a most magnificent bridge to build a cross the sankey valley near newton it will be 70 feet high so as to cross the masts of the ships that navigate that canal. I have drawn a plan on the gothick principal. there will be 20 arches of 40 feet span. It will be quite novel in England as there will be a flat arch sprung from the centre of the tops of the gothick and so on. It has a fine a pearance in the plans. We have also 2 bridges in hand at present, one at the river adjoining chat moss and the other crossing the duckes canal near manchester. 99

Sankey Brook viaduct

This great viaduct was built to carry the railway over the Sankey Brook Navigation. The canal company insisted that there had to be a clearance of 60 ft (over 18 m) to allow the passage of barges such as the one pictured. This engineering work cost £45,000.

SOURCE 6 A painting of the Sankey Brook viaduct, published in 1831

Chat Moss

This was a boggy moorland area near Leigh. In order to cross it Stephenson cut drainage ditches to dry out a strip approximately 15 m across. Over this he built a raft of wooden hurdles and heather. Sand and gravel were laid on top of the raft, followed by the rails themselves.

SOURCE 7 Navvies laying rafts to carry the track over Chat Moss

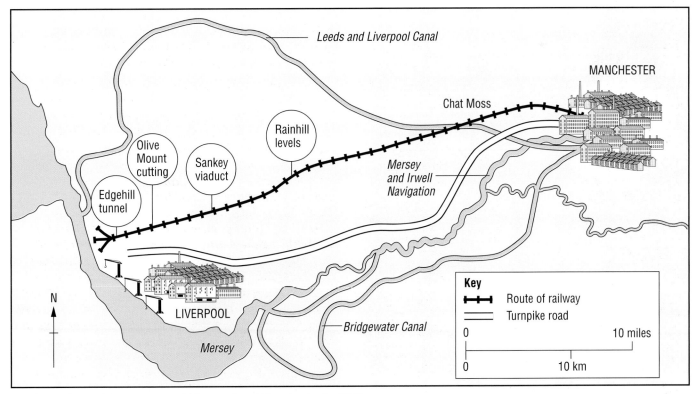

SOURCE 8 The area around Liverpool and Manchester in 1830

The Rainhill Trials, 1829

In 1828 Stephenson persuaded the Company directors that they should use steam locomotives. In order to get the best they organised a competition to be held on the Rainhill levels. The winning locomotive would receive a prize of £500. More importantly, orders for more locomotives to run on the railway would follow.

Certain conditions were laid down for entrants. The locomotive's maximum weight was to be no more than six tons, it had to run on six wheels, the boilers had to be sprung, it had to consume its own smoke and cost less than £550. Each entrant had to undertake a number of tests. They had to make twenty timed runs over a distance of nearly two miles (3 km), the total being roughly the distance for the return journey from Liverpool to Manchester, and pull a weight of wagons three times the weight of their locomotive. They also had to reach a speed of 10 mph (16 kph) and there were other rules relating to how long it took them to get up steam and so on. These were all designed to test how suitable the locomotives would be for the running of the railway.

The competition began on 6 October 1829. Such was the public interest that a crowd of over 10,000 people came to watch. Ten locomotives were originally entered but on the day there were only five entrants.

> **TO ENGINEERS AND IRON FOUNDERS.**
> THE DIRECTORS of the LIVERPOOL and MAN-CHESTER RAILWAY hereby offer a Premium of £500 (over and above the cost price) for a LOCOMOTIVE ENGINE, which shall be a decided improvement on any hitherto constructed, subject to certain stipulations and conditions, a copy of which may be had at the Railway Office, or will be forwarded, as may be directed, on application for the same, if by letter, post paid.
> HENRY BOOTH, Treasurer.
> *Railway Office, Liverpool, April 25, 1829.*

SOURCE 9 An advertisement placed by the Liverpool and Manchester Railway Company in the *Liverpool Mercury* on 1 May 1829, announcing the competition

■ ACTIVITY

Work in groups of three. Imagine you are the competition judges, John Kennedy, John Rastrick and Nicholas Wood.

1. Study the engravings of the locomotives and read the accounts of how each performed.
2. Which one would you declare the winner?
3. Are there any others that you would buy to work on the railway?

CYCLOPED

Owned by: Thomas Brandreth

Powered by: a horse walking on a drive belt

Reached speeds of: 5 mph (8 kph)

Notes: Withdrawn after the horse fell through the floor of the locomotive

---

NOVELTY

Owned by: John Braithwaite and John Ericsson

Powered by: steam

Reached speeds of: 28 mph (45 kph)

Weight: 2 tons 3 cwt (2.2 tonnes)

Notes: Built in six weeks and not tried out before the competition. It performed very well on day one, better than the *Rocket*. On day two a boiler pipe overheated and was damaged. After hasty repairs, the locomotive competed on day three but the cement used in the repairs had not had time to harden. The boiler joints started to blow causing considerable damage. Braithwaite and Ericsson then withdrew their locomotive and left it 'to be judged by the performances it had already exhibited'. The local newspaper, the *Liverpool Mercury*, judged this to be the best locomotive.

PERSEVERANCE

Owned by: Timothy Burstall

Powered by: steam

Reached speeds of: 6 mph (9.5 kph)

Notes: The locomotive was damaged on the way to the trials when the wagon carrying it overturned. Burstall spent five days repairing it. On day six it was ready to take part but after one day Burstall withdrew it.

ROCKET

Owned by: Robert Stephenson

Powered by: steam

Reached speeds of: 29 mph (46 kph)

Notes: Completed all the runs. By day three it was the only engine left in the competition. On that day it covered 56 km in 3 hours 12 minutes. It did not entirely meet the condition to 'consume its own smoke'.

SANS PAREIL

Owned by: Timothy Hackworth

Powered by: steam

Reached speeds of: 16 mph (26 kph)

Weight: 6 tons 2 cwt (6.2 tonnes)

Notes: Completed eight trips, roughly 112 km. Then it broke down with a cracked cylinder. Robert Stephenson's locomotive works had cast this cylinder. Hackworth commented afterwards, 'Neither in construction nor in principle was the engine deficient but circumstances compelled me to put that confidence in others which I found with sorrow was but too implicitly placed.'

Opening day

The Rainhill Trials were won by Stephenson's *Rocket*. Robert Stephenson was awarded the £500 prize and an order for more locomotives. *Sans Pareil* was also purchased by the company and *Perseverance* was given a consolation prize of £25.

The completed railway was opened on 15 September 1830. The Prime Minister – the Duke of Wellington – and a large number of important people attended. The ceremony featured a procession of eight locomotives, including the *Rocket*. After a group of special visitors had been given a ride on the Northumbrian locomotive, William Huskisson, MP for Liverpool, crossed from his own carriage to speak to the Duke of Wellington. Warnings were shouted when people realised that the *Rocket* was coming past but Huskisson failed to move quickly enough. He was knocked down and one of his legs was badly mangled. Despite a doctor's efforts he died later that day.

After the tragic accident it was decided to continue with the procession. However, when it reached Manchester the passenger carriages were pelted with stones by people who remembered the Duke of Wellington's support for the magistrates after the Peterloo Massacre and his strong opposition to parliamentary reform.

SOURCE 11 Lady Wilton's eyewitness description of Huskisson's accident

66 *The locomotive had stopped to take a supply of water, and several of the gentlemen in the directors' carriage had jumped out to look about them. Lord Wilton, Count Batthyany, Count Matuscenitz and Mr Huskisson among the rest were standing talking in the middle of the road, when a locomotive on the other line, which was parading up and down merely to show its speed, was seen coming down upon them like lightning. The most active of those in peril sprang back into their seats; Lord Wilton saved his life only by rushing behind the Duke's carriage, and Count Matuscenitz had but just leaped into it, with the locomotive all but touching his heels as he did so; while poor Mr Huskisson, less active from the effects of age and ill-health, bewildered, too, by the frantic cries of 'Stop the locomotive! Clear the track!' that resounded on all sides, completely lost his head, looked helplessly to the right and left, and was instantaneously prostrated by the fatal machine, which dashed down like a thunderbolt upon him, and passed over his leg, smashing and mangling it in the most horrible way.* 99

SOURCE 10 Closed carriages, open carriages, freight and livestock travelling on the Liverpool and Manchester Railway in 1831

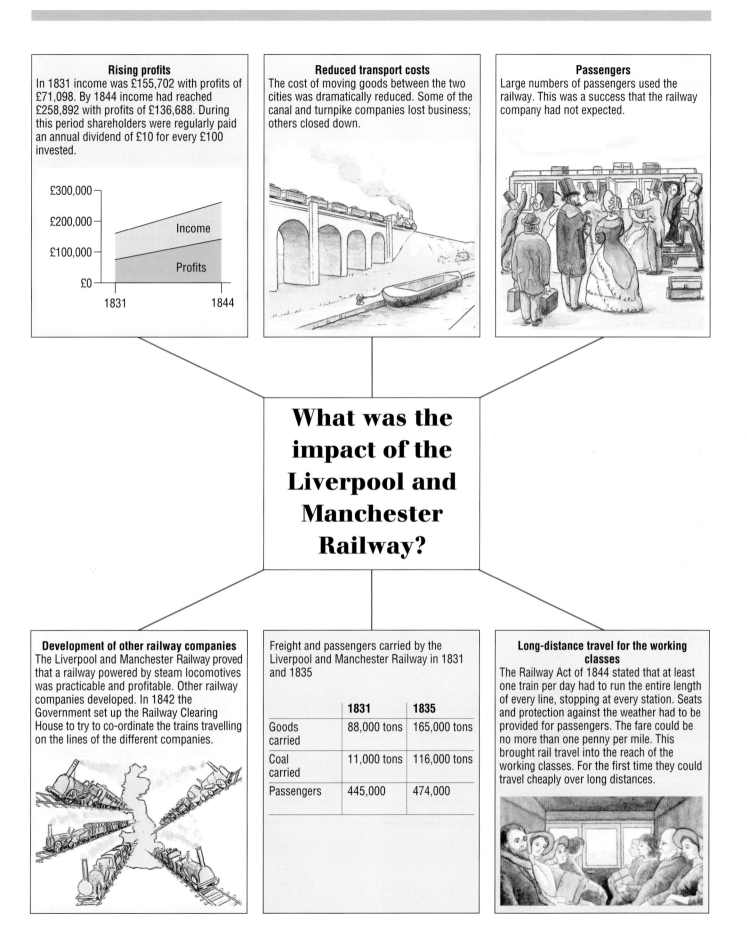

Rising profits

In 1831 income was £155,702 with profits of £71,098. By 1844 income had reached £258,892 with profits of £136,688. During this period shareholders were regularly paid an annual dividend of £10 for every £100 invested.

Reduced transport costs

The cost of moving goods between the two cities was dramatically reduced. Some of the canal and turnpike companies lost business; others closed down.

Passengers

Large numbers of passengers used the railway. This was a success that the railway company had not expected.

What was the impact of the Liverpool and Manchester Railway?

Development of other railway companies

The Liverpool and Manchester Railway proved that a railway powered by steam locomotives was practicable and profitable. Other railway companies developed. In 1842 the Government set up the Railway Clearing House to try to co-ordinate the trains travelling on the lines of the different companies.

Freight and passengers carried by the Liverpool and Manchester Railway in 1831 and 1835

	1831	1835
Goods carried	88,000 tons	165,000 tons
Coal carried	11,000 tons	116,000 tons
Passengers	445,000	474,000

Long-distance travel for the working classes

The Railway Act of 1844 stated that at least one train per day had to run the entire length of every line, stopping at every station. Seats and protection against the weather had to be provided for passengers. The fare could be no more than one penny per mile. This brought rail travel into the reach of the working classes. For the first time they could travel cheaply over long distances.

Who built the railways?

FOLLOWING THE SUCCESS of the Liverpool and Manchester Railway there was a boom in railway building. Four sets of people were involved in the building of each railway: promoters, engineers, contractors and navvies.

■ **Promoters** were the men who financed the railway companies. They made a case for the building of a railway and then persuaded others to invest in it. Two such men were Edward Pease and George Hudson.

■ **Engineers** were the men who planned the railways, surveyed the routes and designed stations, tunnels, viaducts and bridges. Two of the most famous were George Stephenson, whom you have already met, and Isambard Kingdom Brunel. You will learn more about these two men on pages 136–37.

■ **Contractors** were the men who organised the building work. The most famous was Thomas Brassey. Contractors worked through sub-contractors, providing them with all necessary materials and equipment but leaving the hire of labour to them. These sub-contractors hired gangs of navvies.

■ **Navvies** were the men who actually did the physical work of building the railways. You will find out more about them on pages 132–35. Something like 100,000 men worked for twenty years to build some 16,000 km of railway in Britain.

Edward Pease (1767–1858)

At the age of 50 Pease retired from the family wool business and began to concentrate on his idea of starting a public railway. He saw a great need for this in the coal industry in the north east. In 1821, with a group of businessmen from the area, he formed the Stockton to Darlington Railway Company. He was later persuaded by George Stephenson to use a steam locomotive and employed Stephenson as engineer. In 1823 he went into partnership with George and Robert Stephenson to form a company to build steam locomotives.

When the railway opened in 1825 the first train of wagons and passengers was pulled by the *Locomotion*, driven by George Stephenson. So Pease played a key role in promoting this first railway and in developing the production of steam locomotives.

SOURCE 1
A portrait of Edward Pease. Pease was a Quaker who supported the anti-slavery movement and the prison reforms of Elizabeth Fry

Thomas Brassey (1805–70)

Brassey started work as a land surveyor but after meeting George Stephenson became involved in railway building. In 1834 Stephenson helped Brassey to obtain a contract to build a railway viaduct at Bromborough. Soon afterwards the engineer Joseph Locke suggested that Brassey should tender for one of the contracts to build the Grand Junction Railway. He got the contract and this was the start of his long working relationship with Locke.

He was a major employer of navvies and at times had over 10,000 men working for him. In 1845 he had thirteen major contracts under way. He built over 7000 km of railway on three continents, including one-sixth of the British network. He died a rich man, leaving over £3 million.

SOURCE 2
A portrait of Thomas Brassey

George Hudson (1800–71)

Hudson worked in the drapery (fabrics) trade until 1827 when a distant relative left him £30,000. Hudson decided to use this money to buy shares in the North Midland Railway. This was a success and in 1833 he began planning to form his own railway company to link York with other towns in Yorkshire. After £446,000 had been raised the line was completed on 29 May 1839. Hudson went on to promote other lines and by 1844 his companies controlled 1630 km of railway track. He became known as the Railway King and as a result of his involvement with railways was elected Tory MP for Sunderland. He promised to use his influence to help the town to overcome its economic problems and did so.

For a time George Stephenson became his partner but then left as a result of suspicions over Hudson's business methods. Hudson certainly used bribery and some of his deals were not recorded in company books. The Duke of Wellington was friendly with him and took his advice on share dealings. Hudson began to use his inside knowledge to manipulate railway share prices. This period of investment became known as 'Railway mania' (see Source 4). In the short term Hudson made a lot of money but railway shares had become over-priced. Towards the end of 1847 their value fell dramatically.

Those who had invested heavily in railway shares faced financial ruin. There was great hostility towards Hudson as the man who had persuaded them to buy shares. He was forced to resign as chairman of all the railway companies under his control. Eventually his dishonest dealings, such as selling land he did not own and bribing MPs, came out. He spent some time in a debtors' prison until his friends raised enough money for him to be released.

SOURCE 3 A portrait of George Hudson

■ TASK

Write an answer to the question: who contributed most to railway development – Pease, Brassey or Hudson?

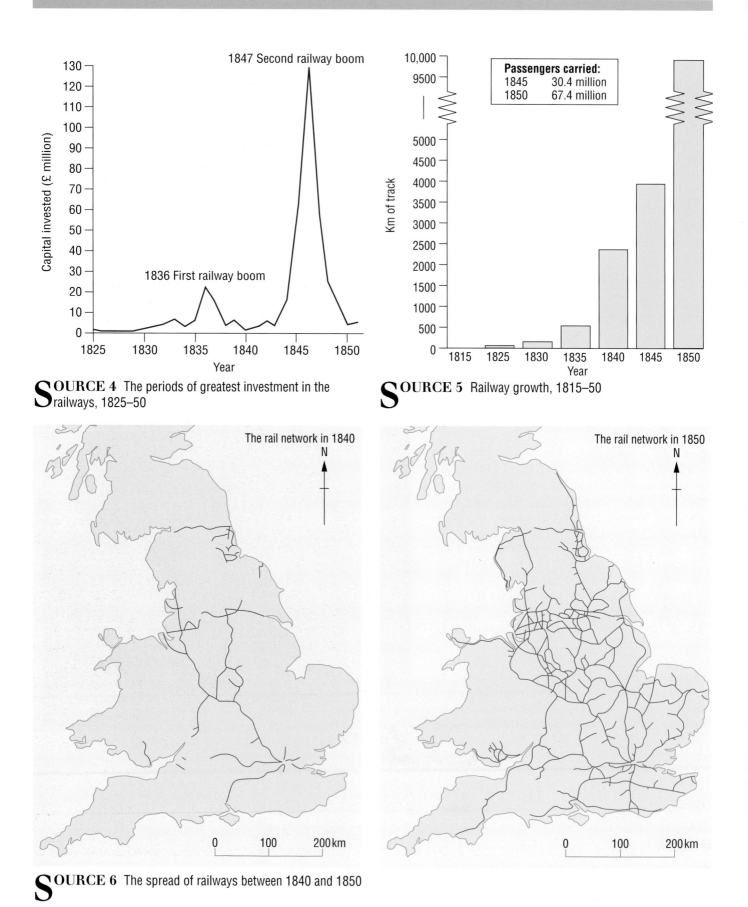

SOURCE 4 The periods of greatest investment in the railways, 1825–50

SOURCE 5 Railway growth, 1815–50

Passengers carried:
1845   30.4 million
1850   67.4 million

SOURCE 6 The spread of railways between 1840 and 1850

The Battle of the Gauges

As the railway network spread across the country, a new problem had to be tackled. The gauge is the distance between the rails. George Stephenson had built his railways with a gauge of 4 feet 8.5 inches (1.4 m), the narrow gauge. He apparently arrived at this figure by measuring the distance between the wheels on farm carts. When Isambard Kingdom Brunel started to build the Great Western Railway he decided to work out a gauge that would allow wagons and coaches to travel quickly and smoothly. The gauge he decided upon was 7 feet (2.1 m), the broad gauge.

The problem arose where the lines of different railway companies came together and the two gauges met. This happened at enough places to make it a serious problem. The locomotives, carriages and wagons of one gauge could not run on the tracks of the other. This meant that people and goods had to be transferred to a different train, a process which added to costs and wasted time (see Source 7).

Brunel suggested sorting out the problem by holding speed trials. These took place in December 1845. The results showed that the broad gauge was faster, safer and allowed carriages to be more comfortable. However, there were only about 480 km of broad gauge track but over 3000 km of narrow gauge track. To widen all of this track would be very expensive, much more expensive than narrowing the broad gauge. So the narrow gauge became the standard gauge, which it still is today.

1. This is a good example of how the best technical solution to a problem is not always the one chosen. Can you think of any other examples from your own experience?

SOURCE 7 'The break of the gauge at Gloucester' by W. J. Linton, from the *Illustrated London News*, 1846. At Gloucester the broad gauge line of the Great Western Railway met the narrow gauge of the Birmingham line

Building a railway

■ ACTIVITY

Work with a partner on this game. You need to roll a die to move around the board. Make a note of what happens to you as you make each move. Keep this as a journal. If you land on a bankruptcy square you must roll the die again, and if you throw a one this time then you are bankrupt and must start all over again.

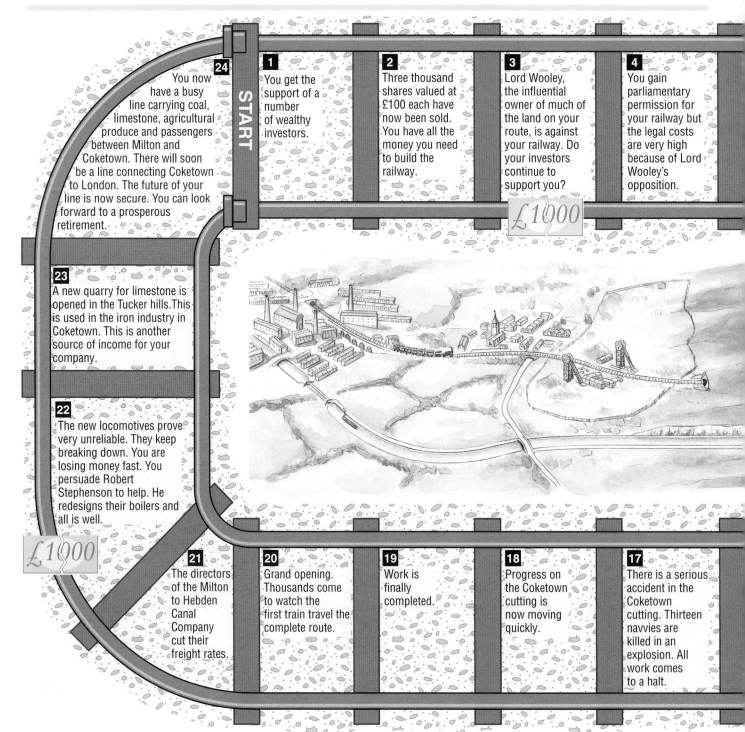

START

24 You now have a busy line carrying coal, limestone, agricultural produce and passengers between Milton and Coketown. There will soon be a line connecting Coketown to London. The future of your line is now secure. You can look forward to a prosperous retirement.

1 You get the support of a number of wealthy investors.

2 Three thousand shares valued at £100 each have now been sold. You have all the money you need to build the railway.

3 Lord Wooley, the influential owner of much of the land on your route, is against your railway. Do your investors continue to support you?

£1000

4 You gain parliamentary permission for your railway but the legal costs are very high because of Lord Wooley's opposition.

23 A new quarry for limestone is opened in the Tucker hills. This is used in the iron industry in Coketown. This is another source of income for your company.

22 The new locomotives prove very unreliable. They keep breaking down. You are losing money fast. You persuade Robert Stephenson to help. He redesigns their boilers and all is well.

£1000

21 The directors of the Milton to Hebden Canal Company cut their freight rates.

20 Grand opening. Thousands come to watch the first train travel the complete route.

19 Work is finally completed.

18 Progress on the Coketown cutting is now moving quickly.

17 There is a serious accident in the Coketown cutting. Thirteen navvies are killed in an explosion. All work comes to a halt.

■ TASK

You are invited to speak to the board of a new railway company. They are anxious to learn from your experience. Summarise the main points of advice you would give them, basing your ideas on your journal.

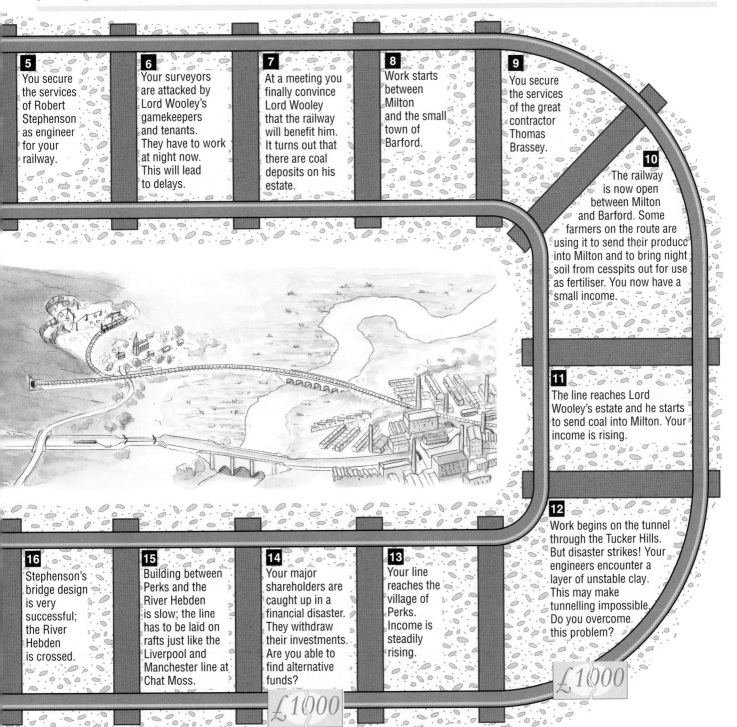

5 You secure the services of Robert Stephenson as engineer for your railway.

6 Your surveyors are attacked by Lord Wooley's gamekeepers and tenants. They have to work at night now. This will lead to delays.

7 At a meeting you finally convince Lord Wooley that the railway will benefit him. It turns out that there are coal deposits on his estate.

8 Work starts between Milton and the small town of Barford.

9 You secure the services of the great contractor Thomas Brassey.

10 The railway is now open between Milton and Barford. Some farmers on the route are using it to send their produce into Milton and to bring night soil from cesspits out for use as fertiliser. You now have a small income.

11 The line reaches Lord Wooley's estate and he starts to send coal into Milton. Your income is rising.

12 Work begins on the tunnel through the Tucker Hills. But disaster strikes! Your engineers encounter a layer of unstable clay. This may make tunnelling impossible. Do you overcome this problem?

13 Your line reaches the village of Perks. Income is steadily rising.

14 Your major shareholders are caught up in a financial disaster. They withdraw their investments. Are you able to find alternative funds?

15 Building between Perks and the River Hebden is slow; the line has to be laid on rafts just like the Liverpool and Manchester line at Chat Moss.

16 Stephenson's bridge design is very successful; the River Hebden is crossed.

£1000

£1000

Why did the navvies have such a bad reputation?

THE MEN WHO physically built the railways were the navvies. There was little machinery; it was mostly done by human muscle, aided by gunpowder in some places. The work was hard and often dangerous: work on the Woodhead tunnel on the Sheffield to Manchester line alone claimed the lives of 32 navvies and left 200 more seriously injured.

The name 'navvy' came from the 'navigators' or builders of the canals, which were also known as 'inland navigations'. Many of the men came from Ireland, Scotland, the West Country and Lincolnshire.

These men lived and worked with the railway, moving as it moved. They worked together in gangs and acquired a reputation as men who worked hard and played hard. The people of towns and villages, sometimes with good reason, feared the arrival of large groups of navvies. In 1842 in the town of Penrith in Cumbria there was a great disturbance involving up to 2000 navvies. The local Yeomanry had to be called out to restore order.

■ SOURCE INVESTIGATION

1. Why did the navvies have such a bad reputation? It is your job to find out, using Sources 1–11 to help you. You should look for evidence about their:

   ■ living conditions
   ■ behaviour.

2. Do you think they entirely deserved their reputation? What evidence can you find to support your answer?

SOURCE 1 An engraving of a navvy from *Punch*, 1855

SOURCE 2 A description of navvies written in 1851

❝ Rude, rugged and uncultivated, with great animal strength, collected in large numbers, living and working entirely together, they are a class by themselves. Unable to read and unwilling to be taught, impulsive and brute-like, they live for the present, care not for the past, are indifferent to the future. Insolent and insulting, they are dreaded by the good and welcomed by the bad. ❞

SOURCE 3 An extract from *A History of the English Railway* by J. Francis, published in 1851

❝ They were in a state of utter barbarism. They made their homes where they got their work. Some slept in huts constructed of damp turf, cut from the wet grass, too low to stand upright in; while small sticks, covered with straw, served as rafters. Barns were better places than the best railway labourers' dwellings. Others formed a room of stones without mortar, placed thatch or flags across the roof, and took possession of it with their families, often making it a source of profit by lodging as many of their fellow workmen as they could crowd into it. It mattered not to them that the rain beat through the roof, and that the wind swept through the holes. If they caught a fever, they died; if they took an infectious complaint, they wandered in the open air, spreading the disease where they went. In these huts they lived; with the space overcrowded; with man, woman and child mixing in promiscuous guilt; with no possible separation of the sexes; in summer wasted by unwholesome heats, and in winter literally hewing their way to work through the snow. In such places from 900 to 1500 men were crowded for six years. Living like brutes, they were depraved, degraded and reckless. Drunkenness and dissoluteness of morals prevailed. There were many women but few wives. ❞

SOURCE 4 An extract from the *Story of the Life of George Stephenson* written by Samuel Smiles, 1862

❝ Joining together in a 'butty gang', some ten or twelve of these men would take a contract to cut out and remove so much 'dirt', fixing their price according to the character of the 'stuff', and the distance to which it had to be wheeled and tipped. The contract taken, every man put himself to his mettle [tried his best]. ❞

SOURCE 5 An extract from *Personal Recollection of English Engineers*, 1868. The writer is commenting on the custom of paying navvies monthly

66 *The argument with which the contractors met the request of the Engineer that the workmen should be paid weekly, or at the farthest fortnightly, was that they never restarted work until they had drunk out the balance of their earnings. It saved time and speeded up the progress of the works to make these seasons of interruption as few as possible.* 99

SOURCE 6 *Rock Cutting at Bishopston* painted by William McKenzie, 1841

SOURCE 7 Brunel's comment on the casualty list of the 131 navvies killed or injured during the building of the Great Western Railway, September 1839–June 1841

66 *Considering the very heavy works and the immense amount of powder used, and some of the heaviest and most difficult works; I am afraid it does not show the whole extent of accidents incurred.* 99

Brunel's comment in 1846 on sub-contractors and navvy work gangs

66 *Frequently [the sub-contractor] runs off, defrauding the other men, rendering them reckless and teaching them to be rascals in their turn. The gang is broken up and the men in debt leave the place to seek work elsewhere. This aggravates the unsettled, roving and consequently reckless habits of the men.* 99

SOURCE 8 An extract from a letter from Thomas Beggs to Edwin Chadwick, 11 April 1846, describing the contractor on the Muirkirk and Ayr Railway

66 *A tall powerful Highlander, a man of brute passions, who drinks, dances and fights with the men. He often incites the men to drink, and provokes them in that state to fight in which amusement he seems to take great delight.* 99

SOURCE 9 The view of the contractor Samuel Peto who employed thousands of navvies

66 *If you pay him well, and show you care for him, he is the most faithful and hardworking creature in existence. He will be your faithful servant . . .* 99

SOURCE 10 The view of J Butler Williams in a letter to Edwin Chadwick, 26 December 1846

66 *On the whole they are fine independent fellows, really fine fellows, who will well repay any amount of care and attention paid to their physical and moral well being.* 99

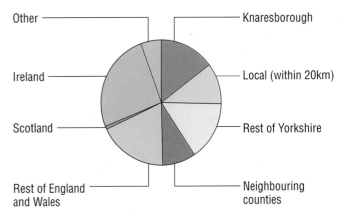

SOURCE 11 The birthplaces of navvies building the East and West Riding Junction Railway, based on information from the 1851 census for Knaresborough. The contractor, George Wilson, employed 270 men, 239 of whom have been identified by the researcher J. A. Patmore (taken from *The Journal of Transport History*). The majority were lodging in the town itself, some in the surrounding villages and a few on the railway construction site. This led to overcrowding, the worst example being the cottage of an agricultural labourer. In his cottage there were his four children plus 19 lodgers: four married couples, three children and eight single men. Eleven of the men were recorded as railway labourers

Saturday night in Kiddy!

■ ACTIVITY

You are going to write a short story set in Kidderminster in 1851. The construction gangs for the Oxford, Worcester and Wolverhampton Railway have almost reached town. You already know a lot about the town and living conditions from your work in Chapter 4. You now also know a lot about the building of the railways and the lives of navvies from this chapter. Discuss with your partner what sort of people might be in the town over the weekend and what they might do.

For your short story you must follow this recipe:

- The year is 1851. It is Saturday night and the navvies building the railway have just been paid.
- Your story can cover a period of no more than two days.
- Your story can have no more than three main characters, one of whom must be female. These can be real people from the trade directory (Source 13) or they can be fictional. You might like to use some of the navvies' names listed in Source 12.
- The events in your story can happen in only two places: the railway construction site and the town centre.

SOURCE 12 Names of navvies

66 *Fancy Bob*
Bellerophon
Fisherman
Fighting Jack
Brummagem
Long Sam 99

SOURCE 13 An edited extract from Pigot & Co's Worcestershire Trade Directory entry for Kidderminster in 1851. Trade directories were the nineteenth-century equivalent of the Thomson Local Directory. Businessmen paid to be included in a publication that was used to advertise their business. This extract includes the listing's for some of the businesses in the town

66 *Kidderminster is a market town and borough in Worcestershire. It is on the eastern bank of the River Stour about three miles from its confluence with the River Severn. The Staffordshire and Worcestershire Canal passes through the town – a conveyance by water being possible to all parts of the kingdom. The town is of an irregular form and contains several well-built and some handsome houses. But the greater part consists of dwellings inhabited by the workmen employed in the different factories. The streets are well lighted with gas, and the inhabitants amply supplied with water.*

By the Act of 1832 the borough is empowered to send one representative to Parliament, the present member is Richard Godson. The carpet industry was introduced in the last century and has been continued with increasing success up to the present day. On the banks of the River Stour are several dye houses in connection with the various factories. 99

SHOPKEEPERS & DEALERS IN GROCERIES & SUNDRIES.

Ball Stephen, Franch
Gowen William, Mill st
Grubham John, Broad st
Long George, Stourbridge st
Mitchelson William, Wolverley
Rogers Richard, Horse fair
Thatcher Sarah, Worcester cross

SURGEONS.

Jothan George William, Mill st
Roden William & Thos. Horse fair

TAVERNS & PUBLIC HOUSES.

Angel, Joseph Nichols, Worcester st
Black Bull, George Ball, Swan st
Black Star, Henry Silkcot, Blackhall st
Cock, Rhoda Renny, Horse fair
Compasses, George Tomkins, Coventry st
Cross Keys, Isaac Chambers, Worcester st
Dolphin, Thomas Mason, Worcester st
Falcon, William Freeman, Mill st
Fox, George Birks, Swan st   [fields
Freemasons' Arms, Edward West, Lion
George & Dragon, John Perry, Trinity lane
Green Man & Still, Edwd. Bradley, Oxford st
Leopard, Wm. Collins, Hoo lane   [butts
Lyttleyton's Arms, Herbert Viney, Park
Market Tavern, Jas Kyres, Worcester st
New Inn, Reuben Hume, Horse fair
Plough, Ann Flinn, Church fields
Red Lion, John Nettleship, Mill st
Seven Stars, Eliz. Jevons, Coventry st
Talbot, John Stockall, Worcester st
Union, James Carter, Worcester st
Vine, George Mills, Horse fair
Wheat Sheaf, William Copner, Worcester st
Woolpack, George Perks, Broad st

WHEELWRIGHTS.

Crundell James, Franch
Crundell William, Franch
Nicholas James, Proud crop

WOOLSTAPLERS.

Best Joseph, Mill st
Collins Charles, Mill st
Randall James, Orchard st

SOURCE 14 Kidderminster town centre in 1851

Stephenson or Brunel: which engineer contributed more to the development of railways up to 1851?

■ SOURCE INVESTIGATION

Historians disagree about which engineer made the greatest contribution to the development of railways between 1815 and 1851. This section invites you to come to your own conclusion – was it George Stephenson or Isambard Kingdom Brunel? Use Sources 1–8 below and the work you have done in the earlier parts of this chapter to help you decide.

Stephenson

SOURCE 1 The back of a modern £5 note, which celebrates the achievements of George Stephenson

SOURCE 2 Biographical details of George Stephenson (1781–1848)

1802   *Began working on colliery winding engines.*

1813   *Became a colliery engine-wright.*

1814   *Built his first locomotive,* Blucher. *Its design was based upon the ideas of pioneers Richard Trevithick, John Blenkinsop and William Hedley, who had all built locomotives.*

1814–21 *Designed and built sixteen more locomotives.*

1815   *Invented a safety lamp for miners (at the same time as Sir Humphrey Davy).*

1821   *Employed as engineer for the Stockton to Darlington Railway. Chose 4 foot 8.5 inches as the gauge, the narrow gauge.*

1824   *Founded his own locomotive works.*

1825   *Opening of Stockton to Darlington Railway.*

1826   *Employed as engineer for the Liverpool and Manchester Railway.*

1829   *George and son Robert's locomotive, the* Rocket, *won the Rainhill Trials.*

1830   *Opening of Liverpool and Manchester Railway. He went on to lay hundreds of kilometres of railway track in the Midlands and north of England.*

1845   *Retired.*

SOURCE 3 A painting of George Stephenson and his family, commissioned by his son Robert in 1857. By the time of its completion all but one of the people in the painting were dead. It shows Stephenson in a family group, holding his safety lamp and with a locomotive in the background. Robert is pictured on his left

SOURCE 4 Historians' views as reported in the *Guardian* newspaper, 11 September 1998. These historians were attending the International Early Railways Conference at Durham University

❝ *John Guy of the Beamish Industrial Open Air Museum has directed five years of research into early railways. His research shows that two other men, William Chapman and John Buddle, played an important role in Stephenson's early locomotive building but received no public credit for their contribution. Of his research he commented, "It is already known that Stephenson was famous for exaggeration. This [research] will show that although he is a key figure, his influence has been exaggerated.'*

Steven Dyke, Curator of the Darlington Railway Centre and Museum said, 'Stephenson often overshadows others who deserve more attention than history gives them.'

Alan Pearce, manager of the Timothy Hackworth Museum in Shildon, County Durham said, 'Within the world of history it is accepted that a lot of the achievements credited to George Stephenson were not his.' ❞

Brunel

SOURCE 5 A photograph of Isambard Kingdom Brunel taken in 1857 by Robert Howlett

SOURCE 6 Biographical details of Isambard Kingdom Brunel (1806–59)

1823   *Began working with his father on the Thames Tunnel.*

1831   *Designed Monkwearmouth docks. Later designed other docks such as Plymouth and Milford Haven. Took his first train ride on the Liverpool and Manchester Railway.*

1833   *Employed as engineer for Great Western railway (GWR). Over the following eight years he built many bridges and tunnels and laid hundreds of kilometres of track. He developed the broad gauge (7 feet between the rails).*

1836   *Designed and began work on the Clifton Suspension Bridge, a road bridge. Due to lack of funding it was not completed until after his death.*

1838   *Designed and built the SS* Great Western, *first steamship to cross the Atlantic.*

1845   *Designed and built the SS* Great Britain, *first large ship to be screw-propelled.*

1855   *Built a hospital for soldiers injured in the Crimean War.*

1858   *Designed and built the SS* Great Eastern, *largest ship ever built at the time.*

1859   *Completion of the Royal Albert Bridge to carry the GWR over the River Tamar.*

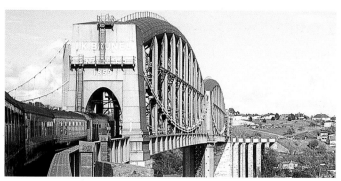

SOURCE 7 A photograph of Brunel's Royal Albert Bridge. Completed in 1859, it still carries the railway over the River Tamar today

SOURCE 8 Adrian Vaughan, author of the biography *Isambard Kingdom Brunel: Engineering Knight-Errant*, published in 1991, gives his view of Brunel's achievements

66 *Isambard's 'extensive ambitions' drove the railway from Paddington to Penzance, Milford Haven and Wolverhampton. His eye for land and his daring genius as a bridge builder are such that we stand in awe of the Maidenhead or Royal Albert bridges to this day. One could say dozens of his bridges, large and small, his viaducts and all his cuttings and embankments are in use, carrying trains at speeds even he did not anticipate – although one of his drivers, John Almond, did ask permission, in May 1847, to drive from Paddington to Bristol in the hour. Without him the routes, with the possible exception of Newton Abbot to Plymouth, would not be capable of the high speeds they now permit.*

His SS Great Western *was the pioneer transatlantic liner, making regular fortnightly crossings between Bristol and New York from April 1838 until December 1846 when she was displaced by larger ships.*

He was indeed a great man, an exceptional man, though he did not, by himself, 'build the railway' but received vital assistance from untold thousands of other men – whose efforts he rarely if ever acknowledged. 99

■ ACTIVITY

Write a letter to the Bank of England suggesting that they revise the £5 note. You must decide whether to celebrate the achievements of Brunel for the first time or to emphasise a different achievement of Stephenson's. Explain why you have made your choice. You should include your design for the new note with your letter.

Demands of industry
Industry needed a cheaper, faster, more efficient method of transporting goods than the roads or canals could provide. Railways were the solution.

Support for local economies
Many towns encouraged the building of railways, as better transport links would provide new opportunities for businesses to develop.

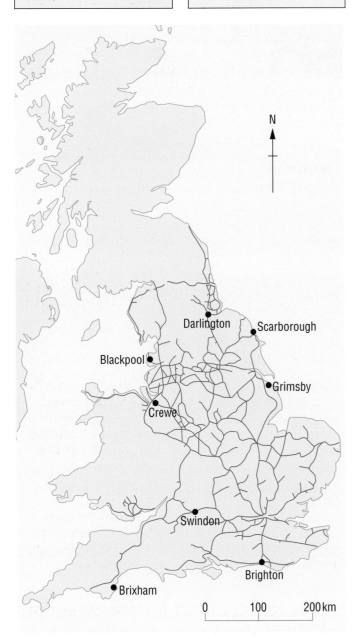

Investment opportunities
The railways offered investors a good opportunity to make money. The financial system was now sophisticated enough to organise large-scale investment.

SOURCE 1 A summary of the reasons for the expansion of the railways. The map shows the rail network in 1850 and some of the towns that benefited from the coming of the railways

■ TASK

What impact did the railways have on Britain? This is a very important historical question, which is sometimes asked by examiners.

You are going to write an answer to his question and in order to do so you need to summarise much of the work that you have been doing throughout this chapter and earlier in the book. As you know, no single historical event has a single consequence. There are a number of consequences that you should consider. They are summarised on the next two pages.

1. Make your own set of consequence cards using just the headings, and then use them to help you think about the following questions.
    a) Are all the consequences relevant?
    b) Can they be grouped into different types?
        i) Try grouping them into economic, political and social consequences. Try fitting them into a Venn diagram. What does that tell you about these consequences?
        ii) Now try splitting them into short-term positive and negative consequences. Will these be different depending upon whose point of view you consider? How does this help you devise an answer to the question?
    c) Are some consequences connected? If so, how are they connected? On a plain sheet of paper try drawing the connections between the other consequences and:

        ■ the spread of ideas
        ■ the growth of cities.

        Now try drawing the connections between the consequence that you think is most important and the other consequences.
    d) Are these consequences all equally important or are some more important than others?

2. Now decide how best to arrange your consequence cards to answer the question: what impact did the new railways have on Britain? Each card or group of cards should provide the basis for a paragraph of your answer. Stick them down. Now you are ready to start writing.

The growth of seaside towns

Cheap day excursions made it possible for people of all classes to visit the seaside on the train for the day or even longer. Popular destinations like Brighton, Scarborough and Blackpool grew into large resorts catering for the day trippers. The travel agent Thomas Cook was one man who spotted the potential of railways. He ran his first excursion in 1841. By booking large numbers of tickets he was able to offer cheap day trips and still make a lot of money.

SOURCE 2 A poster advertising trips to Scarborough

New railway towns

The railway companies needed to set up building and repair works for their locomotives (or wagons) and carriages. Towns grew around the railway works in places such as Darlington and Swindon, the base of the Great Western Railway. Towns also developed around important railway junctions such as Crewe. In 1841 its population was 201 but by 1851 this had grown to 4571.

The spread of ideas

As well as goods and people the railways carried newspapers and letters. Letters were carried by the Liverpool and Manchester Railway from 1830 onwards and by other companies, including the Great Western Railway, from 1839 onwards. The Penny Post, begun in 1840, used the railway network. This meant that news and ideas could spread more quickly. It ultimately led to the development of national newspapers; for example, the *News of the World* was founded as a Sunday newspaper in 1843.

Better diet for town and city dwellers

The speed of the new railways meant that perishable fresh foods, such as fish, and dairy products, such as milk, could be cheaply brought into towns and cities. More people living there could now afford fresh food, so their diet, and in turn their health, improved. The fishing industry grew in ports like Hull, Grimsby and Brixham. Market gardening, the growing of fresh vegetables, developed along the routes of railways.

Benefits for farming

The railways reduced the costs of farming as well as supporting the development of market gardening. For example, it was no longer necessary to walk cattle to market, an expensive and time-consuming process. Now it was possible to send cattle by rail.

Increased employment

The railways needed navvies to build them and more people to run them. This led to an increase in employment. In the census of 1851 65,000 men and 54 women were listed as railway workers.

Increased demand for the iron and coal industries

The railways needed tonnes of iron and steel to build the lines, engines, wagons and carriages. Vast amounts of coal was burned to power the locomotives. In 1848 the railways used more than a quarter of all the iron produced in Britain. This stimulated the iron and coal industries, providing work for miners and iron workers, and profits for the owners.

The development of Chartism

The Chartists (working people who were campaigning to be allowed to vote, see pages 142–56) used the railways to promote their ideas. Chartism flourished in the 1840s. Ordinary members could travel to attend rallies while speakers could travel around the country in order to address meetings.

The development of trade unions

Railways made it possible for the new unions formed by skilled workers to organise on a national level. Officials and members could travel between the branches set up in the industrial towns.

A more unified Britain

In order to run smoothly the railways had to run to time. Until the railways developed, clocks in different parts of the country often showed slightly different times. Now clocks had to show the same time. The railways also brought different parts of Britain closer together. The journey time between places became shorter, so railways made the country seem smaller. At the same time travel was now affordable by all classes, not just the better off. So more people could move about Britain far more easily.

Economic growth

As the railways could carry goods and people quickly and cheaply they helped most other industries and businesses to grow. Businesses could now potentially sell their products throughout the country, not just in their local area.

Strengthening the forces of law and order

The railways and the associated telegraph allowed the quick movement of troops to areas of unrest during disturbances. This strengthened the Government's ability to deal with groups like the Chartists.

Decline in business of canal and turnpike companies

Goods and people could be moved more quickly and cheaply by rail than by canal or road. Where they were in competition, railways won. Long-distance stage routes, turnpike trusts and many canal companies lost money and many went bankrupt. Employees lost their jobs. However, some canal companies survived because their canals carried local goods to the railways, which then carried them over the long distances. The same was true of local road transport.

Areas of economic decline

Some towns resisted the arrival of the railway. A good example of this is Stamford where the BBC filmed *Middlemarch* (see Source 1 on page 27). They chose it as a location because it had changed so little since the early nineteenth century. Once an important market town, it went into economic decline as neighbouring towns on the railway line developed.

SOURCE 3 *Steamed Out or the Starving Stage-Coachman and Boys,* a cartoon by George Cruikshank, published in 1847

REVOLUTION AVERTED

NOT SO *VERY* UNREASONABLE!!! EH?"

WHY WAS THERE NO REVOLUTION IN BRITAIN IN 1848?

DEMANDS FOR POLITICAL reform did not end with the passing of the Reform Act of 1832. Many people wanted more sweeping changes made to the political system. A movement developed in the late 1830s which the authorities feared might trigger a revolution. This was Chartism. In this chapter you are going to find out how and why Chartism developed and how serious a threat it presented to the Government.

Why did people join the Chartists?

CHARTISM WAS ONE of the first mass working-class movements in history. It had its roots in a number of places:

- the Radical tradition which had survived since the French Revolution of 1789
- disappointment with the 1832 Reform Act, under which the middle classes gained the right to vote but the working classes did not
- the working and living conditions of the working classes, which workers had already campaigned to improve, most notably through the Short Time Committees
- opposition to the Poor Law Act of 1834
- the influence of newspapers in favour of reform
- government attacks on trade unionism, seen, for example, in the treatment of the Tolpuddle Martyrs.

Many working men of the time saw gaining the right to vote as an important step towards strengthening their rights at work and gaining improvements in their living conditions.

■ TASK 1

Copy the headings below on to a set of cards and use your own notes or the earlier sections of this book to add supporting points for each factor. Leave space to add new points that emerge as you work through this chapter.

- Radical tradition
- Disappointment with the 1832 Reform Act
- Working and living conditions of the working classes
- Opposition to the Poor Law Act of 1834
- Influence of the press
- Government attacks on trade unionism

How did Chartism develop?

■ TASK 2

As you read this section make notes on how the Chartists campaigned for their Charter and how the government authorities and their allies in the press responded. You will need these notes later.

The Six Points
OF THE
PEOPLE'S
CHARTER.

1. A VOTE for every man twenty-one years of age, of sound mind, and not undergoing punishment for crime.

2. THE BALLOT.—To protect the elector in the exercise of his vote.

3. NO PROPERTY QUALIFICATION for Members of Parliament—thus enabling the constituencies to return the man of their choice, be he rich or poor.

4. PAYMENT OF MEMBERS, thus enabling an honest tradesman, working man, or other person, to serve a constituency, when taken from his business to attend to the interests of the country.

5. EQUAL CONSTITUENCIES, securing the same amount of representation for the same number of electors, instead of allowing small constituencies to swamp the votes of large ones.

6. ANNUAL PARLIAMENTS, thus presenting the most effectual check to bribery and intimidation, since though a constituency might be bought once in seven years (even with the ballot), no purse could buy a constituency (under a system of universal suffrage) in each ensuing twelvemonth ; and since members, when elected for a year only, would not be able to defy and betray their constituents as now.

SOURCE 1 A Chartist handbill listing the six points of the People's Charter

The People's Charter

In 1836 the London Working Men's Association was founded. It was led by William Lovett, Francis Place (whom you met on page 16) and six Radical Members of Parliament. In 1837 it drew up an address to Parliament that became known as the People's Charter. Who the author was is open to dispute; it was either William Lovett or Francis Place. First published in May 1838, the Charter formed the basis of the Association's demands, which were not new. It also gave the movement the name by which it became known – the Chartists.

In the north of England Feargus O'Connor, an Irish landowner and former Member of Parliament, emerged as a leader of those demanding the vote for working men. He gained a reputation as an excellent public speaker and published his newspaper, the *Northern Star*, in Leeds. This use of a newspaper was based upon the success of the earlier papers produced by the Radicals, most notably William Cobbett's *Political Register*. Newspapers were an excellent way of gathering support. The tactic of sending out lecturers which the Methodists had used so successfully to reach the working classes was also used. The mass meetings and rallies on the moors were copied from the factory reform movement.

Birmingham was also an important centre, where the Chartists had the backing of Thomas Attwood and the Birmingham Political Union.

In 1838 all the Chartist groups met at Holloway Head in Birmingham. At this meeting they agreed on the six points of the People's Charter and decided to collect signatures for a national petition supporting the Charter, which they would present to Parliament. If the petition was rejected they would call a general strike. The decision to present a petition illustrates one of the major problems the Chartists faced; they had no real influence among the governing classes. If they had, a petition would not have been necessary.

The Chartists also agreed to hold a national Chartist Convention. The very name alarmed the authorities, as it carried echoes of the People's Convention during the French Revolution.

THE LYING WHIG REFORM BILL;

THE FOLLOWING TABLES EXHIBIT THE MONSTROUS DELUSION THAT THE REFORM BILL DESTROYED THE BOTTEN BOROUGH SYSTEM.

1.—Contested Elections, 1837, and subsequently, at which the votes polled for a successful candidate were less than 200.

	BOROUGH OR COUNTY.	RETURNS	POLLED	CONSTITUENCY FROM WHOM FORMED.	POPULATION.
1	Ashburton	1	98	101 nom. freem. & 342 h.	4,165
2	Arundel	1	176	380 £10 h.	2,803
3	Banbury	1	185	old cor. of 18 & 365 h.	5,906
4	Bandon (Ireland)	1	133	13 f. and 279 h.	9,820
5	Brecon	1	151	350 h.	5,026
6	Caithnesshire	1	198		34,000
7	Carlow (Ireland)	1	167	23 f. and 403 h.	9,012
8	Cockermouth	2	117	burghage holders & 235 h.	6,022
9	Colerain (Ireland)	1	129	52 f. and 240 h.	5,752
10	Devizes	2	109	cor. and 469 h.	6,367
11	Downpatrick (I.)	1	190		4,779
12	Eversham	2	168	130 h.	3,991
13	Frome	1	125	450 h.	12,240
14	Harwich	1	75	cor. and 202 h.	4,297
15	Helston	1	160	cor. and 225 h.	3,293
16	Horsham	1	147	burghage tenants & 365 h	5,105
17	Kidderminster	1	198	500 h.	20,165
18	Kinsale (Ireland)	1	102	301 h.	6,897
19	Knaresborough	2	172	burghage tenants & 369 h	6,252
20	Liskeard	1	113	cor. and 315 h.	4,042
21	Ludlow	2	194	b. and 314 h.	5,252
22	Lyme Regis	1	121	f. and 300 h.	3,345
23	Lymington	2	161	cor. and 189 h.	5,472
24	Petersfield	1	125	freeh. and 305 h.	4,922
25	Sligo (Ireland)	1	178	13 f. and 680 h.	12,762
26	Totness	2	158	f. and 316 h.	3,442
27	Tralee (Ireland)	1	75	13 f. and 354 h.	9,562
28	Wallingford	1	159	cor. and 278 h.	2,467
29	Wareham	1	170	s. and c. and 54 h.	2,566
30	Woodstock	1	126	f. and 373 h.	7,055
31	Youghal (Ireland)	1	158	f. and 479 h.	9,600

2.—Contested Elections, and voters polled under 300.

	BOROUGH OR COUNTY.	RETURNS	POLLED	CONSTITUENCY FROM WHOM FORMED.	POPULATION.
1	Armagh (Ireland)	1	235	13 f. and 520 h.	9,189
2	Ashton-under-Lyne	1	234	610 h.	14,673
3	Banffshire	1	292		48,000
4	Bodmin	1	200	c. and 311 h.	5,228
5	Bridport	2	283	s. and l., and 342 h.	4,242
6	Buckingham	2	235	c. and 225 h.	3,610
7	Bury	1	248	765 h.	15,086
8	Bury St. Edmunds	2	289	719	11,436
9	Clonmell (Ireland)	1	284	94 f. and 752 h.	12,256
10	Gateshead	1	266	750 h.	15,177
11	Guildford	2	252	f. and 431 h.	3,916
12	Haddingshire	1	299		36,100
13	Ditto Districts	1	268	214 h.	
14	Haverfordwest do.	1	247	s. and l., and 584 h.	10,832
15	Honiton	2	294	s. and l., and 318 h.	3,509
16	Hythe	1	243	f. and 537 h.	6,903
17	Inverness-shire	1	254		94,800
18	Kirkaldy Burghs	1	216		
19	Londonderry (I.)	1	214	f. and 735 h.	14,020
20	Newport (I. of W.)	2	264	f. and 445 h.	6,786
21	Peebleshire	1	251		10,600
22	Poole	2	272	f. and 298 h.	6,959
23	Scarborough	2	225	c. and 508 h.	8,760
24	Selkirkshire	1	230		6,800
25	Shaftesbury	1	221	s. and l., and 145 h.	8,518
26	St. Albans	2	252	s. and l., and 286 h.	5,771
27	St. Andrews	1	290	452 h.	
28	Tewkesbury	2	219	f. and 262 h.	5,780
29	Teignmouth	1	259	1,150 h.	23,206
30	Warrington	1	278	973 h.	18,184
31	Weymouth	2	289	c. and 490 h.	8,095
32	Wigan	2	268	b. and 568 h.	20,774
33	Winchester	2	259	b. and 807 h.	9,212

NOTE.—*C., corporation; s. and l., scot and lot voters; f., freeman; h., occupants of houses at an annual rental of £10 and upwards.*

SOURCE 2 An article in a Chartist newspaper, *The Poor Man's Guardian*, criticising the 1832 Reform Act

The Chartist Convention, February 1839

The Chartist Convention took place in London in February 1839. Here the main problem of Chartism emerged. Whilst all could agree on the People's Charter there were great differences in the interpretation of the six demands and, more crucially, on how they could work to achieve them. The movement is often seen as having two main strands.

- The 'physical force' Chartists were led by O'Connor. If their demands were rejected this group wanted to call a general strike, which they saw as leading to an armed uprising.
- The 'moral force' Chartists, led by Lovett, wanted to use public meetings, petitions, newspapers and pamphlets to argue their case and *persuade* the authorities to accept their demands.

Again, the Chartists were hampered by their lack of influence. If they relied on moral persuasion they could be ignored. If they resorted to violence they could be dismissed as rabble-rousers and suppressed. The opponents of Chartism seized upon the threat of violence as an opportunity to demonise the movement, but those labelled as 'physical force Chartists' saw violence only as a last resort. They saw their society, and in particular the political system, as unjust and corrupt. They might use violence to defend themselves but only if all else failed. After all, they did support the Charter and the petitions.

At the end of the debates Lovett and the 'moral force' Chartists walked out in protest at the talk of violence. The Government was so concerned that troops were put on the alert. Major-General Charles Napier was given command of 5000 soldiers and ordered to maintain law and order. He was an interesting choice for the job, as he believed that working men should be given the vote. He was very keen to avoid violence. He made sure that his troops put on displays of their firepower to show their strength and sent personal messages to Chartist leaders in the Manchester area to persuade them that any attempt at an armed rising would fail. He also made it clear to magistrates that he would not support any provocative action on their part. He thus played a key role in ensuring that serious violence did not break out.

Other Chartist groups

There were other groups or divisions within the Chartist movement.

- The Christian Chartists believed that the inequalities between rich and poor should be removed. In some places, such as Birmingham, they set up their own Churches. They faced hostility from some Methodist ministers who warned their congregations against Chartists because they held meetings on Sundays.
- Temperance Chartists thought that drink was a problem for the working classes. They saw it as taking away their self-respect.
- Knowledge Chartists saw education as the way for the working classes to improve their lives. In some areas Chartists set up their own schools.

It is also important to understand that in each area of the country the Chartists had slightly different views about what they were trying to achieve. In a large, national group this was inevitable.

The First Petition, July 1839

The MPs Thomas Attwood and John Fielden presented the first Chartist petition to Parliament in July 1839. It reportedly contained 1,280,000 signatures. Predictably, the House of Commons refused by a vote of 235 to 46 even to receive it. Large numbers of MPs did not even bother to attend the debate. The Chartist leadership now cancelled the proposed general strike; in fact, many Chartists were already out of work due to a trade slump. There were disturbances in many places but the authorities easily dealt with them all (see pages 145–46). More than 500 Chartists, including leaders such as Lovett and O'Connor, were arrested and imprisoned. The sentences passed were usually for short periods of imprisonment, but frequently far from their homes. For the authorities the short sentences were a way of preventing the Chartists from being seen as martyrs. Nevertheless it still meant that the main breadwinners were taken away from their families and prison conditions had a bad effect on some people's health.

SOURCE 3 An extract from a letter from Major-General Charles Napier to his brother in 1839

66 I am for a strong police, but the people should have the vote, the ballot, land to farm and education. England has many bad laws but should everyone arm themselves if they disagree with the law? The Poor cannot go on strike, they will rob and then they will be hanged. Physical force! Fools! What will they do when my cavalry is dancing around them and the cannons are pelting them? Poor men! How little they know of physical force! 99

1. In Source 3 Napier believed that people should not take up arms against a bad or unjust law. Do you think there is ever a situation where it would be right to do so?

Case study: what happened in Newport in 1839?

AFTER THE FAILURE of the First Petition many local groups of Chartists took their own action. There were scattered outbreaks of violence around the country. In Bath on 20 May 1839, for example, the local Chartists tried to hold a mass meeting but 130 police, 600 special constables, a troop of Hussars and six troops of Yeomanry stopped them.

The most serious incident took place in Newport in South Wales. On the night of 3 November 1839 John Frost led several thousand miners and ironworkers in a march on Newport. Some estimates suggest as many as 30,000 men – and a few women – were involved although they did not all go into Newport; many waited in the surrounding villages. When Frost and his followers arrived on the morning of 4 November they found a force of special constables and 32 soldiers of the Forty-fifth Regiment in the town. They were holding prisoner some Chartists who had been arrested the night before. What happened next is for you to decide.

■ ACTIVITY

You have been asked to write a short paragraph for a Year 9 history textbook on the Newport Rising of 1839. Use the background information and Sources 1–4 to help you. Remember that you want to simplify but not distort what happened for your younger audience.

SOURCE 1 A contemporary artist's drawing of the events at Newport

SOURCE 2 An account written by Robert Gammage in his book *History of the Chartist Movement*, published in 1855. Gammage was a Chartist supporter

  A company of the Forty-fifth Regiment was stationed at the Westgate Hotel, and there the multitude marched, loudly cheering as they proceeded through the streets. Arrived in front of the Hotel, an attack was immediately begun; the magistrates, police and special constables were driven from the streets, and fled into the Hotel for refuge. The soldiers were stationed at the windows through which a number of people began to fire... The soldiers, as a matter of course, returned the fire... the consequence was, that in about twenty minutes ten of the Chartists were killed upon the spot, and about fifty others wounded. "

145

SOURCE 3 Evidence given by Edward Patton, a carpenter who lived in Newport, at the trial of John Frost, as reported in the *Northern Star*, 5 July 1840

66 *The parcel of people I saw in the morning of the riot were armed; they had guns, sticks, etc. The sticks had iron points. I did not see many with guns. I saw of this body of 200 or 300. There were not many more. I had full view of those on Stowe Hill... I know the two bow windows in front of the Westgate [Inn]. I never saw anything done to the windows of the Westgate. I did not hear a crash of windows. [The crowd] were not very tumultuous. They drew up in front of the Westgate... The body of the mob stood for a space, and asked for the prisoners who were taken before daylight. None of the mob went forward as a spokesman. They came close to the door. I could only see the steps to which the mob came close up. The first moment or two they asked for the prisoner Smith, then a rush was made. Then I heard firing, and took to my heels. I cannot say whether the mob had guns, or pikes or clubs. I cannot tell whether they were armed for the biggest part. I hears someone say, in a very loud voice, 'No never.' I was distant from the door of the Westgate 25 yards when I heard the words. I heard no groaning. I could not say when the firing began. No man could judge. You nor I could not tell. Saw no smoke outside. It is likely enough that the firing began from the Westgate Inn.* 99

Aftermath

The authorities arrested 90 people, who were tried in Newport in 1840. Eight were sentenced to death but this was commuted to transportation for life to Australia. Most of the rest were found guilty and sentenced to imprisonment. One important feature of the whole affair was the discipline of the Chartists. Despite the large numbers of people involved there were virtually no reports of looting, vandalism or random violence. Also, despite the thousands involved, the authorities found it very difficult to identify and arrest many men, evidence of the strong solidarity in South Wales.

Of course, the significance of the Rising at the time was that Chartism was seen as a violent movement. National leaders like William Lovett, Bronterre O'Brien, Henry Vincent and Feargus O'Connor were imprisoned along with more than 500 other Chartists.

SOURCE 4 Another contemporary artist's drawing of the events in Newport

■ REVIEW ACTIVITY

At a number of places in this book you are 'taking the revolutionary temperature' of Britain to decide how great the danger of revolution was. This is the fourth point, 1839.

1. Look back over the events since 1836 to remind yourself of what the Chartists wanted.

2. Now either sketch the map below or use the copy your teacher gives you and shade in the thermometer. If you believe the danger of revolution was very great, you'll shade all the way to the top. If you think the danger was not so serious, you won't shade so far.

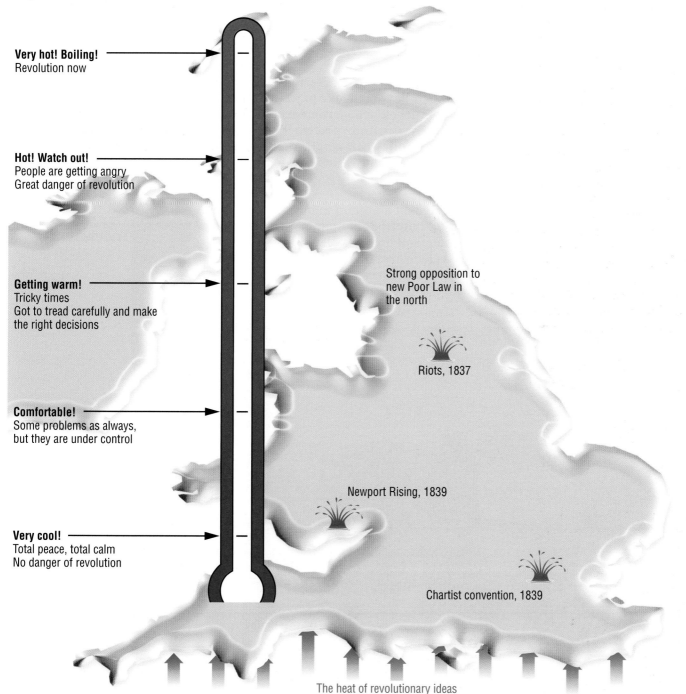

Very hot! Boiling!
Revolution now

Hot! Watch out!
People are getting angry
Great danger of revolution

Getting warm!
Tricky times
Got to tread carefully and make
the right decisions

Comfortable!
Some problems as always,
but they are under control

Very cool!
Total peace, total calm
No danger of revolution

Strong opposition to
new Poor Law in
the north

Riots, 1837

Newport Rising, 1839

Chartist convention, 1839

The heat of revolutionary ideas

How did the Chartists campaign?

The Second Petition and the strike of 1842

After 1839 the Chartists reorganised. Some moved to other organisations and causes. On his release from prison Feargus O'Connor founded the National Charter Association. In 1842 there were about 400 associations with more than 50,000 members. As economic conditions worsened membership grew. Once again the Chartists decided to collect signatures for a petition. In May 1842 the Second Petition was delivered to Parliament. Once again, by a vote of 287 to 49, the MPs refused to receive it. Once again many MPs did not bother to attend the debate.

The Plug Plot

May 1842 also marked the start of a serious industrial depression. Workers were unemployed, on short time or having to take pay cuts. In August a pattern of strikes and meetings developed, particularly in the north of England and the Midlands. These are known as the Plug Plot because the strikers removed the plugs from steam-engine boilers to shut down factories where other workers were unwilling to join the strike. In many instances Chartists and trade unionists were working together.

By the end of a two-week period roughly half a million men were involved in the protests. 'Flying pickets' of hundreds of men moved from one area to the next bringing workers out on strike. It could almost have been called a general strike. However, the strike lacked leadership. Chartist leaders were divided, many were against it. Even the *Northern Star* failed to give its readers advice, merely reporting the events as they happened.

SOURCE 1 An illustration showing the Chartists taking the Second Petition to Parliament in 1842

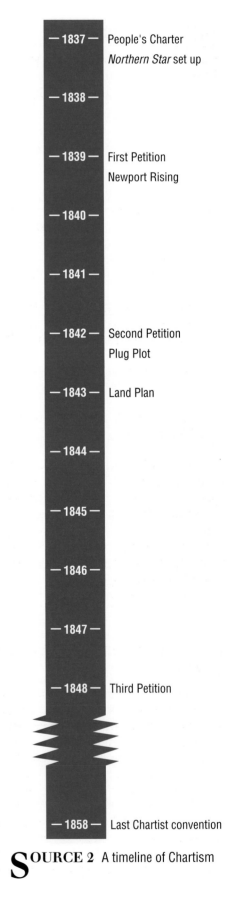

1837	People's Charter / *Northern Star* set up
1838	
1839	First Petition / Newport Rising
1840	
1841	
1842	Second Petition / Plug Plot
1843	Land Plan
1844	
1845	
1846	
1847	
1848	Third Petition
1858	Last Chartist convention

SOURCE 2 A timeline of Chartism

SOURCE 3 An extract from *The Times* of 15 August 1842, describing events in Preston. This incident was reported in the *Illustrated London News* as an Anti-Corn-Law League riot

“ *The mob then proceeded down Lune Street, followed by the military and when near the Corn Exchange halted. The Riot Act was then read and Chief Constable Woodford and Mr Banister, superintendent of police, tried to persuade the mob to retire for fear of the consequences. While they were speaking one of the rioters aimed a stone so surely at Woodford that it felled him to the ground and while he was there he had the brutality to kick him. Large numbers of stones were now thrown at the police and soldiers, many of the former being much hurt. Part of the mob had gone up Fox Street and they then had the advantage of stoning the military from both sides. Under these circumstances orders were given to fire, the soldiers immediately obeyed and several of the mob fell... It is scarcely known how many have been wounded but it is supposed twelve to fifteen, some of them mortally.* ”

1. Read Source 3. From the tone of this report, which side do you think *The Times* supported?

By the end of August the strike was losing momentum and the Government used troops and special constables to arrest pickets and Chartists. By September the strike was over. Over 1500 workers were arrested and tried by magistrates or special commissions. Sentences of transportation and imprisonment were passed on those convicted of riot, conspiracy, felony and sedition. Once again the Government had used the overwhelming force at its disposal to defeat the Chartists.

What happened between 1842 and 1848?

After 1842 economic conditions improved and Chartism was no longer a major force, but it did not disappear altogether. The circulation of the *Northern Star* still averaged 6000 copies per week. Chartists still held meetings and encouraged others to join them.

Other Chartists turned their attention to land. O'Connor set up the National Land Company in which 70,000 Chartists bought shares. The aim was to establish model communities where people would form co-operatives. Two hundred and fifty Chartists actually settled on land bought by the company but ultimately the project ended in

financial disaster. It failed for a number of reasons. Undoubtedly it was poorly organised and badly managed but it finally had to be wound up when a House of Commons committee judged it to be illegal. Meanwhile, it did serve as a rallying point for Chartists in the period when the demands of the Charter seemed impossible to achieve.

Thousands of Chartists put their efforts into other areas such as the Co-operative Societies, workers' education, the Temperance Movement and trade unionism.

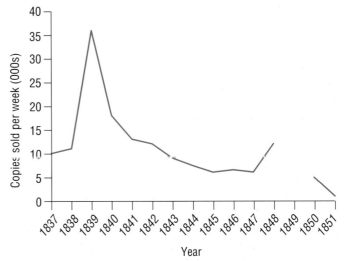

SOURCE 4 Circulation figures for the *Northern Star*, first published on 18 November 1837. The figures are a weekly average. There are no figures for 1849. The paper, which cost 4.5d, was written in a style that made it ideal to be read aloud. In April 1852 O'Connor sold the paper to George Julian Harney

2. Look at Source 4. Do the circulation figures for the *Northern Star* reflect the success of Chartism?

SOURCE 5 An extract from the memoirs of the Chartist Ben Brierley

“ *The* Northern Star *... found its way to the Cut side, being subscribed to by my father and five others. Every Sunday morning these subscribers met at our house to hear what prospect there was of the expected smash-up taking place. It was my task to read aloud so that all could hear at the same time; and the comments that were made on the events foreshadowed would have been exceedingly edifying [uplifting] to me were I to hear them now.* ”

3. Read Source 5. Why do you think the number of readers of the *Northern Star* peaked in 1839?

The Third Petition and the Kennington Common meeting of 1848

The year 1847 was another year of economic depression and once again support for Chartism grew. O'Connor organised another petition, and a public meeting at Kennington Common for 10 April 1848. The Government was afraid of violence, particularly in the light of events elsewhere in Europe (see pages 158–59), and took a number of precautions.

- They got O'Connor to agree that after the meeting the Chartists would not march on Parliament – the crowd would disperse and he alone would take the Petition to Parliament.
- Queen Victoria and the Court were sent to the safety of Osborne House on the Isle of Wight.
- The Government put the Duke of Wellington in charge of military preparations.

On the day there were 8000 soldiers, 4000 London policemen and a reserve of at least 100,000 special constables in position. (Serving among the special constables was Isambard Kingdom Brunel.) At the Tower of London 30 cannon were held in readiness with river steamers ready to move them, while the Bank of England was fortified with sandbags.

The government forces far outnumbered the estimated 20,000 Chartists who attended the meeting. O'Connor had expected 500,000. The meeting passed off without any trouble, the Chartists dispersed and O'Connor delivered the Petition.

Three cabs were needed to carry it and O'Connor claimed it contained 5,706,000 signatures. When these were checked it emerged that there were in fact 1,975,496 and many of these were forgeries.

At the time the meeting and the Petition were regarded as a fiasco, and this marks the end of Chartism as a major force. It did not disappear altogether but gradually its members turned their attention to other causes.

> **SOURCE 7** Two entries from the diary of Charles Cavendish Greville, a government official in London
>
> **9 April 1848**
> *All of London is making preparations to meet a Chartist row tomorrow. I went to the police office with all my clerks and messengers and we were all sworn in as special constables. We have to spend all day at the office tomorrow and I have to send down all my guns. Colonel Harness, of the railway department, is our commander-in-chief. Every gentleman in London has become a special constable and there is an organisation of some sort in every district.*
>
> **13 April 1848**
> *Monday passed off with surprising quiet. Enormous preparations were made, and a host of military, police and special constables were ready if wanted. The Chartist movement was contemptible. Everybody was on the alert. Our office was fortified and all our guns were taken down to be used in defence of the building.*

SOURCE 8 Estimates of the crowd size at the Kennington Common demonstration

Newspaper	Estimated crowd size
Daily papers	
Evening Express	100,000
Evening Standard	9,000–10,000
Evening Sun	150,000
The Times	20,000
Radical weekly papers	
Northern Star	250,000
Weekly Dispatch	50,000 to 200,000

SOURCE 6 A photograph of the Kennington Common demonstration

4. Look at Source 8. Why do you think these figures differ so widely?

SOURCE 9 An extract from the diary of Lady Palmerston, wife of the Foreign Secretary

" It was thought that the people from Kennington Common were going to force their way into the Houses of Parliament and there were frightful reports of these people being armed with guns and pikes and pistols and daggers and knives. But when the Chartists found their own numbers so very far short of what they expected, and no sympathy from the middle classes or soldiers they gave up all hope of revolution. "

SOURCE 10 The House of Commons report on the 1848 Petition

" The number of signatures has been ascertained to be 1,975,496. It is further evident that on numerous consecutive sheets the signatures are in one and the same handwriting. Your Committee also observed the names of distinguished individuals. Among which occurs the name of Her Majesty, Duke of Wellington, Sir Robert Peel, etc., etc. Your Committee have also observed the insertion of numbers of names which are obviously fictitious, such as 'No Cheese', 'Pug Nose', 'Flat Nose'. "

■ REVIEW ACTIVITY

At a number of places in this book you are 'taking the revolutionary temperature' of Britain to decide how great the danger of revolution was. This is the fifth point, 1848.

1. Review all the events in this section on Chartism.

2. Now either sketch the map below or use the copy your teacher gives you and shade in the thermometer. If you believe the danger of revolution was very great, you'll shade all the way to the top. If you think the danger was not so serious, you won't shade so far.

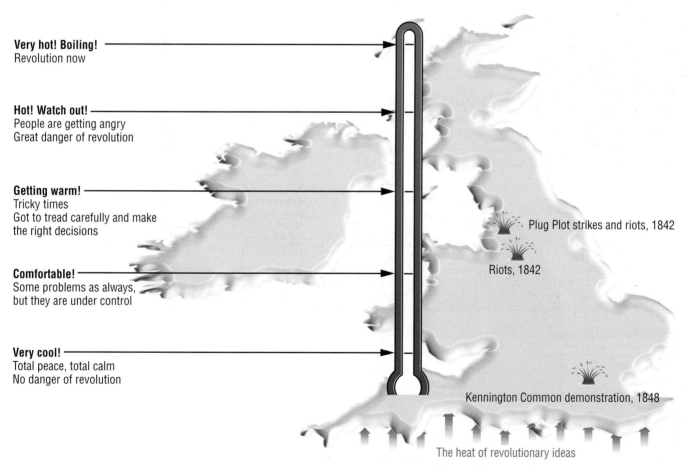

Very hot! Boiling!
Revolution now

Hot! Watch out!
People are getting angry
Great danger of revolution

Getting warm!
Tricky times
Got to tread carefully and make
the right decisions

Comfortable!
Some problems as always,
but they are under control

Very cool!
Total peace, total calm
No danger of revolution

Plug Plot strikes and riots, 1842

Riots, 1842

Kennington Common demonstration, 1848

The heat of revolutionary ideas

Chartist leaders

■ TASK

Consider the mini biographies of the Chartist leaders on these pages and the notes you have compiled on how the Chartists campaigned for their Charter and how the government authorities and their allies in the press responded. Write an answer to the question: would you agree with the statement that the ruling classes used the power of the police, the army, the press, the legal system and the prison system ruthlessly to destroy the Chartist movement? You will need to back up your answer.

William Benbow (1784–1841)

Born in Manchester, he was a shoemaker and Nonconformist preacher. He put forward the theory of the 'Grand National Holiday'. Benbow argued that a month-long general strike would lead to an armed uprising and a change in the political system. This idea lay behind the strike proposed in 1839 and actually carried out in 1842. In 1839 he travelled around England attempting to convince Chartists to strike. He was arrested, tried and convicted of sedition in 1840. He died in prison the following year.

Ernest Jones (1816–69)

He was born in Berlin, the son of an army major. Lawyer, poet and journalist, he became an important Chartist leader. Tried and convicted for sedition after a speech in 1848, he served two years in prison during which time his health was severely damaged. He continued to work in support of Chartism and was influenced by the ideas of Marx and Engels with whom he was in close contact. At his funeral in Manchester in 1869 thousands lined the route to pay their respects.

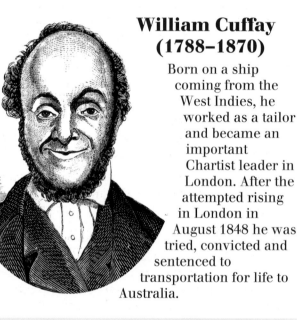

William Cuffay (1788–1870)

Born on a ship coming from the West Indies, he worked as a tailor and became an important Chartist leader in London. After the attempted rising in London in August 1848 he was tried, convicted and sentenced to transportation for life to Australia.

William Lovett (1800–77)

Born in Newlyn, Cornwall, he worked as a cabinet maker in London. He founded the London Working Men's Association in 1836. He was possibly the author of the People's Charter. Arrested in 1839, he was tried and convicted for a speech containing seditious libel. He served twelve months in Warwick gaol. After his release in 1841, his health severely damaged, he dropped out of the Chartist movement and devoted his efforts to improving workers' education whilst running a bookshop. He died in great poverty in 1877.

Robert Gammage (1820–88)

He travelled the country giving political lectures and became part of the national leadership. He wrote the *History of the Chartist Movement*, first published in 1855. He died in 1888 after an accident when he fell off a tram.

James Bronterre O'Brien (1804–64)

Born in County Longford, Ireland, he was a lawyer and then a journalist, working on the *Northern Star*, amongst other papers. In 1840 he was arrested, tried and convicted for making a seditious speech. He served 18 months in Lancaster Castle. On his release, his health severely damaged, he moved away from Chartism. He spent his last years in poverty and ill health supported by money raised by fellow Chartists. Not long before his death he was reportedly seen in a London pub shabbily dressed and offering to debate any subject for the price of a drink.

Joseph Rayner Stephens (?–1879)

Stephens was a Methodist preacher who turned to Chartism after supporting the Short Time Committees. He was a good public speaker. He was arrested in 1839, tried and convicted of sedition. At a meeting on Kersal Moor he referred to a 'war to the knife' and spoke of 'the palace in flames'. He was imprisoned in Chester Castle for eighteen months. On his release he had to promise to behave well for five years. He left Chartism but worked for other workers' causes such as factory conditions and opposition to the Poor Law.

5. What was Stephens threatening by his language on Kersal Moor?

Feargus O'Connor (1796–1857)

Born in County Cork, Ireland, he lived in London from 1833. He joined the Chartists in 1836 and began publishing the *Northern Star* in Leeds in 1837. He was a brilliant public speaker. He was jailed for eighteen months in 1840 for publishing seditious libels. On his release he led the National Charter Association. He was tried, but not convicted, in 1842 for his part in the strikes. In 1843 he launched the Chartist Land Plan which ended in bankruptcy by 1850. He was elected MP for Nottingham in 1847. After the failure of the Third Petition in 1848 he lost credibility. He eventually went mad and ended up in an asylum in Chiswick.

SOURCE 11 George Julian Harney, editor of the *Northern Star* from 1843, writing in *The Operative*, 10 February 1839

66 *I was for six months confined because I dared to give the working classes that untaxed knowledge which they have the right to enjoy. The Tyrants bound me, but they could not subdue me. They sent me away friendless and forlorn; but I return to Derby not as I departed. I come back to look the tyrants in the teeth, in the proud character of a leader of the people – as one of the chosen chieftains of the brave men of the north.* 99

■ CONNECTIONS

In our period you have studied a number of different groups of protesters. Copy the table below and use it to review those protesters, what they were protesting about, how they protested and the response of the authorities. How were these similar and how were they different?

Protesters	Motives	Actions	Govt response
Swing rioters			
Reform rioters (e.g. Bristol 1831)			
Newport Chartists			
Plug Plotters			

What contribution did women make to Chartism?

IN MOST LARGE towns the Chartists had women's sections. They signed the petitions, took part in meetings and strikes and were, for example, reported as facing the soldiers' bayonets in Halifax in 1842. Other examples of individual involvement are also recorded. In 1839 Elizabeth Cresswell was imprisoned for carrying a pistol at a demonstration in Mansfield. In the same year Amy Meredith was arrested for stealing a gun to take part in the Newport Rising.

One important area where women were active was exclusive dealing. This was the attempt by Chartists to deal only with shopkeepers who sympathised with Chartism. Where a choice of shops existed this was possible.

In Scotland exclusive dealing took a different form. There, Chartists did not attend services led by clergy of the Established and Baptist Churches who were hostile to Chartism.

SOURCE 1 Part of a statement issued by the Female Chartists of Aberdeen, 12 November 1841

❝ While we are compelled to share the misery of our fathers, our husbands, our brothers, and our lovers, we are determined to have a share in their struggles to be free, and to cheer them in their onward march for liberty. ❞

SOURCE 2 Part of an 'Address on the system of exclusive dealing' by Robert Lowery in 1839

❝ The middle-class shopkeepers promised that if we assisted to get them the Reform Bill they would get us the vote; they have broken their pledge. What is our remedy against this evil? Exclusive dealing. We have made them and we can unmake them. Our pennies make their pounds. If we cease to deal with them they will become poor and lose their votes. They will then feel the evils they now inflict upon us and cry out for universal suffrage [votes for all]. Thus while ceasing to spend our money in the shops of our enemies, we have destroyed their power. ❞

SOURCE 3 An extract from a letter written by Jane Jones to her husband, the Chartist leader Ernest Jones, in 1851

❝ Better to be the wife of a wandering peddler – at least we could tramp about together, carrying our children on our backs, and enjoy each other's company – than be the wife of a travelling Chartist lecturer. ❞

SOURCE 4 An extract from *Raise Chartism from the Pothouse* written by Ernest Jones in 1852. Not all the Chartists welcomed the involvement of women – some were afraid their presence would be used to discredit the movement

❝ We want the support and countenance of women in our movement – for the Charter must become a domestic spirit, a tutelar [guardian] saint, a household god, before it can arise [as] a legislative power! And what shall make it so – but the support of woman? That which does not emanate from a million homes, will have no lasting basis even amid the cheering of a thousand platforms. It is woman that ever sways the mind of man – it is woman that ever moulds the character of the child. ❞

SOURCE 5 A cartoon published in *Punch* in 1848 (George Sand was a popular female novelist)

1. Compare Sources 3 and 4. What might the atmosphere have been like in the Jones household?

HOW TO TREAT THE FEMALE CHARTISTS.

2. How does the cartoonist in Source 5 attempt to make fun of female Chartists?

Did the Chartists fail?

> The Chartists were a failure, they failed to achieve their political aims. I know all but one of the demands of the People's Charter have since been achieved but that is due to the efforts of those who followed on afterwards.

> That is just not true. Certainly at the time the ruling classes wanted to show Chartism as a failure but that was for obvious reasons. Instead you could argue that for ten years the Chartists flourished as an effective working-class organisation. They ran a widely read newspaper and organised petitions and meetings throughout the country. They made sure that constitutional questions were asked in Parliament and they certainly frightened the ruling classes. Why else did the Government use all those troops, special constables and give so many harsh prison sentences?

> We shouldn't forget the many achievements of individual Chartists. They raised public awareness and had a positive impact on workers' education. They took their organising and speaking skills into other areas that directly benefited the working classes such as education, the Temperance Movement, trade unionism, Co-operative Societies and electoral reform.

> So it can be argued that the Chartists did not fail, they succeeded! It was only because of their political demands that they failed to secure the six points of the Charter. Let's have a look at why; there are a number of reasons to consider.

Lack of middle-class support

These people were either satisfied by the 1832 reforms, hostile to the violence associated with Chartism or campaigning within the Anti-Corn-Law League (see page 157). Whenever there was confrontation these people enrolled as special constables, such as the 100,000 in London in 1848.

The radical nature of their demands

What the Chartists were asking for was very extreme for the Britain of 1838. The historian Asa Briggs wrote in 1959 that the 'cards were too heavily stacked against them'.

The divisions between their leaders over the use of moral or physical force

It was perhaps inevitable that such a large organisation should be full of disagreements but this did contribute to its failure. The violence advocated by the 'physical force' Chartists alienated those very people in the middle and upper classes whom the 'moral force' Chartists were trying to persuade. It did not matter that the 'physical force' Chartists only saw violence as a last resort; Chartism became associated with violence because of events such as the Newport Rising and because of the hostile coverage they received in the press.

Hostility of the press

Newspapers like *The Times* emphasised the violent aspects of Chartism and publications such as *Punch* ridiculed its ideas. This had an important influence on public opinion. It certainly influenced those members of the middle classes who enrolled as special constables to oppose Chartism.

The localised nature of the movement

Despite the growth of towns most people still lived in small, isolated communities and the Chartist supporters tended to be the poorer people with little real power or influence. Added to this was the development of the railway and telegraph system, which made it quicker and easier for the authorities to move troops to trouble spots. Also in an age before mass communication via television, people living in different towns had very different concerns and interests. It was inevitable that a national organisation would be hopelessly fragmented.

Lack of finance

Chartist supporters were mainly working-class people. They had little money and the extremists in Chartism frightened away the middle-class people who did have money. So Chartism never had the necessary funds to mount an effective national campaign.

The efficient use of government power

Most important was the power that the Government had and used: troops, special constables, police and the legal system. Large numbers of Chartist leaders and supporters were arrested and imprisoned for relatively short periods of time. This robbed the movement of leadership. The short sentences themselves meant there was little protest beyond the Chartist movement itself; those imprisoned did not become popular martyrs. The Government had learned the lesson of Tolpuddle. Since most of the men were from the working classes a prison sentence for them meant poverty for their dependants. Whilst some Chartists returned to the movement on their release, others were discouraged or broken by ill health – and of course some actually died of disease in prison. Others chose to emigrate.

That the Government was confident in its power is demonstrated by the repeated refusal to consider petitions that, despite the forgeries, still contained the signatures of thousands of working men and women. Also it is worth remembering that just 28 well-armed and trained soldiers defeated thousands of Chartists in the Newport Rising. General Napier (Source 3, page 144) was not bluffing when he highlighted the futility of using physical force against trained troops.

Improvements in working and living conditions

The Government was beginning to pass laws which benefited working people, such as the repeal of the Corn Laws in 1846 and the 1847 Factory Act which finally introduced a ten-hour working day.

Economic improvement

From 1850 onwards the improving economic situation robbed the movement of support. It is noticeable that the three high points of Chartism in 1839, 1842 and 1848 coincided with periods of economic hardship.

Chartism had achieved its aims

One modern historian, Owen Ashton, has argued that Chartism disappeared simply because it was no longer necessary. It had achieved its aim of forcing the Government to respond to the needs of the people. It had made a corrupt system respond to its demands. Achieving the demands of the Charter itself was never their aim; it was a tool to achieve their social and economic ends.

■ TASK

The following were all equally important reasons why the Chartists failed to achieve their Charter demands:

■ the divisions between their leaders over the use of moral or physical force
■ economic improvement
■ the efficiency of government policy
■ the lack of support from the middle classes
■ the radical nature of their demands.

Do you agree? Explain your answer.

Why did the Anti-Corn-Law League become a legend in Victorian politics?

THE ANTI-CORN-LAW League was founded in 1838 in Manchester and was led by Richard Cobden and John Bright. By 1841 it had become a national organisation with a number of paid travelling lecturers and by 1846 it had achieved its aim. It had the backing of the middle classes, particularly northern manufacturers, and so did not lack funds as the Chartists did.

It was campaigning for one specific aim, the repeal of the Corn Laws, and therefore had just one enemy, the landowners. The Corn Laws, passed in 1815, worked to the advantage of landowners. By banning the import of foreign corn until the cost of home-grown corn had reached £4 per quarter-hundredweight, these laws kept the price of corn high. They were designed to protect income from farming but they also led to high food prices. For the manufacturers this caused two problems:

- they had to pay the higher wages that employees needed to buy food at high prices
- their export market was damaged because foreign countries that had surplus corn could not sell it and therefore did not have the income to buy the exports of British manufacturers.

The League had a wide appeal, particularly with its call for 'cheap bread'. Nonconformists in the League felt they were doing God's will. However its leaders had another agenda. They saw the repeal of the Corn Laws as the first step in destroying the power of the land-owning aristocracy.

The repeal of the Corn Laws, 1846

The repeal was put through by the Tory Prime Minister Sir Robert Peel, against the wishes of many of his own party; they were, after all, the party of the land. He agreed with the argument for repeal but had to get enough support in Parliament. He had two reasons for doing so:

- he believed British agriculture alone could not feed the British population; the Irish Famine brought this argument home strongly
- he feared the political agenda behind the Anti-Corn-Law League.

Peel thought that the repeal of the Corn Laws was actually the best way to protect the power of the landowners. Whilst he did not fear the short-term electoral gains of the league he did fear their growing influence. He said that repeal would '... remove the contest entirely from the dangerous ground upon which it has got – that of a war between the manufacturers, the hungry and the poor against the landed proprietors and the aristocracy, which can only end in the ruin of the latter.'

1838–41 Propaganda
The league published its own newspaper, printed pamphlets and employed travelling lecturers. However it failed to secure the support of the working classes.

1841 Parliamentary politics
The league put forward candidates in parliamentary elections. This was unsuccessful, even in constituencies where they thought they had a realistic chance.

Different campaigning methods used by the league

Electoral manipulation
In 1844 the league tried to ensure that its supporters were registered to vote and that their opponents were not on the electoral rolls. Not many seats were influenced by this sort of tactic.

In 1845 the league bought property valued at 40 shillings per annum in county constituencies. They were thus buying themselves votes in parliamentary elections. This resulted in success in the South Lancashire and West Yorkshire by-elections in February 1846.

■ TASK

With your partner compare the Anti-Corn-Law League to Chartism. You might consider their:

- aims
- membership
- tactics
- political effect.

Which movement do you think had the greatest success?

THE YEAR 1848 is known as the year of revolutions. Sources 1–4 on these pages show you why. Most European countries experienced disturbances which were a response to two major causes: hatred of foreign rule or demands for more democratic government. In some countries these disturbances led to revolution; in others more liberal forms of government were introduced, with less power for hereditary rulers such as princes, kings and emperors. The year came to a tragic end as cholera swept across the continent with devastating effect.

In Britain the Chartists staged a peaceful demonstration on Kennington Common in April. As you have seen on pages 150–51, their protest ended in ridicule.

■ TASK

Why was there no revolution in Britain? Everything that you have studied in this book should help you to answer this question. Your revolutionary temperature maps should provide a helpful summary.

Ireland
The Young Ireland movement preached revolution and nationalism but did not have popular support. The English Government easily suppressed the isolated incidents of violence and disorder.

Belgium
There were riots in cities during March but the middle-class Government made enough concessions to prevent revolution. The vote was given to the lower middle classes and more poor relief to unemployed workers. King Leopold I continued on the throne.

The Netherlands
King William II agreed to changes to the constitution that led to less power for the monarchy.

France

SOURCE 2 Revolutionaries attack a government building in Paris, 24 February 1848

On 22 February workers, students and others set up barricades in the streets of Paris. The disturbances had begun as a protest against government by the middle classes and a demand for social and democratic reform. The killing of demonstrators by soldiers led to revolution. King Louis Philippe was forced to abdicate in March and the Second Republic replaced the monarchy. In June there was some of the bloodiest street fighting that Europe had seen. Louis Napoleon came to power as President of the French Republic.

Switzerland
After a 25-day civil war in 1847 a new liberal constitution was drawn up in 1848. It guaranteed republican government, equality for all before the law and freedom of conscience, speech, press and public meeting.

Spain
Revolts in Madrid in March and in Seville in April were both easily suppressed by the Government.

SOURCE 1 A map of western Europe, showing countries where protests broke out in 1848

SOURCE 3
Protesters in Berlin defend street barricades as Prussian troops advance, March 1848

Germany

Following the fall of Louis Philippe in France there were disturbances throughout the German states in March. In some, barricades were put up and street fighting took place. More liberal forms of government emerged in Baden, Saxony and Wurttemberg and in Bavaria Ludwig I was forced to abdicate. In Prussia there were riots in the capital, Berlin, but the Government of King Frederick William IV stayed in control by granting liberal concessions.

Austria

The fall of Louis Philippe sparked demonstrations throughout the Austrian Empire. All social classes were against the Government of Prince Metternich. He was forced to resign on 13 March and the Emperor Ferdinand had to grant a new constitution. The peoples of the Empire such as the Czechs, Croats and Hungarians tried to throw off Austrian rule. These nationalist struggles continued into 1849.

SOURCE 4
People in Milan prepare barricades against the advancing Austrian army, 22 March 1848

Italy

Italy was not a country at this time but rather a collection of smaller states. On 12 January the people of Palermo in Sicily rebelled against the rule of Ferdinand II of Naples. By February there were riots in all the major Italian cities. This revolution was a popular protest by all classes against foreign rule. In March the people of Milan and Venice drove out the occupying Austrian troops. All the Italian states also set up more liberal governments. By the end of the year the revolutionary movement had been defeated everywhere by Austrian and French troops.

chapter 9

CONCLUSION

Britain in 1851: the Great Exhibition

PRINCE ALBERT, THE husband of Queen Victoria, is credited with the idea of holding the Great Exhibition. A parliamentary commission was set up to investigate the idea and eventually decided it should go ahead. Its intention, in Prince Albert's own words, was 'to give a true test and a living picture of the point of development at which the whole of mankind has arrived.' A building committee that included amongst its members Isambard Kingdom Brunel and Robert Stephenson oversaw the project.

Joseph Paxton produced the design for the building. It combined the use of glass and iron to create a light and airy building which was nicknamed 'the Crystal Palace', a name that stuck. Work began in September 1850 and was completed nine months later. An unexpected problem emerged when pigeons got inside. Queen Victoria reportedly asked the Duke of Wellington how this problem could be solved and he replied, 'Hawks! Ma'am'.

The exhibition contained thousands of exhibits from Britain and other countries, organised under six main headings: raw materials, machinery, manufactures – textiles, manufactures – vitreous and ceramic (glassware and pottery), fine arts and miscellaneous.

Thousands of people came to visit, and for many the journey was made possible by the railways. There was a sliding system of charges on different days, ranging from £1 to a shilling, so that all classes could afford to visit. This also had the effect of ensuring that the different classes of society did not need to meet. Interestingly, extra policemen were on duty on shilling days but whatever trouble the organisers expected never emerged. By the time the exhibition ended over six million people had visited it. These numbers show how much Britain had changed since 1815, a change made possible by the railways.

■ TASK

With a partner, discuss:

■ the choice of exhibits
■ the reaction of the public
■ the reaction of the authorities.

What does the Great Exhibition tell us about Britain in 1851?

SPECIMENS FROM MR. PUNCH'S INDUSTRIAL EXHIBITION OF 1850.
(TO BE IMPROVED IN 1851).

AN INDUSTRIOUS NEEDLE-WOMAN
A LABOURER AGED 75
A DISTRESSED SHOE MAKER
A SWEATER

SOURCE 1 A cartoon from *Punch*, April 1850. The cartoonist is concerned with all those who have not prospered during the period and who are not represented in the Exhibition

Why study Britain 1815–51?

WE HAVE STUDIED Britain 1815–51 for four reasons.

1. What it means to be human

It has helped us to understand what it means to be human. We have concentrated upon the ideas and beliefs, values and attitudes of the men and women in this period. The one thing that all the aristocrats, emigrants, engineers, Evangelicals, Chartists, child labourers, civil servants, factory workers, farm labourers, magistrates, Methodists, mill owners, miners, navvies, landlords, landowners, philanthropists, reformers, Radicals and soldiers had in common was their humanity.

2. Remembering the past

What happened in the past is still important to us today. The events in Tolpuddle in 1834 are, for example, still seen as significant. In 1934, the Trades Union Congress built six cottages and a museum in Tolpuddle in memory of the Tolpuddle trade unionists. Each cottage bears the name of one of the men. Every year the Trades Union Congress organises a march in the village to honour their memory. For those men on the other side of the argument, the landowners and magistrates, there is no rally or memorial.

SOURCE 1 A photograph of the annual Tolpuddle Martyrs' Rally taken in July 1999

Sanitising the past

As all history is an interpretation there will always be differences of opinion between historians about the past. The debate about whether the living standards of the working classes improved in this period is one example, the Irish Famine another. Sometimes, however, people try to use the past for their own purposes. The airbrushing out of Brunel's cigar by an advertising agency, described in Source 2, is a deliberate attempt to sanitise the past. What the advertisers have failed to appreciate is that in order to understand Brunel you must understand the times in which he lived. He was alive at a time when smoking was not seen as the social evil it is today. It was a time when a young boy, working as a trapper in a coal mine, asked by a parliamentary commissioner 'What do you do in the dark all day?' could say, 'I just sits and smokes me pipe'. So do you think the airbrushing out of Brunel's cigar is valid?

PC modernisers make Brunel's cigar invisible

Like Winston Churchill, Groucho Marx and Bill Clinton long after him, the celebrated Victorian engineer Isambard Kingdom Brunel liked nothing better than a good cigar.

The most famous portrait of the genius responsible for some of the greatest feats of 19th century British engineering shows him proudly before the massive anchor chains of one of his ships, favoured brand clamped tightly in mouth.

Not any longer. Cigar chomping, it has been decided, is inappropriate behaviour.

The cigar has been airbrushed out of the picture used in promotional literature for the SS Great Britain, the pioneering iron steam ship built by Brunel in Bristol docks in 1843 and now attracting more than 100,000 visitors each year.

Alex Timms, creative director of the agency that designed the leaflet for the Great Britain's owners, said the cigar had been removed because it was not felt suitable for the young visitors the historic ship was seeking to attract.

Anti-smoking campaigners yesterday welcomed news of the missing cigar. But the airbrushing of history has left the pro-smoking lobby fuming.

Marjorie Nicholson, director of the pressure group Forest, condemned the touched-up picture as the worst kind of censorship. 'This is distorting our history and our traditions.' she said.

SOURCE 2 An extract from the *Guardian* newspaper, 9 October 1998. See Source 5 on page 137, for the photograph of Brunel the article is talking about

3. Getting better at history

This depth study has helped you to get better at doing history. You have used a wide range of sources to gather evidence about the past. You have used artists' illustrations, broadside ballads, buildings, cartoons, diaries, engravings, graphs, historical fiction, paintings, parliamentary reports, photographs, plans, maps, newspapers, tables and statistics. You have considered how useful and reliable those sources are. This ability to use sources is a core skill in history and, you will find, in life. It is particularly important for a time in our past such as Georgian and early Victorian Britain which is sometimes portrayed by the media and politicians as a 'good' time.

It has also enabled you to investigate the lives of some contrasting sets of people. For example, you have seen the differing views of townspeople and navvies, of Utilitarian reformers and the supporters of *laissez-faire*. You have tried to see life through their eyes in order to understand why they acted in the way they did. This is another core skill in history and in life.

It has also helped you to see that events do not always have simple consequences. Do you still think that railways just made travel quicker or do you think that they had far wider social, economic and political effects? Historians need to look beyond the obvious. They need to keep asking 'why? why? why?' and not to be satisfied with easy answers.

4. Learning lessons from history

Finally, there are lessons to be learnt from history, if we choose to learn them. From the distance of today are you shocked at the treatment of the poor by the wealthier members of Georgian and early Victorian society? Is your view of them a fair one? The historian T.S. Ashton has commented that 'a generation that had the enterprise and industry to assemble the facts, the honesty to reveal them, and the energy to set about the task of reform has been held up to obloquy [blame] as the author, not of the Blue Books [reports], but of the evils themselves.' Should we blame them for the problems in factories, towns, mines and the countryside or applaud their efforts to do something about them? And what of their view of us? Would the Evangelicals who founded the RSPCA in 1824 be astonished to find that fox hunting still survives today?

SOURCE 3 The monument to the Irish Famine in Dublin

What view will future historians have of us today, living in a wealthy developed country and doing so little to help the poor in the developing world? Is our concern with AIDS motivated by how it affects us rather than how it affects Africa? Is it valid to compare our response to this issue with the reaction of the Victorian middle classes to the threat of cholera? Laurence Peter, Professor of Education at the University of California, said: 'History repeats itself because nobody listens.' So what do you think? What lessons do you think we might learn from Britain's history between 1815 and 1851, if we listen?

ACT OF PARLIAMENT a law approved by the monarch and both Houses of Parliament

ARISTOCRACY a group of powerful people whose lands, wealth and titles are passed down from one generation to the next

ASSIZES a court held by the King's judges, who travelled around the country hearing cases that were too serious to be dealt with by Justices of the Peace

BILL a proposal for a new Act of Parliament

CANVASSING trying to persuade people to vote for a particular candidate in an election

CAPITAL wealth owned by a business or individual

CHARTISTS members of a movement that developed in the late 1830s to demand votes for the working classes and other political reforms

CHOLERA a disease carried in water supplies contaminated with sewage. It was usually fatal

COLONIES lands or settlements outside a country's borders. Colonies were usually seized or conquered

COMMUTED reduced to a less severe punishment

CONSTITUENCY the area represented by a Member of Parliament. The size of a constituency today is decided according to how many people live in it, so a densely populated inner-city constituency covers a small area and a rural constituency is large

CO-OPERATIVE a business that is owned and funded by a group of people who receive an equal share in the profits

CORPORATION a form of local government, like a town council

DEMOCRACY a political system in which the government is elected by the people, in elections held at regular intervals

DEMOBILISED released from military duty

EXILE forced by the government to live abroad

FRANCHISE the right to vote

FREEHOLD unconditional ownership of land or property

FRENCH REVOLUTION the overthrow of the monarchy and the aristocratic Government in 1789 and its replacement by the rule of the people

GENTRY a group of landowners, less wealthy and powerful than the aristocracy

GUILLOTINE a device used for beheading people, consisting of a sliding, sharp metal blade fixed between two posts

HOUSE OF COMMONS the section of Parliament in which Bills are debated and eventually made into law. Members of the House of Commons (MPs) are chosen in elections

HOUSE OF LORDS the section of Parliament made up of aristocrats who have inherited their right to be there, and senior members of the Church such as bishops. It can send Bills it objects to back to the House of Commons for further debate

HUSTINGS a platform on which speakers stand to make speeches to a gathering of people

INDUSTRIAL REVOLUTION a period during the late eighteenth and early nineteenth century when industry developed rapidly and people began to make goods with machines in factories

JUSTICE OF THE PEACE or **MAGISTRATE** an important member of the local community responsible for maintaining law and order

LAISSEZ-FAIRE the belief that economic or social problems are best left to be sorted out by the individuals concerned, rather than being tackled by governments

LAY PREACHER a member of the Church community who has undergone training to preach, but who has not been ordained

LEASEHOLDERS people who have legal rights over land or property for a fixed number of years (a lease)

LUDDITES workers in the stocking and lace-making trades who smashed looms and attacked businesses as a protest against the introduction of new machinery and ways of working between 1811 and 1816

METHODISTS Christians who used the ways of worship established by John Wesley. Methodism especially appealed to the working classes

NAVVIES railway labourers

NONCONFORMISTS Christians who had broken away from the Church of England to set up their own Churches with different styles of worship

OUTDOOR RELIEF Poor Relief paid to people living in their own homes

PAID OFF a ship was taken out of service and the crew paid and released from the navy

PARISH the main division of local government until the nineteenth century; it was an area, usually an entire village, served by a single church

PARLIAMENTARY REFORM changes to the way in which people were elected to Parliament, so that the interests of a wider range of people would be represented

PENAL SERVITUDE imprisonment

PETERLOO the name given to the protest meeting held in Manchester on 16 August 1819 at which several protesters were killed by soldiers

POOR RELIEF payments made to people who were out of work or too old, young or sick to work

QUAKER a member of the Society of Friends, a Christian religious group formed around 1650 that has very simple religious meetings and works to achieve social reform

QUARTER SESSIONS courts held by Justices of the Peace in the county towns four times a year

RADICALS a group who wanted to make radical changes to the political system

REPRESSIVE very harsh; designed to control

REVOLUTION very drastic changes; in political terms a revolution involves the overthrow of one system of government and its replacement by another

RIOT ACT an Act read by a Justice of the Peace to declare a public meeting illegal. Troops could then be used to break up the meeting

SEDITION behaviour intended to stir up widespread disobedience towards the authorities

SLUMP a period when prices and the level of economic activity fall, often leading to wage cuts and higher unemployment

STEREOTYPE an impression that is shared by many people, but which may not be accurate

SWING RIOTS disturbances led by agricultural workers that took place in southern England from 1830–32

TEETOTAL someone who is teetotal refuses to drink alcohol

TORY a member of the group in Parliament that strongly supported the interests of the aristocracy and tended to oppose political and social reform (now known as the Conservative Party)

TRANSPORTATION being sent to do penal servitude in one of the British colonies, especially Australia

TURNPIKE TRUST a company set up to finance the building and maintenance of roads, which people paid a toll to use

UTILITARIANISM the beliefs set out by Jeremy Bentham, that the right course of action is always the one that brings the greatest good to the greatest number of people

VESTRY members of a parish responsible for organising local affairs

WHIG a member of the group in Parliament that had close links with the industrialists and supported limited political and social reform (now known as the Liberal Democrats)

WORKHOUSE a building in which people who could not support themselves had to live and work

YEOMANRY members of the local ruling class who acted as a police force to maintain law and order in their area

ndex

cknowledgements

The author would like to thank Ian Kellett for suggesting the case study on the Shaftesbury election of 1830, and Frank Crompton for his help with the section on the Worcestershire workhouses.

The Publishers would like to thank the following for permission to reproduce copyright material:

Pictures:
Cover: *l* Manchester City Art Galleries/Bridgeman Art Library, *r* Russell-Cotes Art Gallery/Bridgeman Art Library; **p.3** *l* The Wallace Collection/Bridgeman Art Library, *r* National Maritime Museum, London; **p.4** *t* Philip Mould Historical Portraits Ltd, London/Bridgeman Art Library, *b* James Bird Photographer; **p.5** *t* Mary Evans Picture Library, *b* NMPFT/Science & Society Picture Library; **p.7** Leeds Museums and Art Galleries City Museum, UK/ Bridgeman Art Library; **p.8** Musee Carnavalet Photo Bulloz; **p.9** *t* Trustees of the British Museum, *b* Mary Evans Picture Library; **p.13** *t* Manchester City Art Galleries/ Bridgeman Art Library, *b* Apsley House, The Wellington Museum London/The Bridgeman Art Library; **p.16** *t* The Bridgeman Art Library, *b* Mary Evans Picture Library; **p.20–21** Manchester City Art Galleries/ Bridgeman Art Library; **p.24** Mansell/Time Inc./Katz Pictures; **p.27** BBC; **p.34** Trustees of the British Museum; **p.35** *t* Hulton Getty Picture Library, *b* The Fotomas Index; **p.40** *t* Mary Evans Picture Library, *b* Dorset Natural History and Archaeological Society at the Dorset County Museum Vol 4 (1862), 35, DNHAS at Dorset County Museum, Dorchester; **p.43** Mary Evans Picture Library; **p.45** © Punch Ltd; **p.50** Dorset Natural History and Archaeological Society at the Dorset County Museum SHIPP, W, 1852, Dorsetshire Vol 1, (1852), 89; **p.52** Mansell/Time Inc./Katz Pictures; **p.55** Mary Evans Picture Library; **p.56** © University College London; **p.58–59** Manchester Public Libraries Local Studies Unit; **p.62** Dickens Museum; **p.63** Romulus Films; **p.65** Worcestershire Record Office Ref: b251 BA400/6; **p.67** The Illustrated London News Picture Library; **p.70** Mary Evans Picture Library; **p.72** Christie's Images Ltd; **p.73** *l* Rastrick's Viaduct, London Road, Brighton by John Wilson Carmichael (1800-68) National Railway Museum York, North Yorkshire, UK/Bridgeman Art Library, and Penguin Books, *r* Christie's Images Ltd, and Penguin Books; **p.74–75** Mary Evans Picture Library; **p.81** James Bird Photographer; **p.82** James Bird Photographer; **p.89** Mary Evans Picture Library; **p.91** *t & bl* Mary Evans Picture Library, *br* Ironbridge Gorge Museum Trust; **p.92** Mansell/ Time Inc./Katz Pictures; **p.95** Mary Evans Picture Library; **p.96** *l* The Fotomas Index, *tr & br* Hulton Getty; **p.97** *both* Mary Evans Picture Library; **p.100** Hulton Getty; **p.101** The British Library; **p.103** Mary Evans Picture Library; **p.104** Mansell/Time Inc./Katz Pictures; **p.106** The Fotomas Index; **p.108** Mary Evans Picture Library; **p.109** *tl* Mary Evans Picture Library, *bl & br* Hulton Getty; **p.112** Bradford Art Gallery and Museum/Bridgeman Art Library; **p.114** Mary Evans Picture Library; **p.116** © Punch Ltd; **p.117** Hulton Getty; **p.118** Mary Evans Picture Library; **p.120** *t* NMPFT/Science & Society Picture Library, *b* Hulton Getty; **p.121** *tl* Hulton Getty; **p.122** *l* NMPFT/Science & Society Picture Library, *r* Mary Evans Picture Library; **p.123** *t* NMPFT/Science & Society Picture Library, *c & b* Mary Evans Picture Library; **p.124** National Railway Museum/Science & Society Picture Library; **p.126** *both* Hulton Getty; **p.127** Hulton Getty; **p.129** Mary Evans Picture Library; **p.132** Mansell/Time Inc./Katz Pictures; **p.133** Ironbridge Gorge Museum Trust; **p.136** Science Museum/ Science & Society Picture Library; **p.137** *l* By courtesy of the National Portrait Gallery, London, *r* Robert Harding Picture Library/Jennifer Fry; **p.140** Mary Evans Picture Library; **p.141** © Punch Ltd; **p.145** Mansell/ Time Inc./Katz Pictures; **p.146** By permission of the National Museum of Labour History; **p.148** Weidenfeld & Nicolson Archives; **p.150** The Royal Archives © 2000 Her Majesty Queen Elizabeth II; **p.152** *l* The British Library, *r* Hulton Getty; **p.153** *both* Hulton Getty; **p.154** © Punch Ltd; **p.159** *t* AKG London/Musee Carnavalet, *c* Mary Evans Picture Library, *b* AKG London; **p.160** © Punch Ltd; **p.161** *l* Dorset Evening Echo, *r* © South West News Services; **p.162** Slidefile

Written sources:
p.65 Frank Crompton, *Workhouse Children*, Sutton Publishing, 1997; **p.89** Roger Watson, *Edwin Chdwick: Poor Law and Public Health*, Addison Wesley Longman, 1969; **p.110** *t* E.P. Thompson, *The Making of the English Working Classes*, Victor Gollancz, 1963, *b* Phyllis Deane, *The First Industrial Revolution*, Cambridge University Press, 1980; **p.111** *t* Roderick Floud, 'A Tall Story', *History Today*, Vol 33, 1983, *b* Norman McCord, *British History 1815–1906*, by permission of Oxford University Press, 1991; **p.114** *t* Cormac O'Graídà, *Before and after the Famine: Explorations in Economic History, 1800–1925*, Manchester University Press, 1988, *b* Colm Tóibín, *The Irish Famine*, Profile Books, London, 1999; **p.137** Adrian Vaughan, *Isambard Kingdom Brunel: Engineering Knight-Errant*, John Murray (Publishers) Ltd, 1991; **p.139** East Yorkshire Local History Service; **p.161** Geoffrey Gibbs, 'PC modernisers make Brunel's cigar invisible', *Guardian*, 9 October 1998

l=left, *r*=right, *c*=centre, *t*=top, *b*=bottom

Every effort has been made to trace all copyright holders, but if any have been inadvertently overlooked the Publishers will be pleased to make the neccessary arrangements at the first opportunity.